# EXECUTIVE JAPANESE

**2**

## Beginner's Guide to Corporate Communications

**by Hajime Takamizawa**

Material used in the BUSINESS COLUMN © was contributed by:
Nick Bornoff, Michael Gerlach, Jim Key, Jonathan Lloyd-Owen, Daniel Masler, Terry D. Ragan, John Rivoir, and Brian Smallshaw

English revisions by Robert Shafer

Designed by Douglas Doolittle
Calligraphy by Yoshihiro Watanabe

Published by
ASMIK CORP.
4 Ageba-cho, Shinjuku-ku, Tokyo 162

Distributed by ASK KODANSHA CO., LTD.
1 Shimomiyabi-cho, Shinjuku-ku, Tokyo 162

Phototype set by Bisha CO., LTD.
Printed by Taiyosha CO., LTD.

First edition, October 1986
Printed in Japan

ISBN 4-87032-001

## CONTENTS

# UNIT 11

## *ASKING THE WAY*

地下鉄

ちかてつ

## MODEL CONVERSATION

## SITUATION

*To get to Chiba's office, Kelly decides to take the subway to Toranomon Station. (at the office)*

| | | |
|---|---|---|
| | **dekakemasu** | to go out |
| Yamaguchi | **1 Kerii-san, dekakemasu ka.** | Mr. Kelly, are you going out? |
| Kelly | **2 Ee, Jetoro de Chiba-san ni aimasu.** | Yes, I'll see Mr. Chiba at JETRO. |
| | **de** | by means of |
| | **nan de** | by what means |
| Yamaguchi | **3 Nan de ikimasu ka.** | How are you going? |
| | **basu de** | by bus |
| Kelly | **4 Basu de ikimasu.** | I'll go by bus. |
| | **chikatetsu** | subway |
| | **hoo** | an alternative |
| | **chikatetsu no hoo ga ii desu** | the subway is better |
| | **michi** | way, road, street |
| | **komimasu** | to be crowded |
| | **michi ga konde imasu** | heavy traffic (on the street) |
| Yamaguchi | **5 Chikatetsu no hoo ga ii desu yo. Ima, michi ga konde imasu kara...** | The subway is better. The traffic is heavy right now... |
| | **chikatetsu de** | by subway |
| | **itte kimasu** | good-by (lit. I'll go and return) |
| Kelly | **6 Soo desu ka. Jaa, chikatetsu de ikimasu. Itte kimasu!** | Is that so? I'll go by subway then. Good-by! |
| | **itte (i)rasshai** | good-by (lit. go and come back) |

| | | |
|---|---|---|
| Yamaguchi | **7 Itte (i)rasshai!** | Good-by! |

*(at the subway station)*

| | |
|---|---|
| **made** | as far as |
| **Toranomon made** | as far as Toranomon |

| | | |
|---|---|---|
| Kelly | **8 Sumimasen. Toranomon made ikura desu ka.** | Excuse me. How much is it to Toranomon? |

| | |
|---|---|
| **ni-ban-sen** | track No. 2 |
| **densha** | train |
| **norimasu** | to get on |
| **densha ni norimasu** | to get on the train |
| **Akasaka-mitsuke** | ⟨a place name in Tokyo⟩ |
| **norikaemasu** | to transfer |

| | | |
|---|---|---|
| Station Employee | **9 Hyakurokujuu-en desu. Ni-ban-sen de densha ni notte, Akasaka-mitsuke de norikaete kudasai.** | It's 160 yen. Please board the train at track No. 2 and transfer at Akasaka-mitsuke. |
| Kelly | **10 Doomo arigatoo.** | Thank you. |

*(on the street in Toranomon)*

| | |
|---|---|
| **hoo** | direction |
| **dochira no hoo** | which direction? |

| | | |
|---|---|---|
| Kelly | **11 Sumimasen ga, Jetoro wa dochira no hoo desu ka.** | Excuse me, but which way (lit. direction) is JETRO? |

| | |
|---|---|
| **o** | ⟨location particle⟩ |
| **tsugi** | next |
| **kado** | corner |
| **hidari** | left |
| **migi** | right |
| **magarimasu** | to turn |
| **massugu** | straight |

| | | |
|---|---|---|
| Stranger | **12 Jetoro desu ka. Kono michi o massugu itte, tsugi no kado o hidari e magatte kudasai.** | JETRO? Go straight along this street and turn left at the next corner. |

| | | |
|---|---|---|
| | **haa** | I see |
| Kelly | **13 Haa.** | I see. |
| | **tsukiatari**<br>**de**<br>**temae**<br>**biru** | end of the street<br>⟨gerund of the copula⟩<br>this side<br>building |
| Stranger | **14 Tsukiatari ga Amerika-taishikan de, Jetoro wa sono temae no hidari no biru desu yo.** | The U.S. Embassy is at the end of the street, and JETRO is the building just this way, on the left. |
| Kelly | **15 Wakarimashita. Doomo arigatoo gozaimashita.** | I see. Thank you very much. |
| Stranger | **16 Doo itashimashite.** | You're welcome. |

## ADDITIONAL VOCABULARY

| | | |
|---|---|---|
| 1 | **eki** | station |
| | **A: Tsugi no eki wa Ginza desu ka.** | Is the next stop (lit. station) Ginza? |
| | **Shinbashi**<br>**tsugi no tsugi** | ⟨a place name in Tokyo⟩<br>(one) after next |
| | **B: Iie, tsugi wa Shinbashi desu.**<br>**Ginza wa tsugi no tsugi desu yo.** | No. The next (station) is Shinbashi.<br>Ginza is the stop after next. |
| 2 | **Yokohama-iki (-yuki)**<br>**nan-ban-sen** | for Yokohama<br>what track number? |
| | **A: Yokohama-iki (-yuki) wa nan-ban-sen de norimasu ka.** | On what track can I get on (the train) for Yokohama? |

| | |
|---|---|
| **yon-ban-sen** | track No. 4 |
| **B: Yon-ban-sen desu.** | It's track No. 4. |

**3** **orimasu** — to get off

| | |
|---|---|
| **A: Doko de orimasu ka.** | Where will you get off? |

| | |
|---|---|
| **kokuden** | national railway train |
| **B: Shinjuku de orite, kokuden ni norikaemasu.** | I'll get off at Shinjuku and transfer to a national railway train. |

**4**

| | |
|---|---|
| **Shinkansen** | bullet train |
| **kippu** | ticket |
| **A: Shinkansen no kippu wa doko de kaimasu ka.** | Where can (lit. do) I buy a ticket for the *Shinkansen*? |

| | |
|---|---|
| **madoguchi** | window |
| **midori no madoguchi** | green window for reservations |
| **B: Ano midori no madoguchi desu yo.** | At the green window over there. |

**5**

| | |
|---|---|
| **Kyuushuu** | Kyushu |
| **A: Kyuushuu e nan de ikimashita ka.** | How did you go to Kyushu? |

| | |
|---|---|
| **iki** | on one's way to |
| **hikooki** | airplane |
| **hikooki ni notte ikimasu** | go by airplane (lit. by riding on) |
| **kaeri** | going home |
| **B: Iki wa hikooki ni notte ikimashita ga kaeri wa Shinkansen deshita.** | Going, I went by airplane, but I came back by *Shinkansen.* |

**6**

| | |
|---|---|
| **byooin** | hospital |
| **Tookyoo Byooin** | Tokyo Hospital |
| **kochira no hoo** | this direction |

| | |
|---|---|
| **A: Tookyoo Byooin wa kochira no hoo desu ka.** | Is the Tokyo Hospital in this direction? |

**sochira** — that one
**sochira no hoo** — that direction
**kooen** — park
**mukoo** — over there, the far side

| | |
|---|---|
| **B: Iie, chigaimasu. Sochira no hoo desu yo. Ano kooen no mukoo desu.** | No, (lit. you're wrong) it's in that direction. It's beyond that park. |

7 **yuubinkyoku** — post office

| | |
|---|---|
| **A: Sumimasen ga, kono hen ni yuubinkyoku wa arimasen ka.** | Excuse me, but isn't there a post office in this area? |

**achira** — that (one) over there
**gasorin-sutando** — gasoline station
**ushiro** — back, behind

| | |
|---|---|
| **B: Arimasu yo. Achira no gasorin-sutando no ushiro ni arimasu.** | There is. It's behind the gasoline station over there. |

8 **manshon** — apartment building (from the English word mansion)
**tatemono** — building

| | |
|---|---|
| **A: Anata no manshon wa ano shiroi tatemono desu ka.** | Is your apartment building that white building over there? |

**sono tonari** — next door
**kooban** — police box

| | |
|---|---|
| **B: Iie, sono tonari desu. Ano kooban no mae desu yo.** | No. It's next to that (building). It's in front of that police box. |

## GRAMMATICAL NOTES

**1** New use for the **TE** form

The -**te** form is also used to connect two or more sentences. As you saw in the MODEL CONVERSATION, the -**te** form combined two sentences ending with **kudasai** meaning 'please.'

separate sentences:

**Ni-ban-sen no densha ni *notte kudasai.***
"Please get on the train at track No. 2."
**Akasaka-mitsuke de *norikaete kudasai.***
"Please transfer at Akasaka-mitsuke."

combined: **Ni-ban-sen no densha *ni notte*, Akasaka-mitsuke de *norikaete kudasai.***
"Please get on the train at track No. 2 and transfer at Akasaka-mitsuke."

Other ways to combine sentences using the -**te** form:
separate sentences:

**Ashita Oosaka e Ikimasu.** "I'll go to Osaka tomorrow."
**Buraun san ni aimasu.** "I'll meet Mr. Brown."

combined: **Ashita Oosaka e *itte*, Buraun-san ni aimasu.**
"I'll go to Osaka tomorrow and meet Mr. Brown."

The -**te** form of the copula is **de**. It is also used to combine sentences.
separate sentences:

**Ano hito wa ekiin desu.** "That person is a station employee."
**Shinbashi-eki de hataraite imasu.**
"(He/she) is working at Shinbashi Station."

combined: **Ano hito wa ekiin *de*, Shinbashi-eki de hataraite imasu.**
"That person is a station employee, working at Shinbashi Station."

Note that the **de** immediately after **Shinbashi-eki** is not the -**te** form of the copula, but the location particle meaning 'at, on, or in.'

**2** Particle **DE**

Particle **de** is also used to indicate how an action takes place and means 'by means of' or 'with.'

Examples:
**Chikatetsu *de* ikimasu.** "I'll go by subway."
**Enpitsu *de* kakimashita.** "I wrote it with a pencil."
**Denwa *de* kikimashita.** "I asked by telephone."

**3** Particle **O**

Particle **o** following a location noun may be used to show where an action takes place.

Examples:
**Kono michi *o* ikimasu.** "I'll go along this street."
**Tsugi no kado *o* magarimashoo.** "Let's turn (at) the next corner."

Note that this particle **o** is different from the particle **o** indicating a direct object.

Compare: **Atarashii uchi *o* kaimashita.** "I bought a new house."(direct object)
**Go-ji ni uchi *o* demasu.** "I'll leave (from) my house." (place of an action)

**4** Particle **MADE**

When **made** follows a location noun, it means 'as far as.'

Examples: **Konban Yokohama *made* ikimasu.**
"This evening, I'll go as far as Yokohama."
**Kinoo doko *made* ikimashita ka.**
"How far (lit. as far as what place) did you go yesterday?"

Compare with particle **made** 'until' introduced in Unit 7.

**5** **KOCHIRA/SOCHIRA/ACHIRA/DOCHIRA**

In this unit, the **kochira** series is used to refer to directions:

**kochira** 'this direction'
**sochira** 'that direction'
**achira** 'that direction over there'
**dochira** 'which direction?'

This series is often followed by **no hoo** to more clearly indicate direction.

Example: **Jetoro wa kochira *(no hoo)* desu ka.** "Is JETRO in this direction?"

This is also used to indicate other meanings as well. **Kochira** may refer to 'this person' (introduced in Unit 2) and 'this side' or 'I' (introduced in Unit 10).

**6** **~NO HOO GA II**

A noun + **no hoo ga ii** is used to indicate something is better, compared to other things. **Chikatetsu no hoo ga ii desu** means "the subway is better than other transportation," while **chikatetsu ga ii desu** means "the subway is good."

**7** **ITTE KIMASU ~ ITTE (I)RASSHAI**

**Itte kimasu** is customarily used by the person who is leaving his home or office, while **Itte (i) rasshai** is used by the person remaining behind, to someone who is leaving.

## PRACTICE

**1** Usage drill

Basic Pattern: **Sumimasen. Toranomon made ikura desu ka.**
"Excuse me. How much is it to Toranomon?"

| | |
|---|---|
| **Tookyoo-eki** | **Ginza** |
| **Yokohama** | **Oosaka** |
| **Akasaka-mitsuke** | (places you would like to go) |

**2** Response drill

Pattern: Teacher: **Nan de ikimasu ka./basu/** "How will you go?"/bus/
Student: **Basu de ikimasu.** "I'll go by bus."

| | |
|---|---|
| 1) Nan de ikimashita ka./takushii/ | Takushii de ikimashita. |
| 2) Nan de kimashita ka./chikatetsu/ | Chikatetsu de kimashita. |
| 3) Kyuushuu e nan de ikimasu ka. /hikooki/ | Hikooki de ikimasu. |
| 4) Oosaka kara nan de kimasu ka. /Shinkansen/ | Shinkansen de kimasu. |
| 5) Jimusho made nan de kimashita ka. /densha/ | Densha de kimashita. |

**3** Transformation drill

Pattern: Teacher: **Basu de ikimasu.** "I'll go by bus."
Student: **Basu ni notte ikimasu.** "I'll go by (riding on the) bus."

| | |
|---|---|
| 1) Shinkansen de ikimashita. | Shinkansen ni notte ikimashita. |
| 2) Kyoo chikatetsu de kimashita. | Kyoo chikatetsu ni notte kimashita. |
| 3) Oosaka e hikooki de ikimasu. | Oosaka e hikooki ni notte ikimasu. |
| 4) Yokohama made densha de ikimasu. | Yokohama made densha ni notte ikimasu. |
| 5) Kaisha e kuruma de kimasu. | Kaisha e kuruma ni notte kimasu. |
| 6) Takushii de ikimashoo. | Takushii ni notte ikimashoo. |

**4** Response drill

Pattern: Teacher: **Sumimasen ga, Jetoro wa dochira no hoo desu ka./kochira/**
"Excuse me, but which way is JETRO?"/this way/
Student: **Jetoro desu ka. Kochira (no hoo) desu yo.**
"JETRO? It's this way (or direction)."

| | |
|---|---|
| 1) Sumimasen ga, Toranomon wa dochira no hoo desu ka./achira/ | Toranomon desu ka. Achira (no hoo) desu yo. |
| 2) Sumimasen ga, Amerika-taishikan wa dochira no hoo desu ka./sochira/ | Amerika-taishikan desu ka. Sochira (no hoo) desu yo. |
| 3) Sumimasen ga, Tookyoo Hoteru wa dochira no hoo desu ka. /kono michi no tsukiatari/ | Tookyoo Hoteru desu ka. Kono michi no tsukiatari desu yo. |
| 4) Sumimasen ga, yuubinkyoku wa dochira no hoo desu ka. /ano ginkoo no mukoo/ | Yuubinkyoku desu ka. Ano ginkoo no mukoo desu yo. |
| 5) Sumimasen ga, Tookyoo Byooin wa dochira no hoo desu ka. /tsugi no kado/ | Tookyoo Byooin desu ka. Tsugi no kado desu yo. |
| 6) Sumimasen ga, chikatetsu no eki wa dochira no hoo desu ka. /ano biru no ushiro/ | Chikatetsu no eki desu ka. Ano biru no ushiro desu yo. |

**5** Communication drill
Use the following patterns to describe the neighborhood around your office or home.

1) **Watakushi no jimusho** (or **uchi) no mae wa (　　　) desu.**
2) **Watakushi no jimusho** (or **uchi) no hidari ni (　　　) ga arimasu.**
3) **Watakushi no jimusho** (or **uchi) no migi wa (　　　) desu.**
4) **Watakushi no jimusho** (or **uchi) no ushiro ni (　　　) ga arimasu.**
5) **Watakushi no jimusho** (or **uchi) wa (　　　) no mae desu.**
6) **Watakushi no jimusho** (or **uchi) wa (　　　) no tonari ni arimasu.**

**6** Transformation drill
Pattern: Teacher: **Kono michi o itte kudasai.** "Please go along this street."
**Tsugi no kado o hidari e magatte kudasai.**
"Please turn left at the next corner."
Student: **Kono michi o itte, tsugi no kado o hidari e magatte kudasai.**
"Please go along this street and turn left at the next corner."

| | |
|---|---|
| 1) **Jetoro e itte kudasai.**<br>**Chiba-san ni atte kudasai.** | **Jetro e itte, Chiba-san ni atte kudasai.** |
| 2) **Kono densha ni notte kudasai.**<br>**Shinbashi de norikaete kudasai.** | **Kono densha ni notte,**<br>**Shinbashi de norikaete kudasai.** |
| 3) **Tsugi no nichiyoobi kaisha e kite kudasai.**<br>**Hataraite kudasai.** | **Tsugi no nichiyoobi kaisha e kite,**<br>**hataraite kudasai.** |
| 4) **Ano kado o magatte kudasai.**<br>**Tsukiatari made itte kudasai.** | **Ano kado o magatte, tsukiatari made itte kudasai.** |
| 5) **Kinoo Ginza e ikimashita.**<br>**Kaban o kaimashita.** | **Kinoo Ginza e itte, kaban o kaimashita.** |
| 6) **Shinkansen ni norimasu.**<br>**Kyuushuu e ikimasu.** | **Shinkansen ni notte, Kyuushuu e ikimasu.** |
| 7) **Ano hito ga Nakano-san desu.**<br>**Kochira ga Doi-buchoo desu.** | **Ano hito ga Nakano-san de,**<br>**kochira ga Doi-buchoo desu.** |
| 8) **Yamaguchi-san ni denwa-bangoo o kikimashita.**<br>**Nakano-san ni denwa-shimashita.** | **Yamaguchi-san ni denwa-bangoo o kiite,**<br>**Nakano-san ni denwa-shimashita.** |
| 9) **Shinbashi de chikatetsu ni norimashita.**<br>**Toranomon de orimashita.** | **Shinbashi de chikatetsu ni notte,**<br>**Toranomon de orimashita.** |

**7** Response drill
Pattern: Teacher: **Basu de ikimashoo ka. Chikatetsu de ikimashoo ka.**
"Shall we go by bus or (shall we go) by subway?"
*(Select the second choice)*
Student: **Chikatetsu no hoo ga ii desu.** "The subway is better."

| | |
|---|---|
| 1) **Ookii chizu o kaimashoo ka.**<br>**Chiisai chizu o kaimashoo ka.** | **Chiisai hoo ga ii desu.** |

**2) Tanaka-san ni kikimashoo ka.**
**Nakano-san ni kikimashoo ka.**
**Nakano-san no hoo ga ii desu.**

**3) Shinbashi de orimashoo ka.**
**Ginza de orimashoo ka.**
**Ginza no hoo ga ii desu.**

**4) Kyoo denwa-shimashoo ka.**
**Ashita denwa-shimashoo ka.**
**Ashita no hoo ga ii desu.**

**5) Koko de machimashoo ka.**
**Jimusho de machimashoo ka.**
**Jimusho no hoo ga ii desu.**

**6) Huransugo o oshiemashoo ka.**
**Eego o oshiemashoo ka.**
**Eego no hoo ga ii desu.**

## EXERCISES

**1** Study the map and answer the following questions as if you were the person in front of the hotel.

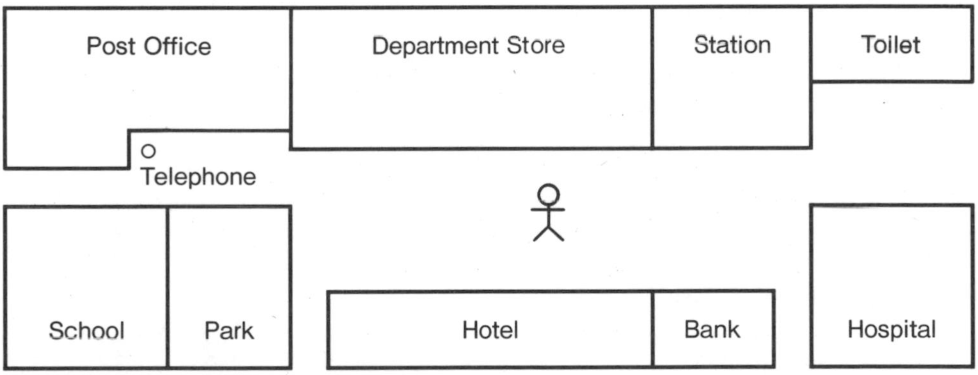


Questions:
**1) Depaato no mae ni nani ga arimasu ka.**
**2) Ginkoo no migi ni nani ga arimasu ka.**
**3) Kooen no ushiro ni nani ga arimasu ka.**
**4) Eki no hidari ni nani ga arimasu ka.**
**5) Denwa wa doko ni arimasu ka.**
**6) Ginkoo no mae wa yuubinkyoku desu ka.**
**7) Kooen wa hoteru no migi no hoo desu ka.**
**8) Byooin no hidari ni nani ga arimasu ka.**

**2** Translate the following sentences into Japanese:
1) Tom Kelly came from America by airplane last week.
2) Let's go by bus as far as Shinbashi and transfer to a national railway train.
3) Excuse me, but is that big building JETRO?

4) Tomorrow morning I'll go to Asian Electric and see Mr. Doi.
5) Please go along this street and turn (to the) right at the corner by the bank.
6) There is no subway (station) in this area, so please go by taxi.
7) Mr. Tanaka's company is in the building behind that hotel.
8) Mr. Yamaguchi bought a ticket at the green window in Tokyo Station.
9) Mr. Chiba got on the *Shinkansen* at track No. 2 and went to Kyoto.
10) I got off the train at Shinjuku and transferred to a bus.

## FOR REFERENCE

### 〔MODEL CONVERSATION〕

| | | |
|---|---|---|
| Yamaguchi | **Kerii-san, dekakemasu ka.** | ケリーさん、でかけます か。 |
| Kelly | **Ee, Jetoro de Chiba-san ni aimasu.** | ええ、ジェトロ で 千葉さん に 会います。 |
| Yamaguchi | **Nan de ikimasu ka.** | なん で 行きます か。 |
| Kelly | **Basu de ikimasu.** | バス で 行きます。 |
| Yamaguchi | **Chikatetsu no hoo ga ii desu yo. Ima, michi ga konde imasu kara...** | 地下鉄 の ほう が いい です よ。 いま、道 が 混んで います から… |
| Kelly | **Soo desu ka. Jaa, chikatetsu de ikimasu. Itte kimasu!** | そう です か。 じゃあ、地下鉄 で 行きます。 いって きます! |
| Yamaguchi | **Itte (i)rasshai!** | いって(い)らっしゃい! |
| Kelly | **Sumimasen. Toranomon made ikura desu ka.** | すみません。 虎ノ門 まで いくら です か。 |
| Station Employee | **Hyakurokujuu-en desu. Ni-ban-sen de densha ni notte, Akasaka-mitsuke de norikaete kudasai.** | 160円 です。2番線 で 電車 に 乗って、赤坂見附 で 乗り換えて ください。 |
| Kelly | **Doomo arigatoo.** | どうも ありがとう。 |
| Kelly | **Sumimasen ga, Jetoro wa dochira no hoo desu ka.** | すみません が、ジェトロ は どちら の ほう です か。 |
| Stranger | **Jetoro desu ka. Kono michi o massugu itte, tsugi no kado o hidari e magatte kudasai.** | ジェトロ です か。 この 道 を まっすぐ 行って、 次 の かど を 左 へ 曲がって ください。 |
| Kelly | **Haa.** | はあ。 |
| Stranger | **Tsukiatari ga Amerika-taishikan de, Jetoro wa sono temae no hidari no biru desu yo.** | つきあたり が アメリカ大使館 で、 ジェトロ は その 手前 の 左 の ビル です よ。 |
| Kelly | **Wakarimashita. Doomo arigatoo gozaimashita.** | わかりました。 どうも ありがとう ございました。 |
| Stranger | **Doo itashimashite.** | どう いたしまして。 |

## 〔ADDITIONAL VOCABULARY〕

**1** A: Tsugi no eki wa Ginza desu ka.
B: Iie, tsugi wa Shinbashi desu.
Ginza wa tsugi no tsugi desu yo.

次 の 駅 は 銀座 です か。
いいえ、次 は 新橋 です。
銀座 は 次 の 次 です よ。

**2** A: Yokohama-iki (-yuki) wa nan-ban-sen de norimasu ka.
B: Yon-ban-sen desu.

横浜いき(ゆき)は 何番線 で 乗ります か。
4番線 です。

**3** A: Doko de orimasu ka.
B: Shinjuku de orite, kokuden ni norikaemasu.

どこ で 降ります か。
新宿 で 降りて、 国電 に 乗り換えます。

**4** A: Shinkansen no kippu wa doko de kaimasu ka.
B: Ano midori no madoguchi desu yo.

新幹線 の 切符 は どこ で 買います か。
あの 緑 の 窓口 です よ。

**5** A: Kyuushuu e nan de ikimashita ka.
B: Iki wa hikooki ni notte ikimashita ga kaeri wa Shinkansen deshita.

九州 へ なん で 行きました か。
行き は 飛行機 に 乗って 行きました が 帰り は 新幹線 でした。

**6** A: Tookyoo Byooin wa kochira no hoo desu ka.
B: Iie, chigaimasu. Sochira no hoo desu yo. Ano kooen no mukoo desu.

東京病院 は こちら の ほう です か。
いいえ、違います。 そちら の ほう です よ。 あの 公園 の 向こう です。

**7** A: Sumimasen ga, kono hen ni yuubinkyoku wa arimasen ka.
B: Arimasu yo. Achira no gasorin-sutando no ushiro ni arimasu.

すみません が、この 辺 に 郵便局 は ありません か。
あります よ。 あちら の ガソリン スタンド の 後ろ に あります。

**8** A: Anata no manshon wa ano shiroi tatemono desu ka.
B: Iie, sono tonari desu.
Ano kooban no mae desu yo.

あなた の マンション は あの 白い 建物 です か。
いいえ、 その 隣り です。
あの 交番 の 前 です よ。

## BUSINESS COLUMN

## WELL, YES AND NO...

"Would somebody please just give me a straight answer?" If you find yourself asking this question, you won't be the first in Japan to be confronted with what seems to be a tendency to be evasive, give contradictory information and avoid the issues that a non-Japanese might consider to be the most vital. Language and culture are inseparable and much of what strikes foreigners as vague and ambiguous is built into the Japanese language. This is not a nation of wishy-washy people—as you probably realize in your calmer moments—they just have a different way of doing things.

Words as simple as 'yes' and 'no' reflect the ambiguity inherent in the Japanese language. '*Hai*' and '*ee*' take the place of 'yes' in English; however the former can take on a whole range of implied meanings depending on the context. Though it sometimes means the speaker is agreeing with what was just said, it can also merely confirm that what was said was understood, or even, "yes, I heard you what you said, but don't necessarily agree." When you suggest to your Japanese friend that he be the company representative in charge of electric toilet plunger sales, he might reply '*hai*' several times while you're speaking, only implying that the communication is getting through, not that he agrees with, or will act upon, what you're saying. Keep listening for more agreement in phrases like '*ee, soo desu ne*', if you want to be sure that your statement is finding agreement.

'No', on the other hand, is rarely heard. With a cultural tendency to avoid the confrontation suggested by a blunt and direct '*iie*', a native speaker of Japanese is much more likely to reply, 'it's different' or '*chigaimasu*', when asked if it was him that ate the egg rolls you had been saving in the refrigerator. A favorite way to say no without actually saying 'no' is to suck air in through your teeth and slowly say, "*Saa... muzukashii desu nee...*", or "Hmm... seems difficult..." This phrase is useful for a whole range of situations. Keep it handy.

In Japan, to strongly assert your opinion is to appear somewhat pushy or aggressive. In English you might say, "We should start selling our automatic navel lint removers by the first of next month", however a Japanese speaker would probably preface the statement with something like, "I'm not at all sure, but perhaps starting the sales campaign sometime next month would be a good idea." Phrases like '*to omoimasu*'—'I think', and ending statements with '*no hoo ga ii*'—'that way would be better', are common ways for the Japanese to deliberately soften the impact of what they are saying. English speakers tend to admire clear, direct speech. Japanese speakers prefer a gentler approach.

Do not confuse vagueness of speech with lack of direction or resolve. For the Japanese, a vaguer, looser style of speaking gives greater play to instinct and feeling, and may give their language a certain flexibility that others lack. In any case, you are certain to encounter times when almost nothing seems clear. Relax and try to remember that from their standpoint, your way of communication is as much a mystery.

**by Brian Smallshaw**
(Senior Editor, Tradescope)

# UNIT 12

*VISITING*

訪問

ほうもん

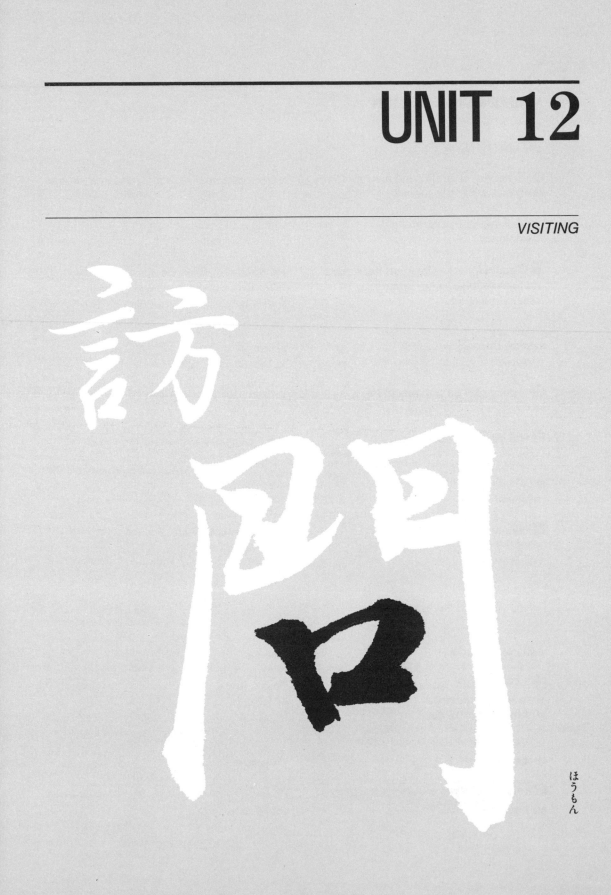

## MODEL CONVERSATION

## SITUATION

*Kelly arrives at JETRO and asks for Chiba at the reception desk. Chiba arrives and shows Kelly to a reception room.*

| | | |
|---|---|---|
| | **irasshaimasu** | to be ⟨respectful⟩ |
| Kelly | **1 Watakushi, Ajia Denki no Kerii desu. Joohoo-saabisubu no Chiba-san, irasshaimasu ka.** | I'm Kelly from Asian Electric. Is Mr. Chiba of the Information Service Department in? |
| | **yakusoku/oyakusoku** ⟨polite⟩<br>**gozaimasu** | appointment, promise<br>to have, there is ⟨polite⟩ |
| Receptionist | **2 Oyakusoku ga gozaimasu ka.** | Do you have an appointment? |
| Kelly | **3 Hai, ni-ji no yakusoku desu.** | Yes, I've an appointment at two. |
| | **sugu**<br>**mairimasu** | soon, right away<br>to come ⟨humble⟩ |
| Receptionist | **4 Shooshoo omachi kudasai.** (after telephoning) **Chiba wa sugu mairimasu.** | Just a moment please. Chiba will be right here. |

*(Chiba arrives at the reception desk)*

| | | |
|---|---|---|
| | **yoku irasshaimashita** | welcome! |
| Chiba | **5 Aa, Kerii-san desu ne? Yoku irasshaimashita. Watakushi, Chiba desu.** | Oh, Mr. Kelly? Welcome! I'm Chiba. |
| | **oisogashii tokoro** | while you're so busy |
| Kelly | **6 Kerii desu. Kyoo wa oisogashii tokoro sumimasen.** | I'm Kelly. I'm sorry (to disturb you) today, while you're so busy. |

| | | |
|---|---|---|
| | **tondemo gozaimasen** | please don't mention it. <polite> |
| Chiba | **7 Iya, tondemo gozaimasen.**<br>**Maa, kochira e doozo.** | Please don't mention it.<br>Well, please come this way. |
| Kelly | **8 Shitsuree-shimasu.** | Excuse me. |

*(in the reception room after the discussion)*

| | | |
|---|---|---|
| | **taihen** | very |
| | **sankoo** | reference |
| | **narimasu** | to become |
| | **sankoo ni narimasu** | to be of value for reference |
| Kelly | **9 Chiba-san, iroiro arigatoo gozaimashita.**<br>**Taihen sankoo ni narimashita.** | Mr. Chiba, thank you very much.<br>You've been very helpful (lit. your information is valuable for reference purposes). |
| | **orimasu** | to be, exist <for animate objects, polite> |
| Chiba | **10 Soo desu ka. Watakushi wa taitee Saabisubu ni orimasu kara, mata itsu de mo irasshatte kudasai.** | Is that so? I'm usually here at the Information Service Department, so please come (to JETRO) again any time (you need to see me). |
| | **jama** | intervention, interference |
| | **ojama-shimasu** | to interrupt, visit <humble> |
| Kelly | **11 Arigatoo gozaimasu.**<br>**Mata, ojama-shimasu.** | Thank you very much.<br>I'll come again. |
| | **omachi-shite orimasu** | to wait <polite> |
| Chiba | **12 Omachi-shite orimasu.** | I'll be waiting (for your call). |
| | **kore de** | with this, now |
| Kelly | **13 De wa, kyoo wa kore de shitsuree-shimasu.** | Well, (as for) today I'll leave now. |

**yoroshiku** — to say hello (to), give my best regards (to)

Chiba 14 **Soo desu ka. De wa, Yamaguchi-san ni yoroshiku.** — Is that so? Well, please give my regards to Mr. Yamaguchi.

**itashimasu** — to do 〈humble〉

Kelly 15 **Shoochi-itashimashita.** — (Yes,) I will (lit. I understand).

Chiba 16 **De wa, doozo kochira e.** — Well, please (come) this way.

## ADDITIONAL VOCABULARY

1 **uketsuke** — reception area (or desk)

**A: Sumimasen ga, uketsuke wa dochira desu ka.** — Excuse me, but where is the reception desk?

**genkan** — entrance
**migi-gawa** — right side

**B: Genkan no migi-gawa desu yo.** — It's to the right of the entrance.

2 *(a visitor at the reception desk)*

**yoo/goyoo** 〈polite〉 — business affairs

Receptionist **Nani ka goyoo deshoo ka.** — May I help you? (lit. What is your business?)

**Oosaka Kookoku** — Osaka Advertising Co.
**Nakamura-san no shookai de** — through the introduction of Mr. Nakamura

Kimura **Watakushi, Oosaka Kookoku no Kimura desu. Chiyoda Kookoku no Nakamura-san no shookai de ukagaimashita. Koohoobu no Yamaguchi-san wa irasshaimasu ka.** — I'm Kimura from Osaka Ad Co. I came through an introduction by Mr. Nakamura of Chiyoda Advertising Co. Is Mr. Yamaguchi of the P.R. Department in?

| | | |
|---|---|---|
| | **Yamaguchi de gozaimasu ka** | is it Yamaguchi? |
| | **gaishutsu-shimasu** | to be out |
| Receptionist | **Yamaguchi de gozaimasu ka. Tadaima gaishutsu-shite orimasu ga...** | Yamaguchi? He is out now. |

| | | |
|---|---|---|
| | **donata** | who? 〈polite〉 |
| | **donata ka** | someone/anyone 〈polite〉 |
| | **kata** | person 〈polite〉 |
| | **de kekkoo desu** | would be fine |
| Kimura | **Jaa, donata ka onaji ka no kata de kekkoo desu ga...** | Then, anyone from the same section will be fine, but... |
| Receptionist | **Shooshoo omachi kudasai.** | Just a moment please. |

| | | |
|---|---|---|
| **3** | **ocha** | tea |
| Host | **Ocha wa ikaga desu ka.** | Would you care for some tea? (lit. How about some tea?) |

| | | |
|---|---|---|
| | **iie, kekkoo desu** | no thank you |
| | **okamai-naku** | don't trouble yourself |
| Guest | **Iie, kekkoo desu. Doozo okamai-naku.** | No thank you. Please don't trouble yourself. |

## GRAMMATICAL NOTES

**1** Japanese speech levels

In Japanese there are several different levels of speech, each used for different social occasions.

1) Ordinary

This is the general category used in Japanese society and is often referred to as the **desu/masu** level. Up until now you have been studying this level, which is ordinarily used for talking with people you don't know well, or on formal occasions with those you do. This would be the proper level for ordinary business conversations.

2) Formal
This level is for addressing superiors, respected seniors and business clients. The MODEL CONVERSATION in this unit introduces this level of speech.
It is helpful even for foreign businessmen to learn to use this level correctly for establishing good relations with Japanese counterparts. Details will be discussed in the following section of GRAMMATICAL NOTES.

3) Informal
This level is used for addressing subordinates, young people and intimate friends and will be introduced in detail in a later section. It is recommended that this level be learned initially for comprehension only. Used improperly, this level may unintentionally be offensive. It is used generally for communications between members of the family, colleagues, and close friends. However, intonation clearly differs between these situations and when addressing subordinates.

**2** Formal
This level is divided into three categories:

1) Respectful or honorific expressions
Used to express respect by elevating the relative status of the listener above your own. **Irasshaimasu** 'to be, come or go' belongs in this division.

2) Modest or humble expressions
For referring to yourself or to members of your group when speaking with outsiders. In the MODEL CONVERSATION the receptionist uses this kind of expression in referring to Mr. Chiba, her superior at JETRO. In **Chiba wa sugu mairimasu** "Chiba is coming soon" she omits the honorific -**san** and uses the humble verb **mairimasu** 'to come or go.' This is because Chiba is within her group and Kelly is an outsider.

**Orimasu** an equivalent of **imasu** 'to be' is also used in the pattern of 'verb gerund + **imasu** to express humbleness by the speaker.
Example: **Omachi-shite *orimasu.*** (Sentence 12, MODEL CONVERSATION)
"I'll be expecting you. ( lit. I'm waiting for you.)"

3) Polite Expressions
There are a number of ways to express things more politely. For example, **kashi** 'cake, candy, sweets' is often expressed with the polite prefix **o** as **okashi**.
This is a polite way to say cake and does not necessarily express respect for the listener. (Note 5 of this unit.) **Gozaimasu** is a polite equivalent for **arimasu** 'to be, have.' The copula gerund, **de** + **gozaimasu** is used as the polite equivalent of copula **desu**. The polite equivalent of a negative copula (i.e. **ja arimasen**) is **de wa gozaimasen**. Remember that the particle **wa** always occurs between **de** and **gozaimasen**.

Compare: **Are ga wagasha no jimusho *de gozaimasu.*** "That is our company's office."
**Yamaguchi wa kachoo *de wa gozaimasen.*** "Yamaguchi is not the manager."

Carefully study the following chart:

| ORDINARY | FORMAL | | |
|---|---|---|---|
| | Respectful | Humble | Polite |
| **imasu** 'be' | **irasshaimasu** | **orimasu** | |
| **ikimasu** 'go' | **irasshaimasu** | **mairimasu**<br>**ukagaimasu** | |
| **kimasu** 'come' | **irasshaimasu** | **mairimasu**<br>**ukagaimasu** | |
| **arimasu** 'be, have' | | | **gozaimasu** |
| **desu** 'be' | | | **de gozaimasu** |

Note that the verb **ukagaimasu** 'to visit' is also a modest or humble verb, and is used in referring to the speaker or the speaker's group visiting the listener. **Mairimasu** conveys visiting someone of respect.

Compare: **Ashita otaku e *ukagaimasu*** (or ***mairimasu***).
"I'll go to your house tomorrow."
**Ashita shachoo no otaku e *mairimasu* kara, asatte *ukagaimasu.***
"I'll go to the president's house tomorrow, so I'll call (on you) the day after tomorrow."

### 3 ~NI NARIMASU

A noun + **ni narimasu** usually means 'become~' or 'get to be~.'

Examples: **Doi-san ga buchoo *ni narimashita.*** "Mr. Doi became a general manager."
**Ano tatemono wa ginkoo *ni narimasu*.** "That building will be a bank."
**Moo go-ji *ni narimashita* yo.** "It's already five o'clock."

**Sankoo ni narimashita** in the MODEL CONVERSATION of this unit literally means 'became a reference', but here it means '(the information given by Chiba) was of value for reference.'

### 4 KEKKOO

**Kekkoo** basically means 'good, fine, nice', but it can also be used to convey other meanings as well:

1) **DE KEKKOO DESU**

A noun + **de kekkoo desu** is used to mean 'it will be fine if it's (noun).'

Example: *(at a Japanese restaurant)*

Diner: **Wain, onegai-shimasu.** "I'd like wine."

Waitress: **Sumimasen. Wain wa arimasen. Biiru wa ikaga desu ka.** "I'm sorry, we have no wine. How about beer."

Diner: **Jaa, biiru *de kekkoo desu.*** "Well, beer will have to do."

Note that **biiru de kekkoo desu** implies that beer is acceptable but not the desired selection. ~**De ii desu** is also used for similar situaition.

2) **IIE, KEKKOO DESU**

This is commonly used to politely refuse something.

Examples: A: **Koohii, ikaga desu ka.** "Would you care for coffee?"

B: ***Iie, kekkoo desu.*** "No, thank you."

A: **Hoteru made annai-shimashoo ka.** "Shall I take you to the hotel?"

B: ***Iie, kekkoo desu.*** "No, thank you."

**5** Polite prefix **O**

A prefix **o** occurs directly before a noun, adjective or verb stem (an ordinary verb minus -**masu**; **machimasu**-**masu** = **machi**) and conveys politeness or respect.

| | |
|---|---|
| **yakusoku** 'appointment' | **oyakusoku** ⟨respectful⟩ |
| **isogashii** 'busy' | **oisogashii** ⟨polite⟩ |
| **matte kudasai.** "Please wait." | **omachi kudasai.** ⟨respectful⟩ |
| ⟨Gerund + **kudasai**⟩ | ⟨**o** + stem + **kudasai**⟩ |

**O** often makes the following word polite but not necessarily respectful.
This is especially common for feminine expressions.

| Example: | | |
|---|---|---|
| | **kusuri** 'medicine' | ***o*kusuri** ⟨polite⟩ |
| | **niku** 'meat' | ***o*niku** ⟨polite⟩ |
| | **denwa** 'telephone' | ***o*denwa** ⟨polite⟩ |

Note that **ogenki** 'well, fine' introduced in Unit 2, **onegai** 'request,' in Unit 10 and **osewa** 'trouble,' in Unit 7 use this prefix plus a noun or verb stem. For adjectives, **oisogashii** was introduced in this unit.

**6** **(X-san) NI YOROSHIKU**

This is a popular expression for having someone convey the speaker's regards to others.

Examples: ***Nakamura-san ni yoroshiku.***

"Please give my best regards to Mr. Nakamura."

**Shisha no *minasan ni yoroshiku.***

"Say hello to everyone at the branch office."

Note also that **yoroshiku** (or **doozo yoroshiku**) without ⟨**X-san**⟩ **ni** is used for meeting someone for the first time and means "Nice to meet you."

**7** **DE** in **(X-san) NO SHOOKAI DE**

**De** is a particle meaning 'by means of' introduced in Unit 11 and literally means '(to come) by means of someone's introduction'.

## PRACTICE

**1** Level drill (ordinary to polite; **arimasu** to **gozaimasu**)

Example: Teacher: **Yakusoku ga arimasu ka.** "Do you have an appointment?"
Student: **(O) yakusoku ga gozaimasu ka.** "Do you have an appointment?"

| | |
|---|---|
| **1) Denwa wa tonari no heya ni arimasu.** | **Denwa wa tonari no heya ni gozaimasu.** |
| **2) Tookyoo no chizu wa arimasen.** | **Tookyoo no chizu wa gozaimasen.** |
| **3) Shisha wa Nyuuyooku ni arimasu.** | **Shisha wa Nyuuyooku ni gozaimasu.** |
| **4) Meeshi ga arimasu ka.** | **(O) meeshi ga gozaimasu ka.** |

**2** Level drill (ordinary to polite; **desu** to de **gozaimasu**)

Example: Teacher: **Watakushi no meeshi desu.** "(This is) my business card."
Student: **Watakushi no meeshi de gozaimasu.** "(This is) my business card."

| | |
|---|---|
| **1) Watakushi wa Buraun desu.** | **Watakushi wa Buraun de gozaimasu.** |
| **2) Yakusoku no jikan wa nan-ji desu ka.** | **(O) yakusoku no jikan wa nan-ji de gozaimasu ka.** |
| **3) Daigaku wa Haabaado ja arimasen deshita.** | **Daigaku wa Haabaado de wa gozaimasen deshita.** |
| **4) Kerii wa eegyoobu ja arimasen.** | **Kerii wa eegyoobu de wa gozaimasen.** |

**3** Level drill (ordinary to respectful/honorific)

Example: Teacher: **Chiba-san wa imasu ka.** "Is Mr. Chiba in?"
Student: **Chiba-san wa irasshaimasu ka.** "Is Mr. Chiba in?"

| | |
|---|---|
| **1) Nakamura-shachoo ga kimashita.** | **Nakamura-shachoo ga irasshaimashita.** |
| **2) Kyoo wa doko e ikimasu ka.** | **Kyoo wa dochira e irasshaimasu ka.** |
| **3) Nakano-san wa Amerika e ikimasu.** | **Nakano-san wa Amerika e irasshaimasu.** |
| **4) Ashita nan-ji ni kimasu ka.** | **Ashita nan-ji ni irasshaimasu ka.** |
| **5) Ima Tanaka-san wa imasen yo.** | **Ima Tanaka-san wa irasshaimasen yo.** |
| **6) Buchoo wa kyoo kaisha e kimasen.** | **Buchoo wa kyoo kaisha e irasshaimasen.** |
| **7) Shachoo wa kinoo no paatii e ikimasen deshita.** | **Shachoo wa kinoo no paatii e irasshaimasen deshita.** |
| **8) Doyoobi wa otaku ni imasen ka.** | **Doyoobi wa otaku ni irasshaimasen ka.** |

**4** Level drill (ordinary to modest/humble)

Example: Teacher: **Kyoo Oosaka e ikimasu.** "I'm going to Osaka today."
Student: **Kyoo Oosaka e mairimasu.** "I'm going to Osaka today."

| | |
|---|---|
| **1) Ashita mata kimasu.** | **Ashita mata mairimasu/ukagaimasu.*** |
| **2) Sengetsu Nihon e kimashita.** | **Sengetsu Nihon e mairimashita.** |
| **3) Ni-ji made ni ikimasu.** | **Ni-ji made ni mairimasu/ukagaimasu.*** |
| **4) Go-ji made kaisha ni imasu.** | **Go-ji made kaisha ni orimasu.** |
| **5) Konban no paatii e (wa) ikimasen.** | **Konban no paatii e (wa) mairimasen/ukagaimasen.*** |

| | |
|---|---|
| 6) **Itsu jimusho e ikimashoo ka.** | **Itsu jimusho e mairimashoo/ ukagaimashoo* ka.** |
| 7) **Shinkansen de kimashita.** | **Shinkansen de mairimashita.** |
| 8) **Kinoo wa ichi-nichi kaisha ni imashita.** | **Kinoo wa ichi-nichi kaisha ni orimashita.** |

*Either **mairimasu** or **ukagaimasu** may be used depending on the situation.

**5** Response drill (ordinary levels for questions, respectful or modest levels for replies).
Example: Teacher: **Buchoo wa doko ni imasu ka./yakuin-shokudoo/**
"Where is the general manager?"/executive dining room/
Student: **Yakuin-shokudoo ni irasshaimasu.**
"He's in the executive dining room."

| | |
|---|---|
| 1) **Kerii-san wa nan-ji ni kimasu ka. /san-ji goro/** | **San-ji goro irasshaimasu.** |
| 2) **Ashita dare ga Oosaka e ikimasu ka. /watakushi/** | **Watakushi ga mairimasu.** |
| 3) **Kachoo wa itsu Amerika e ikimasu ka. /mokuyoobi/** | **Mokuyoobi ni irasshaimasu.** |
| 4) **Nan-ji made jimusho ni imasu ka. /taitee roku-ji/** | **Taitee roku-ji made orimasu.** |
| 5) **Itsu Nihon e kimashita ka./senshuu/** | **Senshuu mairimashita.** |
| 6) **Ashita dare ga kimasu ka. /Nakamura-shachoo/** | **Nakamura-shachoo ga irasshaimasu.** |
| 7) **Ima koohoobu ni dare ga imasu ka. /Doi-buchoo/** | **Doi-buchoo ga irasshaimasu.** |
| 8) **Dare ga paatii e kimasen deshita ka. /Yamaguchi-san/** | **Yamaguchi-san ga irasshaimasen deshita.** |
| 9) **Nichiyoobi ni doko e ikimashita ka. /Ginza/** | **Ginza e mairimashita.** |
| 10) **Tanaka-san wa nan-ji ni kimashita ka. /san-ji sugi/** | **San-ji sugi ni irasshaimashita.** |

**6** Transformation drill (ordinary to humble)
Example: Teacher: **Ima hookoku o kaite imasu.** "Now I'm writing a report."
Student: **Ima hookoku o kaite orimasu.** "Now I'm writing a report."

| | |
|---|---|
| 1) **Eegyoobu no shigoto o shite imasu.** | **Eegyoobu no shigoto o shite orimasu.** |
| 2) **Ima buchoo o matte imasu.** | **Ima buchoo o matte orimasu.** |
| 3) **Kerii wa Amerika e kaette imasu.** | **Kerii wa Amerika e kaette orimasu.*** |
| 4) **Yunyuu no deeta o mite imasu.** | **Yunyuu no deeta o mite orimasu.** |
| 5) **Senshuu made ginkoo de hataraite imashita.** | **Senshuu made ginkoo de hataraite orimashita.** |

*This sentence implies Kelly belongs to the speaker's group.

**7** Communication drill
Practice formal levels of speech using the following patterns:

**Watakushi wa** (your company) **no** (your name) **de gozaimasu.**
**Honsha wa** (place name) **ni gozaimasu.**
**Shisha wa** (place name) **ya** (place name) **ni gozaimasu.**
**Shachoo wa** (full name) **de gozaimasu.**
**Watakushi wa** (year and month) **kara kono kaisha de hataraite orimasu.**
(Year, month and date) **ni Nihon e mairimashita.**
(Year and month) **goro made Nihon ni orimasu.**

**8** Usage drill
Practice making sentences using the following pattern.
Basic pattern: **Kono hon wa sankoo ni narimashita.**
"This book was valuable for reference."

| | |
|---|---|
| **Doi-san** | **buchoo** |
| **Ano biru** | **byooin** |
| **Tanaka-san** | **genki** |
| **Kimura-san** | **ekiin** |
| **Nakano-san** | **bosu** |
| **tsugi no shigoto** | **eegyoo** |

**9** Transformation drill (positive preference to passive acceptance)
Example: Teacher: **Biiru ga ii desu.**"Beer would be fine."
Student: **Biiru de kekkoo desu.** "Beer will have to do."

| | |
|---|---|
| **1) Nichiyoobi ga ii desu.** | **Nichiyoobi de kekkoo desu.** |
| **2) Kono hoteru ga ii desu.** | **Kono hoteru de kekkoo desu.** |
| **3) Takushii ga ii desu.** | **Takushii de kekkoo desu.** |
| **4) Go-ji han ga ii desu.** | **Go-ji han de kekkoo desu.** |
| **5) Kono jisho ga ii desu.** | **Kono jisho de kekkoo desu.** |
| **6) Nakano-san ga ii desu.** | **Nakano-san de kekkoo desu.** |

**10** Response drill
Example: Teacher: **Machimashoo ka.** "Shall I wait?"
Student: **Ee, omachi kudasai.** "Yes, please wait."

| | |
|---|---|
| **1) Kore o kaimashoo ka.** | **Ee, okai kudasai.** |
| **2) Buchoo ni kikimashoo ka.** | **Ee, okiki kudasai.** |
| **3) Shiryoo o misemashoo ka.** | **Ee, omise kudasai.** |
| **4) Tsugi no eki de norikaemashoo ka.** | **Ee, onorikae kudasai.** |
| **5) Shachoo ni aimashoo ka.** | **Ee, oai kudasai.** |

## EXERCISES

**1** Give the appropriate polite expression for the following situations:

| As a host or hostess: | As a guest: |
|---|---|
| 1) Welcome Mr. Chiba to your office. | Apologize to your host for visiting while he/she is busy. |
| 2) Tell someone to come this way. | Thank him or her. |
| 3) Ask if Mr. Chiba would like coffee. | Refuse coffee (politely). |
| 4) Ask if someone would like tea. | Thank him or her. |

**2** Translate the following sentences into Japanese:

1) My office is in Ginza and my house is in Shibuya. (use the gerund **de**)
2) I don't have an appointment, but is the general manager in? (humble)
3) I'll call at your company by 10:30 tomorrow morning. (humble)
4) President Nakamura went to New York last week. (respectful)
5) How long were you in England? (respectful)
6) I was in London for about three years. (humble)
7) I was working at a Japanese bank in London. (humble)
8) Mr. Tanaka came to my office by introduction from Mr. Chiba. (respectful)
9) Please give my best regards to General Manager Doi.
10) Mr. Yamaguchi's report was very instructive.

## FOR REFERENCE

### 〔MODEL CONVERSATION〕

| | | |
|---|---|---|
| Kelly | **Watakushi, Ajia Denki no Kerii desu. Joohoo-saabisubu no Chiba-san, irasshaimasu ka.** | わたくし、アジア 電機 の ケリー です。 情報サービス部 の 千葉さん、いらっしゃいます か。 |
| Receptionist | **Oyakusoku ga gozaimasu ka.** | お約束 が ございます か。 |
| Kelly | **Hai, ni-ji no yakusoku desu.** | はい、2時 の 約束 です。 |
| Receptionist | **Shooshoo omachi kudasai. Chiba wa sugu mairimasu.** | 少々 お待ちください。 千葉 は すぐ まいります。 |
| Chiba | **Aa, Kerii-san desu ne? Yoku irasshaimashita. Watakushi, Chiba desu.** | ああ、ケリーさん です ね? よく いらっしゃいました。 わたくし、千葉 です。 |
| Kelly | **Kerii desu. Kyoo wa oisogashii tokoro sumimasen.** | ケリー です。 今日 は お忙しい ところ すみません。 |
| Chiba | **Iya, tondemo gozaimasen. Maa, kochira e doozo.** | いや、とんでも ございません。 まあ、こちら へ どうぞ。 |

| | | |
|---|---|---|
| Kelly | **Shitsuree-shimasu.** | 失礼します。 |
| Kelly | **Chiba-san, iroiro arigatoo gozaimashita. Taihen sankoo ni narimashita.** | 千葉さん、いろいろ ありがとう ございました。 たいへん 参考 に なりました。 |
| Chiba | **Soo desu ka. Watakushi wa taitee saabisubu ni orimasu kara, mata itsu de mo irasshatte kudasai.** | そう です か。 わたくし は たいてい サービス部 に おります から、また いつ で も いらっしゃって ください。 |
| Kelly | **Arigatoo gozaimasu. Mata, ojama-shimasu.** | ありがとう ございます。 また、おじゃまします。 |
| Chiba | **Omachi-shite orimasu.** | お待ちして おります。 |
| Kelly | **De wa, kyoo wa kore de shitsuree-shimasu.** | で は、今日 は これ で 失礼します。 |
| Chiba | **Soo desu ka. De wa, Yamaguchi-san ni yoroshiku.** | そう です か。で は、山口さん に よろしく。 |
| Kelly | **Shoochi-itashimashita.** | 承知いたしました。 |
| Chiba | **De wa, doozo kochira e.** | で は、どうぞ こちら へ。 |

## 〔ADDITIONAL VOCABULARY〕

**1**

| | | |
|---|---|---|
| | **A: Sumimasen ga, uketsuke wa dochira desu ka.** | すみません が、受付 は どちら です か。 |
| | **B: Genkan no migi-gawa desu yo.** | 玄関 の 右側 です よ。 |

**2**

| | | |
|---|---|---|
| Receptionist | **Nani ka goyoo deshoo ka.** | 何 か ご用 でしょう か。 |
| Kimura | **Watakushi, Oosaka Kookoku no Kimura desu. Chiyoda Kookoku no Nakamura-san no shookai de ukagaimashita. Koohoobu no Yamaguchi-san wa irasshaimasu ka.** | わたくし、大阪 広告 の 木村 です。 千代田 広告 の 中村さん の 紹介 で うかがいました。 広報部 の 山口さん は いらっしゃいます か。 |
| Receptionist | **Yamaguchi de gozaimasu ka. Tadaima gaishutsu-shite orimasu ga...** | 山口 で ございます か。 ただいま 外出して おります が… |
| Kimura | **Jaa, donata ka onaji ka no kata de kekkoo desu ga...** | じゃあ、どなた か おなじ 課 の かた で 結構 です が… |
| Receptionist | **Shooshoo omachi kudasai.** | 少々 お待ち ください。 |

**3**

| | | |
|---|---|---|
| Host | **Ocha wa ikaga desu ka.** | お茶 は いかが です か。 |
| Guest | **Iie, kekkoo desu. Doozo okamai-naku.** | いいえ、結構 です。 どうぞ おかまいなく。 |

## BUSINESS COLUMN

## "ZANGYOO": OBLIGATORY OVERTIME

The Japanese are famous, or perhaps infamous, as hard workers. The shop floor in a Japanese factory is buzzing with continual motion as workers go about their tasks. In department stores, a simple request may lead to a chain reaction of activity as it moves through different departments, until the desired item is finally located. And it is not unusual to see people on the streets running to their appointments.

It is not surprising, therefore, that overtime is an important part of white-collar life in Japan. However, the significance of overtime goes beyond simply hard work, for its prevalence says much about the important role that the company plays in organizing the lives of its employees. During the week, company employees consider all their time to be that of the company.

Pay is not the main reason for working overtime. Nor even is the need to finish one's own work necessarily the motivation. Instead, it reflects the need to show commitment to one's own work group and to the company as a whole. Most white collar workers, as with their blue collar counterparts, are organized into work teams. These teams are charged with collective responsibility of carrying out various functions. Where others within one's own group need to stay late to complete a project, oftentimes the whole group stays late. If no work is being done by some members, they punch out so they are not getting paid for remaining in the office. But they stay around to indicate symbolically their affiliation with the others who must stay. When the last work is finally completed—sometimes not until 9 or 10 o'clock—all work group members may go out together for drinks and food before making the long commute home.

This shows basic differences in how work is viewed in Japan and in the West. Rather than merely reflecting a set of functions and tasks that must be completed work is a social commitment to the company and to one's co-workers. Ironically, this means that employees may be in the office or at their desk, but not doing anything. It is not unusual in a Japanese office to see employees even in the middle of the day reading newspapers or drinking tea while chatting with co-workers over nothing in particular. While this may strike Westerners as a waste of employee time, and a paradox given the vaunted efficiency of the Japanese firm, it should be understood that the company and the work team, rather than the job itself, plays a central role for the Japanese employee.

Since the mid-1970's, there has been a trend toward shorter working hours and less overtime. Honda Motors, for example, now has a policy stating that all employees at the head office must leave by 5:30 on Wednesdays and days before holidays. Additionally, Japanese officials now talk about the 'leisure revolution' and the need to improve office efficiency if this is to come about. Whether this revolution actually materializes will depend on the extent to which employees' views of the company change. As long as the company is primary, staying in the office late will remain common and leisure will be secondary.

**by Michael Gerlach**

(Assistant Professor of Business Administration, University of California at Berkeley)

# UNIT 13

*REPORT*

報告

ほうこく

## MODEL CONVERSATION

## SITUATION

*When Kelly returns from JETRO, he sees General Manager Doi and they discuss the visit.*

| | | |
|---|---|---|
| | **tadaima** | hello, I'm back |
| Kelly | **1 Tadaima.** | I'm back. |
| | **okaerinasai** | welcome back |
| Yamaguchi | **2 Okaerinasai, Kerii-san. Gokuroosama.** | Hello Mr. Kelly, thanks for your trouble. |
| | **to** | 〈quotative particle〉 |
| | **iimasu** | to say |
| | **yoroshiku to iimasu** | to say hello |
| Kelly | **3 Chiba-san ga yoroshiku to itte imashita.** | Mr. Chiba sends his regards.(lit. Mr. Chiba said to tell you hello.) |
| | **yobimasu** | to call, wish to see |
| Yamaguchi | **4 Soo desu ka. Aa, Kerii-san, buchoo ga yonde imashita yo.** | Is that so? Oh, Mr. Kelly, the general manager wants to see you. (lit. the general manager was calling you.) |
| | **itte mimasu** | to go and see, try to go |
| Kelly | **5 Soo desu ka. Sugu itte mimasu.** | Is that so? I'll go and see him right now. |

*(at the general manager's desk)*

| | | |
|---|---|---|
| | **oyobi** | wanting to see someone |
| | **oyobi desu** | to want to see someone |
| Kelly | **6 Buchoo, oyobi deshita ka.** | General manager, did you want to see me? |
| Doi | **7 Aa, Kerii-san, Jetoro wa doo deshita?** | Oh, Mr. Kelly, how was JETRO? |

| | | |
|---|---|---|
| | **iroiro /na/** | various |
| | **moraimasu** | to receive |
| Kelly | **8 Joohoo-saabisubu no Chiba-san kara iroiro na shiryoo o moraimashita.** | I received various material from Mr. Chiba of the Information Service Department. |
| | **yokatta** | was good 〈past adjective〉 |
| | **ii hito deshoo?** | (he) is a good person, isn't he? |
| Doi | **9 Sore wa yokatta desu nee. Chiba-san wa ii hito deshoo?** | That's (lit. was) good! Mr. Chiba is a good person, isn't he? |
| | **shinsetsu /na/** | kind, kind hearted |
| Kelly | **10 Hai, taihen shinsetsu na kata deshita.** | Yes, he is (lit. was) a very kind person. |
| | **donna koto** | what kind of things? |
| | **shirabemasu** | to check, investigate, study |
| Doi | **11 Jetoro de donna koto o shirabemashita ka.** | What were you looking for at JETRO? (lit. What kind of things were you checking?) |
| | **aishii** | IC, integrated circuit |
| Kelly | **12 Aishii no yushutsu ni tsuite shirabemashita.** | I was looking for information on IC exports. |
| Doi | **13 Soo desu ka.** | Is that so? |
| | **shijoo** | market |
| | **yushutsu-shijoo** | export market |
| | **hookoku** | report |
| Kelly | **14 Ato de, aishii no yushutsu-shijoo ni tsuite hookoku o kakimasu.** | I 'm going to (lit. later) write a report on the IC export market. |
| Doi | **15 Sore wa ii desu ga, yunyuu ni tsuite mo kaite kudasai.** | That's good. Please write about (IC) imports also. |

| | | |
|---|---|---|
| | **dandan** | gradually |
| | **huemasu** | to increase |
| Kelly | **16 Soo desu ne. Chiba-san mo aishii no yunyuu wa dandan huete imasu to itte imashita.** | That's right. Mr. Chiba also said IC imports are gradually increasing. |
| | **sonna koto** | such things |
| | **kaite mimasu** | to try to write |
| | **hookokusho** | a (written) report |
| | **yomimasu** | to read |
| Doi | **17 Jaa, sonna koto ni tsuite mo hookokusho ni kaite mite kudasai. Ato de yomimasu kara.** | Well, please write about that also. (lit. Please try to write about such things as that in the report also.) I'll read it later. |
| Kelly | **18 Kashikomarimashita.** | Certainly. |

## ADDITIONAL VOCABULARY

| | | |
|---|---|---|
| 1 | **hanashi** | story, news, talk |
| | **kikimasu** | to hear |
| | **A: Sono hanashi wa dare kara kikimashita ka.** | From whom did you hear that news? |
| | **shiriai** | acquaintance |
| | **hanashimasu** | to talk, tell |
| | **B: Ginkoo no shiriai ga hanashite imashita.** | A bank acquaintance told me. |
| | **hookoku-shimasu** | to report |
| | **A: Soo desu ka. Jaa, sugu kachoo ni hookoku-shimashoo.** | Is that right? Let's tell (lit. report it to) the manager right away. |

| | |
|---|---|
| **2** konna | this kind of |
| techoo | notebook |
| benri/na/ | easy-to-use, convenient, handy |
| urimasu | to sell |

| | |
|---|---|
| **A: Konna techoo wa benri desu nee. Doko de utte imasu ka.** | This kind of notebook is easy-to-use, isn 't it? Where (are they) selling? |

| | |
|---|---|
| kuremasu | to give (to the speaker) |

| | |
|---|---|
| **B: Depaato de utte imasu ga, kore wa shiriai ga kuremashita.** | (They are) selling at department stores, but an acquaintance gave me this one. |

| | |
|---|---|
| **3** anna | that kind of... over there |
| gaisha | foreign cars |
| zuibun | very |

| | |
|---|---|
| **A: Anna gaisha wa zuibun takai deshoo?** | Those kind of foreign cars are very expensive, aren't they? |

| | |
|---|---|
| mae wa | formerly |
| sonna ni | so, that much |

| | |
|---|---|
| **B: Mae wa zuibun takakatta desu ga, ima wa sonna ni takaku arimasen yo.** | They used to be very expensive but now not so much. (lit. aren't so expensive) |

| | |
|---|---|
| **4** katarogu | catalog |

| | |
|---|---|
| **A: Kono katarogu wa mada arimasu ka.** | Do you still have this catalog? |

| | |
|---|---|
| agemasu | to give (to someone) |
| herimasu | to decrease |

| | |
|---|---|
| **B: Ee, mada arimasu ga, iroiro na kata ni agemashita kara, zuibun herimashita.** | Yes, We do, ( lit. have) but we gave so many away there's hardly any left. ( lit. gave them to various people so the number has decreased.) |

## GRAMMATICAL NOTES

**1** **~TO IIMASU** 'to say that~'

Particle **to** is quotative and indicates the preceding word or phrase is a quotation. The name of the person being quoted usually occurs before the quotation as the topic or subject of the sentence.

| Person being quoted | Quotation | Quotative + **iimasu** |
|---|---|---|
| **Doi-san wa/ga** | **sore wa yokkatta** | ***to iimashita.*** |
| | Mr. Doi said that was good. | |

Examples: **Chiba-san wa Yamaguchi-san ni yoroshiku *to iimashita.***
"Mr. Chiba said please remember him to Mr. Yamaguchi."
**Kachoo wa takai *to iimashita.***
"The manager said (it)'s expensive."
**Nakano-san wa ashita denwa-shite kudasai *to iimashita.***
"Mr. Nakano told (me) to telephone (him) tomorrow."

The person's name who receives the information usually appears before the particle ***ni*** :
**Watakushi wa Kerii-san *ni* sore wa dame desu to iimasu.**
"I'll tell Mr. Kelly that it's no good."
In colloquial speech, **tte** is often used instead of the quotative **to**.
**Omoshiroi tte iimashita.** "(He) said it's interesting."
**To itte imashita** literally means '(someone) was saying,' but it is often used to indicate the past as illustrated in Sentence 3 and 16 of the MODEL CONVERSATION.
Note that when **~to iimasu** occurs directly after ordinary forms of verbs, adjectives or the copula, it is regarded as a direct quotation. However, when an informal verb, adjective or copula, discussed in Unit 17, is followed by this combination **~to iimasu**, it can be considered an indirect quotation in English.

**2** **NA** Nouns

Among Japanese nouns, there is a special group called **na** nouns. These are followed by **na**, when they modify another noun:

| | |
|---|---|
| **shinsetsu *na* hito** | 'kind person' |
| **genki *na* hito** | 'healthy person ' |
| **dame *na* hito** | 'useless person (lit. bad person)' |
| **benri *na* techoo** | 'handy notebook ' |
| **kaiteki *na* ryokoo** | 'pleasant trip' |
| **iroiro *na* shiryoo*** | 'various data ' |

***Iroiro** is a **na** noun, but it can sometimes occur with the particle **no**.
Hereafter all **na** nouns will be indicated by the sign/**na**/as they are introduced.

**3** Gerund + **MIMASU**

A verb gerund + **mimasu** means 'to do and see (or find out)' or 'to try doing'

Examples: **Ashita Yokohama no koojoo e itte *mimasu.***
"I'll go and see the Yokohama factory tomorrow."
**Denki-seehin no shijoo shirabete o*mimashita.***
"I tried to investigate the electrical appliance market.
**Ano hito ni michi o kiite *mimashoo.***
"Let's try and ask that person the way."

**4 DESHOO?**

**Deshoo** was introduced in Unit 7 with the meaning, 'maybe.' But when it occurs with a question-mark intonation, it becomes a question that anticipates agreement from the listener, much like the sentence particle **ne?**

Examples: **Chiba-san wa ii hito *deshoo?*** "Mr. Chiba is a good person, isn't he?"
**Ano hoteru wa takai *deshoo?*** "That hotel is expensive, isn't it?"
**Kaigi wa ni-ji kara *deshoo?*** "The meeting is from two, isn't it?"

**5 KONNA/SONNA/ANNA/DONNA**

**Konna/sonna/anna/donna** are also **ko-so-a-do** words and mean 'this kind of,' 'that kind of, 'that kind of (...over there)' and 'what kind of. '

Note that **konna/sonna/anna/donna** always refer to kinds of things, while **kono/sono/ano/dono** refer to something specific.

Compare: **Kono kaban wa takai desu.** "This bag is expensive."
***Konna* kaban wa takai desu.** "This kind of bag is expensive."

**6 TADAIMA〜OKAERINASAI**

**Tadaima** which literally means 'just now' is a greeting used by someone returning. The greeting in reply is **okaerinasai**.

## PRACTICE

**1** Usage drill

Basic pattern: **Chiba-san ga yoroshiku to iimashita.**
"Mr. Chiba sends his regards (to you).
(lit. Mr. Chiba told me to say hello to you.)"
**Nakano-san**
**Tanaka-kachoo**
**Doi-buchoo**
**Nakamura-shachoo**
(friend's name)

**2** Transformation drill (non-past→ past)

Example: Teacher: **Sore wa ii desu nee.** "That's good!"
Student: **Sore wa yokatta desu nee.** "That was good!"

| | |
|---|---|
| **1) Sono waapuro wa takai desu yo.** | **Sono waapuro wa takakatta desu yo.** |
| **2) Kyoo wa isogashii desu nee.** | **Kyoo wa isogashikatta desu nee.** |
| **3) Ano kaisha wa ookii desu yo.** | **Ano kaisha wa ookikatta desu yo.** |
| **4) Kono hoteru wa yasui desu ne.** | **Kono hoteru wa yasukatta desu ne.** |
| **5) Sumimasen. Watakushi ga warui desu.** | **Sumimasen. Watakushi ga warukatta desu.** |

**3** Response drill

Example: Teacher: **Ano kata wa shinsetsu desu ka.** "Is that person kind?"
Student: **Ee, shinsetsu na kata desu.** "Yes, (he)'s a kind person."

| | |
|---|---|
| **1) Kono chizu wa benri desu ka.** | **Ee, benri na chizu desu.** |
| **2) Sono shiryoo wa atarashii desu ka.** | **Ee, atarashii shiryoo desu.** |
| **3) Tanaka-san no kaisha wa chiisai desu ka.** | **Ee, chiisai kaisha desu.** |
| **4) Ano hito wa genki desu ka.** | **Ee, genki na hito desu.** |
| **5) Anata no heya wa kaiteki desu ka.** | **Ee, kaiteki na heya desu.** |
| **6) Ano kuruma wa dame desu ka.** | **Ee, dame na kuruma desu.** |
| **7) Kono manshon wa takai desu ka.** | **Ee, takai manshon desu.** |
| **8) Ano sensee wa joozu desu ka.** | **Ee, joozu na sensee desu.** |
| **9) Sono shigoto wa isogashii desu ka.** | **Ee, isogashii shigoto desu.** |
| **10) Kyoo no kaigi wa taisetsu desu ka.** | **Ee, taisetsu na kaigi desu.** |

**4** Transformation drill

Example: Teacher: **Kono shiryoo ga irimasu.** "I need this material."
Student: **Konna shiryoo ga irimasu.** "I need this kind of material."

| | |
|---|---|
| **1) Sono jisho wa dame desu ka.** | **Sonna jisho wa dame desu ka.** |
| **2) Ano nekutai wa ii desu nee.** | **Anna nekutai wa ii desu nee.** |
| **3) Dono omocha o kaimashita ka.** | **Donna omocha o kaimashita ka.** |
| **4) Kono waapuro wa benri desu yo.** | **Konna waapuro wa benri desu yo.** |
| **5) Ano shigoto wa taisetsu desu ne.** | **Anna shigoto wa taisetsu desu ne.** |
| **6) Sono kaban wa doko de utte imasu ka.** | **Sonna kaban wa doko de utte imasu ka.** |
| **7) Dono hon o kaimasu ka.** | **Donna hon o kaimasu ka.** |
| **8) Kono tsukue wa takai deshoo?** | **Konna tsukue wa takai deshoo?** |

**5** Transformation drill

Example: Teacher: **Chiba-san wa ii hito desu ka.** "Is Mr. Chiba a good person?"
Student: **Chiba-san wa ii hito deshoo?**
"Mr. Chiba is a good person, isn't he?"

| | |
|---|---|
| 1) **Yamaguchi-san wa Koohoobu desu ka.** | **Yamaguchi-san wa Koohoobu deshoo?** |
| 2) **Kore wa buchoo no kooto desu ka.** | **Kore wa buchoo no kooto deshoo?** |
| 3) **Are wa yuubinkyoku desu ka.** | **Are wa yuubinkyoku deshoo?** |
| 4) **Kono hookoku wa dame desu ka.** | **Kono hookoku wa dame deshoo?** |
| 5) **Buchoo no heya wa nana-kai desu ka.** | **Buchoo no heya wa nana-kai deshoo?** |
| 6) **Chikatetsu no hoo ga benri desu ka.** | **Chikatetsu no hoo ga benri deshoo?** |
| 7) **Nakamura-shachoo wa ogenki desu ka.** | **Nakamura-shachoo wa ogenki deshoo?** |
| 8) **Ryokoo wa yokatta desu ka.** | **Ryokoo wa yokatta deshoo?** |

**6** Response drill

Example: Teacher: **Aishii no shijoo ni tsuite shirabete kudasai.**
"Please look into the IC market."
Student: **Hai, sugu shirabete mimasu.**
"Yes, I'll try to check (it) right now."

| | |
|---|---|
| 1) **Kono hookoku o kaite kudasai.** | **Hai, sugu kaite mimasu.** |
| 2) **Kono shiryoo o yonde kudasai.** | **Hai, sugu yonde mimasu.** |
| 3) **Tanaka-san ni denwa o kakete kudasai.** | **Hai, sugu kakete mimasu.** |
| 4) **Kerii-san ni kono eego o kiite kudasai.** | **Hai, sugu kiite mimasu.** |
| 5) **Watakushi no shiriai ni atte kudasai.** | **Hai, sugu atte mimasu.** |
| 6) **Doi-san no denwa-bangoo o shirabete kudasai.** | **Hai, sugu shirabete mimasu.** |

**7** Transformation drill

Example: Teacher: **Ashita ikimasu./Kerii-san/**
"I'll come tomorrow."/Mr. Kelly/
Student: **Kerii-san wa ashita kimasu to iimashita.**
Mr. Kelly said that he'll come tomorrow."

| | |
|---|---|
| 1) **Buchoo ga yonde imasu. /Yamaguchi-san/** | **Yamaguchi-san wa buchoo ga yonde imasu to iimashita.** |
| 2) **Hookokusho o yonde kudasai. /kakarichoo/** | **Kakarichoo wa hookokusho o yonde kudasai to iimashita.** |
| 3) **Ato de shiryoo o agemasu. /Chiba-san/** | **Chiba-san wa ato de shiryoo o agemasu to iimashita.** |
| 4) **Kono deeta wa dame desu. /Kerii-san/** | **Kerii-san wa kono deeta wa dame desu to iimashita.** |
| 5) **Atarashii waapuro o kaimashita. /Nakamura-san/** | **Nakamura-san wa atarashii waapuro o kaimashita to iimashita.** |
| 6) **Aishii no yunyuu wa huete imasu. /Doi-san/** | **Doi-san wa aishii no yunyuu wa huete imasu to iimashita.** |
| 7) **Chikatetsu no hoo ga benri desu. /Yamaguchi-san/** | **Yamaguchi-san wa chikatetsu no hoo ga benri desu to iimashita.** |
| 8) **Koohoo no shigoto wa taisetsu desu. /shachoo/** | **Shachoo wa koohoo no shigoto wa taisetsu desu to iimashita.** |

## EXERCISES

**1** Complete the sentences using the following patterns:
1) **Shachoo wa itsu mo (   ) to itte imasu.** "The president always says..."
2) **Watakushi wa tomodachi ni (   ) to iimashita.** "I said (   ) to my friend."
3) **Tanaka-san ni (   ) to itte kudasai.** "Please tell Mr. Tanaka (   )"
4) **Ano hito ni (   ) to iimashoo ka.** "Shall I tell that person (   )"
5) **Buchoo ni (   ) kudasai to iimashita.** "I asked the general manager to (do)"

**2** Translate the following sentences into Japanese:
1) Mr. Kelly said to Mr. Yamaguchi, "I'm back."
2) Yesterday, I tried to read the report on the IC market, but I didn't understand it.
3) General Manager Doi is checking important data.
4) I received a book about American history from Mr. Brown.
5) I'll give Mr. Brown a very expensive notebook.
6) Mr. Nakamura gave me a handy word-processer.
7) (The number of ) executives in our company is gradually increasing.
8) What are you writing? I'm writing a report on sales and marketing.
9) Mr. Chiba gave me various materials. (He) is a kind person.
10) Let's try to investigate the electrical appliance market in America.

## FOR REFERENCE

### 〔MODEL CONVERSATION〕

| | | |
|---|---|---|
| Kelly | **Tadaima.** | ただいま。 |
| Yamaguchi | **Okaerinasai, Kerii-san. Gokuroosama.** | おかえりなさい、ケリーさん。ごくろうさま。 |
| Kelly | **Chiba-san ga yoroshiku to itte imashita.** | 千葉さん が よろしく と いって いました。 |
| Yamaguchi | **Soo desu ka. Aa, Kerii-san, buchoo ga yonde imashita yo.** | そう です か。 ああ、ケリーさん、部長 が 呼んで いました よ。 |
| Kelly | **Soo desu ka. Sugu itte mimasu.** | そう です か。 すぐ いって みます |
| Kelly | **Buchoo, oyobi deshita ka.** | 部長、お呼び でした か。 |
| Doi | **Aa, Kerii-san, Jetoro wa doo deshita?** | ああ、ケリーさん、ジェトロ は どう でした？ |
| Kelly | **Joohoo-saabisubu no Chiba-san kara iroiro na shiryoo o moraimashita.** | 情報サービス部 の 千葉さん から いろいろ な 資料 を もらいました。 |
| Doi | **Sore wa yokatta desu nee. Chiba-san wa ii hito deshoo?** | それ は よかった です ねえ。千葉さん は いい 人 でしょう？ |

| | | |
|---|---|---|
| Kelly | **Hai, taihen shinsetsu na kata deshita.** | はい、たいへん 親切 な かた でした。 |
| Doi | **Jetoro de donna koto o shirabemashita ka.** | ジェトロ で どんな こと を 調べました か。 |
| Kelly | **Aishii no yushutsu ni tsuite shirabemashita.** | ICの 輸出 に ついて 調べました。 |
| Doi | **Soo desu ka.** | そう です か。 |
| Kelly | **Ato de, aishii no yushutsu-shijoo ni tsuite hookoku o kakimasu.** | あと で、IC の 輸出市場 に ついて 報告 を 書きます。 |
| Doi | **Sore wa ii desu ga, yunyuu ni tsuite mo kaite kudasai.** | それ は いい です が、輸入に ついて も 書いて ください。 |
| Kelly | **Soo desu ne. Chiba-san mo aishii no yunyuu wa dandan huete imasu to itte imashita.** | そう です ね。 千葉さん も IC の 輸入 は だんだん 増えて います と 言って いました。 |
| Doi | **Jaa, sonna koto ni tsuite mo hookokusho ni kaite mite kudasai. Ato de yomimasu kara.** | じゃあ、そんな こと に ついて も 報告書 に 書いて みて ください。 あと で 読みます から。 |
| Kelly | **Kashikomarimashita.** | かしこまりました。 |

## 〔ADDITIONAL VOCABULARY〕

**1** **A: Sono hanashi wa dare kara kikimashita ka.**
その 話 は 誰 から 聞きました か。

**B: Ginkoo no shiriai ga hanashite imashita.**
銀行 の 知り合い が 話して いました。

**A: Soo desu ka. Jaa, sugu kachoo ni hookoku-shimashoo.**
そう です か。じゃあ、すぐ 課長 に 報告しましょう。

**2** **A: Konna techoo wa benri desu nee. Doko de utte imasu ka.**
こんな 手帳 は 便利 です ねえ。 どこ で 売って います か。

**B: Depaato de utte imasu ga, kore wa shiriai ga kuremashita.**
デパート で 売って います が、これ は 知り合い が くれました。

**3** **A: Anna gaisha wa zuibun takai deshoo?**
あんな 外車 は ずいぶん 高い でしょう？

**B: Mae wa zuibun takakatta desu ga, ima wa sonna ni takaku arimasen yo.**
前 は ずいぶん 高かった です が、 今 は そんな に 高く ありません よ。

**4** **A: Kono katarogu wa mada arimasu ka.**
この カタログ は まだ あります か。

**B: Ee, mada arimasu ga, iroiro na kata ni agemashita kara, zuibun herimashita.**
ええ、まだ あります が、いろいろ な かた に あげました から、 ずいぶん 減りました。

## BUSINESS COLUMN

## "HONNE" AND "TATEMAE": INNER AND OUTER OPINIONS

Social interaction in Japan is a kind of stage performance, with all of the actors knowing their roles as the drama unfolds. As with all acting, the important thing is to express the proper lines for the proper situation, rather than one's true feelings. This is the difference between *honne* and *tatemae*. *Honne* is what the person actually feels—his 'real sound,' as the Japanese translates—but what the audience hears is the *tatemae*, or the performance. *Tatemae* originally referred to the ceremony associated with the construction of a house. In the context here, it is also a kind of ceremony of construction—for the building of human relationships.

One form of *tatemae* that often confuses foreigners is the Japanese predilection to apologize, for the apology is a far more important social lubricant in Japan than it is in the West. For example, where Westerners might introduce a speech before an audience with a joke, Japanese typically introduce it with an apology (something on the order of "I do not feel worthy of standing before this group"). Similarly, where Westerners say 'thank you' for having the door opened for them, for having their beer glasses refilled, or for receiving gifts, the Japanese apologize (*doomo, sumimasen*—"I'm so sorry"). The mistake is to attribute to the speaker real feelings of apology, humbleness, or guilt, for this is only the surface meaning. The real importance is in the act of saying it, not in actually believing it. It is in this sense *tatemae*.

*Tatemae* is important in the world of business. Both within the office and in relationships between companies, there are rituals that must be performed in day-to-day interaction. Within the company, there is an informal order based on seniority, age, position and other factors. Levels of politeness and seating arrangements at meetings, must conform to this hierarchy. Even if one dislikes a coworker in one's *honne*, these true feelings must not be shown, for this would disrupt the atmosphere of harmony that must be maintained in the group, just as saying the wrong lines in the middle of the play would disrupt a stage performance. Reliance on *tatemae* allows everyone to share common expectations in social situations, so no one is out of place or loses face. It is a means for avoiding direct confrontations.

While *tatemae* is important, the ideal in Japanese interpersonal relationships is to move away from pure *tatemae* to communicate at the 'gut level'—the *honne-honne* connection. Office hours are marked by considerable *tatemae*; after work, when employees go out together, the *tatemae* drops and the *honne* takes over. The boss may tell his employees that the gathering is *bureikoo*—without ceremony. As libations lubricate interaction, employees relax from the formalities of office life and may even go so far as to tell their boss what they really think of him or of how they think the company should be run. In times like these, *honne* is allowed expression, and even if a person throws himself into this with too much relish, all is forgiven as the result of having had a little too much sake. As long as the on-the-job requirements of *tatemae* are maintained afterwards, the group will continue to function effectively.

**by Michael Gerlach**

# UNIT 14

*LUNCH*

昼食

ちゅうしょく

## MODEL CONVERSATION

## SITUATION

*A week later Kelly visits JETRO again and takes Chiba to lunch at a neighborhood restaurant.*

| | | |
|---|---|---|
| Waitress | 1 **Irasshaimase.**<br>*(hands a menu to Kelly)* **Doozo.** | Welcome!<br>Please! |
| | **nan ni shimasu** | to decide on what? |
| Kelly | 2 *(while looking over the menu)*<br>**Nan ni shimashoo ka.** | What shall we have ( lit. decide on)? |
| | **ebi-hurai** | fried prawns |
| Chiba | 3 **Soo desu nee. Boku wa ebi-hurai ni shimasu.** | Let me see. I'll have fried prawns. |
| | **biiru** | beer |
| Kelly | 4 **Jaa, watakushi mo. Biiru wa ikaga desu ka.** | Well, me too. How about beer? |
| Chiba | 5 **Ee, ii desu nee.** | Yes, (that's) good. |
| Kelly | 6 *(to the waitress)* **Ebi-hurai, sore kara biiru mo onegai-shimasu.** | Fried prawns, and then we'd like beer also. |
| | **ip-pon** | a bottle |
| Waitress | 7 **Kashikomarimashita.**<br>**Ebi-hurai to biiru ip-pon desu ne?** | Certainly, sir.<br>Fried prawns and a bottle of beer, right? |

| | | |
|---|---|---|
| | **ni-hon** | two bottles |
| | **washoku** | Japanese food |
| | **yooshoku** | Western food |
| | **dochira** | which one? |
| | **suki/na/** | like (something), pleasing |
| Kelly | **8 Iie, ni-hon onegai-shimasu.** *(to Mr. Chiba)* **Chiba-san wa washoku to yooshoku to dochira ga suki desu ka.** | No, we'd like two bottles. Which do you like, Japanese (food) or W estern food, Mr. Chiba? |
| Chiba | **9 Boku wa yooshoku no hoo ga suki desu ga, Kerii-san wa?** | I like Western food (more than Japanese food). How about you? |
| | **washoku mo yooshoku mo** | both Japanese food and Western food |
| Kelly | **10 Boku wa washoku mo yooshoku mo suki desu.** | I like both ( lit. Japanese food and Western food). |
| | **sashimi/osashimi** 〈polite〉 | *sashimi* (raw fish) |
| | **tabemasu** | to eat |
| Chiba | **11 Sashimi mo tabemasu ka.** | Do you eat *sashimi* too? |
| | **mochiron** | of course |
| | **Nyuuyooku de mo** | In New York too |
| | **sushi/osushi** 〈polite〉 | *sushi* |
| | **yoku** | often |
| Kelly | **12 Ee, mochiron. Nyuuyooku de mo yoku osushi o tabemashita yo.** | Yes, of course. I often ate *sushi* in New York too. |
| | *(the waitress brings beer)* | |
| | **omachidoosama deshita** | I'm sorry ( I ) kept you waiting |
| Waitress | **13 Omachidoosama deshita.** | I'm sorry ( I ) kept you waiting. |
| Kelly | **14 Saa, Chiba-san, Doozo.** | Well, Mr.Chiba, please. |

*(pours beer for Chiba)*

| | | |
|---|---|---|
| Chiba | **15 Aa, doomo. Kerii-san, doozo.** | Oh,thanks. Mr. Kelly, please. |

*(in return, Chiba pours beer for Kelly)*

| | | |
|---|---|---|
| Kelly | **16 Jaa, kanpai !** | Well, cheers! |
| Chiba | **17 Kanpai.** | Bottoms up! |

*(after eating)*

| | | |
|---|---|---|
| | **oishii** | delicious, tasty |
| Chiba | **18 Aa, oishikatta desu nee. Doomo gochisoosama deshita.** | Ah, it was delicious, a real feast! (lit. it was a feast.) |
| | **koohii** | coffee |
| Kelly | **19 Koohii wa ikaga desu ka.** | How about coffee? |
| Chiba | **20** *(while looking at his watch)* **Jikan ga arimasen kara...** | There is no time, so... |
| | **okanjoo** | bill, payment |
| Kelly | **21 Soo desu ka.** *(to the waitress)* **Okanjoo onegai-shimasu.** | Is that so? Give me the bill. |
| | **reji** | cashier, cash register |
| Waitress | **22** *(handing the bill to Kelly)* **Arigatoo gozaimashita.** | Thank you very much.<br>Please pay the cashier. |

**Okanjoo wa reji de onegai-shimasu.**

| | | |
|---|---|---|
| Kelly | 23 **Jaa, ikimashoo.** | Well, let's go. |

## ADDITIONAL VOCABULARY

1 **A: Niku to sakana to dochira (no hoo) ga suki desu ka.** — Which do you like, meat or fish?

| | |
|---|---|
| **yori** | (more) than |
| **niku yori** | (more) than meat |

**B: Boku wa niku yori sakana no hoo ga suki desu.** — I like fish more than meat.

2

| | |
|---|---|
| **ryoori** | cooking, dishes, food |
| **Nihon-ryoori** | Japanese food |
| **no naka de** | among |
| **no uchi de** | among |
| **Nihon-ryoori no naka de (***or* **uchi de)** | among Japanese foods |
| **ichi-ban** | first, best |

**A: Nihon-ryoori no naka de, nani ga ichi-ban ii desu ka.** — What would be best among Japanese foods?

| | |
|---|---|
| **sukiyaki** | *sukiyaki* |

**B: Boku wa sukiyaki ga ichi-ban suki desu.** — I like *sukiyaki* best.

| | |
|---|---|
| **okusan** <honorific> | (your) wife |
| **goshujin** <honorific> | (your) husband |

**A: Okusan mo sukiyaki ga suki desu ka.** — Your wife also likes *sukiyaki?*

| | |
|---|---|
| **kanai** | (my) wife |
| **shujin** | (my) husband |
| **kirai/na/** | dislike |
| **B: Iie, kanai wa niku wa kirai desu kara...** | My wife dislikes meat so... |

**3** **restoran** — restaurant

| | |
|---|---|
| **A: Ano restoran de tabemashoo ka.** | Shall we eat at that restaurant over there? |

| | |
|---|---|
| **tabemono** | food |
| **mazui** | bad-tasting |
| **B: Asoko no tabemono wa taitee mazui desu yo.** | Food at that (place) is generally bad. (lit. The food over there, usually tastes bad.) |

| | |
|---|---|
| **onaka** | abdomen, stomach |
| **onaka ga sukimasu** | to feel hungry |
| **A: Soo desu ka. Jaa, doko e ikimashoo ka. Boku wa onaka ga sukimashita yo.** | Is that so? Well, where shall we go? I'm ( lit. I've become) hungry. |

| | |
|---|---|
| **ura** | behind |
| **yuumee/na/** | famous |
| **ryooriya** | Japanese-style restaurant |
| **B: Ano biru no ura ni, hurui yuumee na ryooriya ga arimasu kara, soko e ikimashoo.** | There is an old and famous restaurant behind that building, so let's go there. |

| | |
|---|---|
| **soo shimasu** | to decide on |
| **A: Jaa, soo shimashoo.** | Well, let's. (lit. decide on) |

**4**

| | |
|---|---|
| **nodo** | throat |
| **nodo ga kawakimasu** | to become thirsty |
| **ip-pai** | one glass |
| **yarimasu** | to do |
| **ip-pai yarimashoo** | let's have a drink |

| | |
|---|---|
| **A: Nodo ga kawakimashita yo.** | I'm thirsty. |
| **Ip-pai yarimashoo.** | Let's have a drink! |

| | |
|---|---|
| **nama-biiru** | draft beer |
| **nama-biiru de mo** | draft beer or something similar |
| **nomimasu** | to drink |

| | |
|---|---|
| **B: Ii desu nee.** | That's good. |
| **Nama-biiru de mo nomimashoo.** | Let's have something like a draft beer. |

**5** Additional restaurant terms

| | | | |
|---|---|---|---|
| **gohan** | cooked rice | **suteeki** | steak |
| **pan** | bread | **tenpura** | tempura |
| **soba/udon** | Japanese noodles | **sarada** | salad |
| **sake/osake** <polite> | Japanese *sake* | **gyuuniku** | beef |
| **uisukii** | whisky | **butaniku** | pork |
| **juusu** | juice | **toriniku** | chicken |
| **ocha** | green tea | **tamago** | egg |
| **koocha** | black tea | **gyuunyuu/miruku** | milk |
| **oyu** | hot water | **bataa** | butter |
| **mizu** | (cold) water | **chiizu** | cheese |
| **shio** | salt | **dezaato** | dessert |
| **satoo** | sugar | **kudamono** | fruit |
| **soosu** | sauce | **okashi** | cake, sweets |
| **shooyu** | soy sauce | | |

**6** Adjectives used for describing meals

| | | | |
|---|---|---|---|
| **amai** | sweet | **suppai** | sour, acidic |
| **karai** | hot, spicy | **shoppai** | salty |
| **nigai** | bitter | **shiokarai** | salty |
| **atsui** | hot | **katai** | hard, tough |
| **tsumetai** | cold | **yawarakai** | soft, tender |

## GRAMMATICAL NOTES

**1** **DOCHIRA**

Unit 11 introduced **dochira** for asking directions. It can also be used when asking someone to choose between two items as in:
**A to B to, dochira ga... desu ka.**

Examples: **Oosaka *to* Yokohama *to, dochira ga* ookii *desu ka.***
"Which is larger, Osaka or Yokohama?"
**Osake *to* uisukii *to, dochira ga* ii *desu ka.***
"Which is better, *sake* or whisky?"

## 2 ~YORI~NO HOO

In replying to an alternative, the following pattern can be used:

| Topic | Rejected alternative | Preferred alternative | Predicate |
|---|---|---|---|
| **Watakushi wa** | **osake *yori*** | **uisukii *no hoo* ga** | **suki desu.** |
| I like whisky more than *sake.* | | | |

The preferred alternative is usually followed by **no hoo ga,** but sometimes **ga** by itself is sufficient.

Examples: **Tenpura *yori* sashimi (no hoo) *ga* ii desu.**
"*Sashimi* is better than *tempura* (for me)."
**Boku *yori* Nakano-san (no hoo) *ga* eego ga joozu desu.**
"Mr. Nakano is better at English than me."

In actual conversation, when selecting an alternative, the unselected choice is often omitted:

Question: **Gyuuniku to butaniku to, dochira ga takai desu ka.**
"Which is more expensive, beef or pork?"
Answer: **Gyuuniku *no hoo* ga takai desu.** "Beef is more expensive."

## 3 ICHI-BAN

**Ichi-ban** which can mean 'the first, the best and the most' is used to designate one's choice among three or more alternatives:

**Nihon-ryoori de wa sukiyaki ga *ichi-ban* suki desu.**
"Among Japanese foods, I like *sukiyaki* best."

Note that when asking about one's choice between three or more alternatives, **dore, dare, doko** and **itsu** are usually used as the question word, and **dochira** is used only for an alternative between two items.

Examples: **Kono ryoori no naka de *dore* ga ichi-ban suki desu ka.**
"Which do you like best among these foods?"
**Doi-san to Nakano-san to Yamaguchi-san no uchi de *dare* ga ichi-ban eego ga joozu desu ka.**
"Who is the best English speaker, among Mr. Doi, Mr. Nakano and Mr. Yamaguchi?"

## 4 ~NI SHIMASU

**Ni shimasu,** literally meaning 'to make something into...' also can mean 'decide on...'

Examples: **Ryoori wa suteeki *ni shimashita.*** "As for food, we decided on steaks."
**Dono hoteru *ni shimashoo* ka.** "Which hotel shall we decide on?"

Note that a noun + **ni shimasu** refers to one's decision, while a noun + **ni narimasu** specifies a result.
Compare: **Nakano-san o kachoo *ni shimashita.*** "We made Mr. Nakano a manager."
**Nakano-san ga kachoo *ni narimashita.*** "Mr. Nakano became a manager."

**5** -**BON**/-**HON**/-**PON** and -**BAI**/-**HAI**/-**PAI**

Counters, -**bon**/-**hon**/-**pon** are used for counting long and cylindrical objects such as bottles, pens, trees, legs, etc. These counters occur with numerals of Chinese origin, except for 4 and 7:

| | | | |
|---|---|---|---|
| **ip-pon** | 1 long, cylindrical object | **nana-hon** | 7 long, cylindrical objects |
| **ni-hon** | 2 long, cylindrical objects | **hap-pon** | 8 long, cylindrical objects |
| **san-bon** | 3 long, cylindrical objects | **kyuu-hon** | 9 long, cylindrical objects |
| **yon-hon** | 4 long, cylindrical objects | **jup-pon** | 10 long, cylindrical objects |
| **go-hon** | 5 long, cylindrical objects | **nan-bon** | how many long, cylindrical objects? |
| **rop-pon** | 6 long, cylindrical objects | | |

-**Bai**/-**hai**/-**pai** are counters for counting full containers and are also used with numerals of Chinese origin, except for 4 and 7:

| | | | |
|---|---|---|---|
| **ip-pai** | 1 glassful | **nana-hai** | 7 glassfuls |
| **ni-hai** | 2 glassfuls | **hap-pai** | 8 glassfuls |
| **san-bai** | 3 glassfuls | **kyuu-hai** | 9 glassfuls |
| **yon-hai** | 4 glassfuls | **jup-pai** | 10 glassfuls |
| **go-hai** | 5 glassfuls | **nan-bai** | how many glassfuls? |
| **rop-pai** | 6 glassfuls | | |

**6** **KANJOO/OKANJOO**

**Kanjoo** or with the polite prefix **o** + **kanjoo** literally means 'counting'or 'calculation,' but in restaurants, it can refer to 'bill' or 'payment:'
***Okanjoo* wa ikura desu ka.** "How much is my bill?"
***Okanjoo* wa mada desu.** "Your payment is not ready yet."

## PRACTICE

**1** Usage drill

Basic pattern: **Watakushi wa ebi-hurai ni shimasu.** "I'll have (decide on) fried prawns."

**tenpura**
**osashimi**
**sukiyaki**
**nama-biiru**
**soba**

**2** Response drill

Example: Teacher: **Washoku ga suki desu ka./yooshoku/**
"Do you like Japanese food?"/Western food/
Student: **Washoku mo yooshoku mo suki desu.**
"I like both Japanese food and Western food."

| | |
|---|---|
| **1) Osashimi o tabemashita ka./osushi/** | **Osashimi mo osushi mo tabemashita.** |
| **2) Nakano-san ga ikimasu ka./Doi-san/** | **Nakano-san mo Doi-san mo ikimasu.** |
| **3) Biiru wa nomimasen ka./sake/** | **Biiru mo sake mo nomimasen.** |
| **4) Buchoo wa irasshaimasu ka./kachoo/** | **Buchoo mo kachoo mo irasshaimasu.** |
| **5) Gyuuniku wa kirai desu ka./butaniku/** | **Gyuuniku mo butaniku mo kirai desu.** |
| **6) Eego ga joozu desu ka./doitsugo/** | **Eego mo doitsugo mo joozu desu.** |

**3** Usage drill

Basic pattern: ***Washoku* to *yooshoku* to, dochira ga *suki* desu ka.**
"Which do you like better, Japanese food or Western food?"

| | | |
|---|---|---|
| **toriniku,** | **sakana,** | **oishii** |
| **kono jisho,** | **ano jisho,** | **takai** |
| **kono waapuro,** | **tonari no waapuro,** | **atarashii** |
| **Tanaka-san,** | **Nakamura-san,** | **genki** |
| **kono shiryoo,** | **sono shiryoo,** | **taisetsu** |
| **kokuden,** | **chikatetsu,** | **benri** |

**4** Response drill

Example: Teacher: **Washoku to yooshoku to dochira ga suki desu ka.**
"Which do you like best, Japanese food or Western food?"
(select the second choice)
Student: **Washoku yori yooshoku no hoo ga suki desu.**
"I like Western food more than Japanese food."

| | |
|---|---|
| **1) Toriniku to butaniku to dochira ga yawarakai desu ka.** | **Toriniku yori butaniku no hoo ga yawarakai desu.** |
| **2) Biiru to uisukii to dochira ga ii desu ka.** | **Biiru yori uisukii no hoo ga ii desu.** |
| **3) Basu to chikatetsu to dochira ga benri desu ka.** | **Basu yori chikatetsu no hoo ga benri desu.** |
| **4) Doi-san to Chiba-san to dochira ga shinsetsu desu ka.** | **Doi-san yori Chiba-san no hoo ga shinsetsu desu.** |
| **5) Kono biiru to ano biiru to dochira ga tsumetai desu ka.** | **Kono biiru yori ano biiru no hoo ga tsumetai desu.** |

| | |
|---|---|
| 6) Kono ryoori to ano ryoori to dochira ga oishii desu ka. | Kono ryoori yori ano ryoori no hoo ga oishii desu. |
| 7) Kochira no osake to sochira no osake to dochira ga karai desu ka. | Kochira no osake yori sochira no osake no hoo ga karai desu. |
| 8) Sono kudamono to ano kudamono to dochira ga amai desu ka. | Sono kudamono yori ano kudamono no hoo ga amai desu. |

**5** Usage drill

Basic pattern: ***Niku*** **to** ***sakana*** **to** ***yasai*** **no uchi de dore ga ichi-ban** ***suki*** **desu ka.**

**"Which do you like best, meat, fish or vegetables?"**

| | | | |
|---|---|---|---|
| eego, | doitsugo, | huransugo, | joozu |
| kono seehin, | sono seehin, | ano seehin, | takai |
| takushii, | chikatetsu, | basu, | benri |
| gyuuniku, | toriniku, | sakana, | mazui |
| juusu, | miruku, | koohii, | kirai |
| kono shinbun, | sono shinbun, | ano shinbun, | dame |

**6** Response drill

Example: Teacher: **Nihon-ryoori no naka de nani ga ichi-ban suki desu ka. /sashimi/**
"What do you like best among Japanese foods? "/*sashimi*/

Student: **Sashimi ga ichi-ban suki desu.** "I like *sashimi* best."

| | |
|---|---|
| 1) Kono shiryoo no uchi de dore ga ichi-ban atarashii desu ka./sore/ | Sore ga ichi-ban atarashii desu. |
| 2) Tookyoo no hoteru no naka de doko ga ichi-ban benri desu ka. /Tookyoo Hoteru/ | Tookyoo Hoteru ga ichi-ban benri desu. |
| 3) Niku no naka de nani ga ichi-ban takai desu ka./gyuuniku/ | Gyuuniku ga ichi-ban takai desu. |
| 4) Washoku to yooshoku to Chuugoku-ryoori no uchi de nani ga ichi-ban suki desu ka./washoku/ | Washoku ga ichi-ban suki desu. |
| 5) Sukii to sukeeto to tenisu no uchi de nani ga ichi-ban joozu desu ka. /sukii/ | Sukii ga ichi-ban joozu desu. |
| 6) Doitsu to Huransu to Supeln no uchi de doko ga ichi-ban ii desu ka. /Supein/ | Supein ga ichi-ban ii desu. |

**7** Response drill

Example: Teacher: **Nyuuyooku de osushi o tabemashita ka.**
"Have you eaten *sushi* in New York?"

Student: **Ee, Nyuuyooku de mo yoku tabemashita.**
"Yes, I often ate (it) in New York too."

| | |
|---|---|
| 1) Ginza de ip-pai yarimasu ka. | Ee, Ginza de mo yoku ip-pai yarimasu. |

| | |
|---|---|
| **2) Otaku de paatii o shimasu ka.** | **Ee, uchi de mo yoku paatii o shimasu.** |
| **3) Ano hoteru de osake o nomimasu ka.** | **Ee, ano hoteru de mo yoku osake o nomimasu.** |
| **4) Kaisha de Doi-san ni aimasu ka.** | **Ee, kaisha de mo yoku Doi-san ni aimasu.** |
| **5) Amerika de kooen ni ikimashita ka.** | **Ee, Amerika de mo yoku kooen ni ikimashita.** |
| **6) Shikago de basu ni norimashita ka.** | **Ee, Shikago de mo yoku basu ni norimashita.** |

**8** Response drill (review of respectful-humble usages)

Example: Teacher: **Okusan wa ogenki desu ka.** "Is your wife well? "
Student: **Hai, kanai wa genki desu.** "Yes, my wife is well."

| | |
|---|---|
| **1) Goshujin wa sakana ga kirai desu ka.** | **Hai, shujin wa sakana ga kirai desu.** |
| **2) Okusan wa Kyooto e irasshaimashita ka.** | **Hai, kanai wa Kyooto e mairimashita.** |
| **3) Goshujin wa otaku ni irasshaimasu ka.** | **Hai, shujin wa uchi ni orimasu.** |
| **4) Okusan mo kyoo no paatii ni irasshaimasu ka.** | **Hai, kanai mo kyoo no paatii ni mairimasu.** |

**9** Response drill (review of negative answers)

Example: Teacher: **Kono niku wa takakatta desu ka.** "Was this meat expensive?"
Student: **Iie, takaku arimasen deshita.** "No, (it) wasn't expensive."

| | |
|---|---|
| **1) Konban no ryoori wa mazukatta desu ka.** | **Iie, mazuku arimasen deshita.** |
| **2) Kinoo wa onaka ga sukimashita ka.** | **Iie, onaka ga sukimasen deshita.** |
| **3) Konna sarada wa kirai desu ka.** | **Iie, kirai ja arimasen.** |
| **4) Nodo ga kawaite imasu ka.** | **Iie, nodo ga kawaite imasen.** |
| **5) Ano ryooriya wa yuumee desu ka.** | **Iie, yuumee ja arimasen.** |
| **6) Kanjoo wa yasukatta desu ka.** | **Iie, yasuku arimasen deshita.** |
| **7) Buraun-san no okusan wa Amerikajin desu ka.** | **Iie, Amerikajin ja arimasen.** |
| **8) Kono sakana wa hurui desu ka.** | **Iie, huruku arimasen.** |

**10** Response drill

Example: Teacher: **Kono tenpura wa oishii desu nee.** "This tempura is delicious!"
Student: **Ee, oishii tenpura desu nee.** "Yes, it's delicious tempura!"

| | |
|---|---|
| **1) Kono juusu wa amai desu nee.** | **Ee, amai juusu desu nee.** |
| **2) Kono udon wa shoppai desu nee.** | **Ee, shoppai udon desu nee.** |
| **3) Kono kudamono wa suppai desu nee.** | **Ee, suppai kudamono desu nee.** |
| **4) Kono ryoori wa karai desu nee.** | **Ee, karai ryoori desu nee.** |
| **5) Kono sake wa atsui desu nee.** | **Ee, atsui sake desu nee.** |
| **6) Kono miruku wa tsumetai desu nee.** | **Ee, tsumetai miruku desu nee.** |

**7) Kono suteeki wa yawarakai desu nee.** **Ee, yawarakai suteeki desu nee.**
**8) Kono pan wa katai desu nee.** **Ee, katai pan desu nee.**

## EXERCISES

**1** Fill in the blanks with the word(s) that best describe what you like to do:
1) **Watakushi wa asa itsumo ( ) o nomimasu.**
2) **Watakushi wa konogoro yoku ( ) o tabemasu.**
3) **Yooshoku no naka de ( ) ga ichi-ban suki desu.**
4) **Watakushi wa ( ) yori ( ) no hoo ga suki desu.**
5) **Nihon-ryoori wa tabemasu ga, ( ) wa kirai desu.**
6) **Taitee ( )-ji goro onaka ga suite imasu.**
7) **Ichi-ban mazui ryoori wa ( ) deshoo.**
8) **Watakushi yori ( )-san no hoo ga ( ) ga joozu desu.**
9) **Tenisu mo suki desu ga, ( ) wa motto suki desu.**
10) **Nodo ga kawakimashita kara, ( ) o nomimashoo ka.**

**2** Translate the following sentences into Japanese:
1) Mr. Chiba said, "Bottoms up! "
2) I like both *tempura* and *sukiyaki,* but ( I ) like *sushi* best.
3) There is no good food served at that cafeteria over there.
4) Mr. Nakamura's wife drinks neither beer nor sake.
5) Who is the best at (speaking) Japanese, Mr. Kelly, Mr. Brown or Mr. Smith?
6) Which is older, the Tokyo Hotel or the Kyoto Hotel?
7) Mr. Nakano asked Mr. Kelly, "Do you eat *sushi?"*
8) Mr. Kelly said, "Please give us a bottle of beer and a glass of draft beer."
9) Mr. Chiba did not drink coffee, because he had no time.
10) I feel hungry. Let's go to the famous restaurant behind the post office.

## FOR REFERENCE

### 〔MODEL CONVERSATION〕

Waitress **Irasshaimase.** いらっしゃいませ。
**Doozo.** どうぞ。
Kelly **Nan ni shimashoo ka.** なん に しましょう か。

| | | |
|---|---|---|
| Chiba | **Soo desu nee.**<br>**Boku wa ebi-hurai ni shimasu.** | そう です ねえ。<br>ぼく は エビフライ に します。 |
| Kelly | **Jaa, watakushi mo. Biiru wa ikaga desu ka.** | じゃあ、わたくし も。 ビール は いかが です か。 |
| Chiba | **Ee, ii desu nee.** | ええ、いい です ねえ。 |
| Kelly | **Ebi-hurai, sore kara biiru mo onegai-shimasu.** | エビフライ、それ から ビール も お願いします。 |
| Waitress | **Kashikomarimashita. Ebi-hurai to biiru ip-pon desu ne?** | かしこまりました。 エビフライ と ビール 一本 で すね。 |
| Kelly | **Iie, ni-hon onegai-shimasu.**<br>**Chiba-san wa washoku to yooshoku to dochira ga suki desu ka.** | いいえ、二本 おねがいします。<br>千葉さん は 和食 と 洋食 と どちら が 好き です か。 |
| Chiba | **Boku wa yooshoku no hoo ga suki desu ga, Kerii-san wa?** | ぼく は 洋食 の ほう が 好き です が、ケリーさん は? |
| Kelly | **Boku wa washoku mo yooshoku mo suki desu.** | ぼく は 和食 も 洋食 も 好き です。 |
| Chiba | **Sashimi mo tabemasu ka.** | 刺身 も 食べます か。 |
| Kelly | **Ee, mochiron. Nyuuyooku de mo yoku osushi o tabemashita yo.** | ええ、もちろん。 ニューヨーク で も よく お寿司 を 食べました よ。 |
| Waitress | **Omachidoosama deshita.** | おまちどうさま でした。 |
| Kelly | **Saa, Chiba-san. Doozo.** | さあ、千葉さん。 どうぞ。 |
| Chiba | **Aa, doomo. Kerii-san, doozo.** | ああ、どうも。 ケリーさん、どうぞ。 |
| Kelly | **Jaa, kanpai!** | じゃあ、乾杯! |
| Chiba | **Kanpai.** | 乾杯。 |
| Chiba | **Aa, oishikatta desu nee.**<br>**Doomo gochisoosama deshita.** | ああ、おいしかった です ねえ。<br>どうも ごちそうさま でした。 |
| Kelly | **Koohii wa ikaga desu ka.** | コーヒー は いかが です か。 |
| Chiba | **Jikan ga arimasen kara...** | 時間 が ありません から… |
| Kelly | **Soo desu ka.**<br>**Okanjoo onegai-shimasu.** | そう です か。<br>お勘定 お願いします。 |
| Waitress | **Arigatoo gozaimashita.**<br>**Okanjoo wa reji de onegai-shimasu.** | ありがとう ございました。<br>お勘定 は レジ で お願いします。 |
| Kelly | **Jaa, ikimashoo.** | じゃあ、行きましょう。 |

## 〔ADDITIONAL VOCABULARY〕

| | | |
|---|---|---|
| 1 | **A: Niku to sakana to dochira (no hoo) ga suki desu ka.**<br>**B: Boku wa niku yori sakana no hoo ga suki desu.** | 肉 と 魚 と どちら (のほう) が 好き です か。<br>ぼく は 肉 より 魚 の ほう が 好き です。 |
| 2 | **A: Nihon-ryoori no naka de, nani ga ichi-ban ii desu ka.** | 日本料理 の なか で、何 が いちばん いい です か。 |

| | |
|---|---|
| B: Boku wa sukiyaki ga ichi-ban suki desu. | ぼく は すきやき が いちばん 好き です。 |
| A: Okusan mo sukiyaki ga suki desu ka. | 奥さん も すきやき が 好き です か。 |
| B: Iie, kanai wa niku wa kirai desu kara... | いいえ、家内 は 肉 は 嫌い です から… |

**3**

| | |
|---|---|
| A: Ano resutoran de tabemashoo ka. | あの レストラン で 食べましょう か。 |
| B: Asoko no tabemono wa taitee mazui desu yo. | あそこ の 食べ物 は たいてい まずい です よ。 |
| A: Soo desu ka. Jaa, doko e ikimashoo ka. Boku wa onaka ga sukimashita yo. | そう です か。 じゃあ、どこ へ 行きましょう か。 ぼく は おなか が すきました よ。 |
| B: Ano biru no ura ni, hurui yuumee na ryooriya ga arimasu kara, soko e ikimashoo. | あの ビル の 裏 に、古い 有名 な 料理屋 が あります から、 そこ へ いきましょう。 |
| A: Jaa, soo shimashoo. | じゃあ、そう しましょう。 |

**4**

| | |
|---|---|
| A: Nodo ga kawakimashita yo. Ip-pai yarimashoo. | のど が かわきました よ。 一杯 やりましょう。 |
| B: Ii desu nee. Nama-biiru de mo nomimashoo. | いい です ねえ。 生ビール で も 飲みましょう。 |

**5**

| | | | |
|---|---|---|---|
| gohan | ご飯 | suteeki | ステーキ |
| pan | パン | tenpura | てんぷら |
| soba/udon | そば/うどん | sarada | サラダ |
| sake/osake | 酒/お酒 | gyuuniku | 牛肉 |
| uisukii | ウイスキー | butaniku | 豚肉 |
| juusu | ジュース | toriniku | 鶏肉 |
| ocha | お茶 | tamago | 卵 |
| koocha | 紅茶 | gyuunyuu/miruku | 牛乳/ミルク |
| oyu | お湯 | bataa | バター |
| mizu | 水 | chiizu | チーズ |
| shio | 塩 | dezaato | デザート |
| satoo | 砂糖 | kudamono | くだもの |
| soosu | ソース | okashi | お菓子 |
| shooyu | しょうゆ | | |

**6**

| | | | |
|---|---|---|---|
| amai | 甘い | suppai | すっぱい |
| karai | 辛い | shoppai | しょっぱい |
| nigai | にがい | shiokarai | 塩からい |
| atsui | 熱い | katai | かたい |
| tsumetai | 冷たい | yawarakai | 柔らかい |

## BUSINESS COLUMN

## "SENTOO": THE PUBLIC BATH

"Rub-a-dub-dub, all together in the tub" might seem fitting on your first visit to the public bathhouse. Recalling my boarding school days, when two to a shower for two minutes with compulsory cold shower afterward were all that was deemed necessary for body and soul, the daily soak in the *sentoo* tubs now seems as necessary as dinner. From age, infirmity, lumbago, stiff shoulders and even jet-lag I, find relief and renewal in the swirling hot water.

*Sentoo*'s are becoming scarcer as new apartment houses and the '*Mai Hoomu*' drive promote private baths. Rising fuel costs contribute to higher bathhouse prices. Despite stories of Okinawa and Kyushu *sentoos* capitalizing on solar power, most Tokyo baths are heated by oil, and they cater to fewer and fewer customers.

To off-set the odds against them, *Sentoos* are being modernized, superfically at least, with the introduction of new features: sauna's, sports-centers, and the inevitable '*karaoke*' corner. Jacuzzi pools are injected with 'micro-bubbles', and 'ultra-sound', as means of relaxation. The newcomer should be warned about one of these new conveniences; on a winter business trip a few years ago, I went to a *sentoo* near my guest-house. Of three pools, one was unoccupied. I tested it with my finger and the temperature seemed just right. I couldn't understand why it was being left unused.

"Aaaaah!" I screamed, while the locals laughed. For, running at regular intervals through the water were bursts of electrical current. At rare *sentoos,* this, apparently, is another new-fangled way to unwind.

To find the *sentoo*, look for the tall chimney first. Older *sentoos* usually have a wooden carved gate and beautiful grey tile roof facades, but a newer one may be packed in the rear of an apartment building. If you are renting an older, bathless apartment, checking the distances from all local bathhouses is a good idea. Since bath holidays can vary, knowledge of two neighborhood public baths is recommended.

Shoes and umbrellas are left in lockers at the entrance. Once you decide which side is appropriate (you quickly learn the *kanji* for male and female here), you enter and pay your money. Those tall enough can also get a quick peep over the partition.

At the entrance, you can buy soap, shampoo, a razor and underwear—everything you could need for a bath. Lockers, or in some older areas, simple baskets are available for your clothes. The large changing room is also furnished with a mirror, scale, coin-operated hair-dryers, and massage chairs.

Inside the main bathroom are rows of taps, mirrors, and overhead shower-heads at squatting level; small stools and basins are available. Here you can soap down, scrub, rinse, shave, even brush your teeth, in preparation for the major event, soaking in the swirling hot tub.

Soaking is just that. Soap is never brought into these communal tubs, and be sure the suds are thoroughly rinsed from your body before immersing yourself. You may also want to test the water with your hand. If it's too hot, don't hesitate to add cold water from a tap in the corner of the tub.

Then, enter slowly. The water is generally hot. But, once you get used to it, the resultant feeling of contentment will tell you exactly how the *sentoo* has remained essentially the same in a changing world.

**by Jim Key** (Australian financier and scholar of Shintoism)

# UNIT 15

*MEETING A FRIEND*

友達

ともだち

## MODEL CONVERSATION

## SITUATION

*One evening Kelly agrees to meet Yamaguchi at his favorite bar for drinks. However, Yamaguchi arrives a little late.*

| | |
|---|---|
| **osoi** | late, slow |
| **osoku narimasu** | to be late |
| **moo** | already |
| **chuumon-shimasu** | to order |

| | | |
|---|---|---|
| Yamaguchi | **1 Osoku narimashita. Moo nani ka chuumon-shimashita ka.** | I was late. Did you already order something? |

| | |
|---|---|
| **nani mo**/+negative/ | nothing, not...anything |
| **tanomimasu** | to ask, order |

| | | |
|---|---|---|
| Kelly | **2 Iie, mada nani mo tanomimasen.** | No, I haven't ordered anything yet. |

| | |
|---|---|
| **nasaimasu** | to do ⟨honorific form of **shimasu**⟩ |
| **ni nasaimasu** | to decide on |

| | | |
|---|---|---|
| Bartender | **3 Nan ni nasaimasu ka.** | What would you like, sir? |

| | |
|---|---|
| **mizu-wari** | whisky and water |

| | | |
|---|---|---|
| Yamaguchi | **4 Boku wa mizu-wari.** | I'd like whisky and water. |

| | |
|---|---|
| **baabon** | bourbon |
| **on-za-rokku** | on the rocks |

| | | |
|---|---|---|
| Kelly | **5 Baabon no on-za-rokku, onegai-shimasu.** | I'll have a bourbon on the rocks please. |

| | |
|---|---|
| **tsumami/otsumami** ⟨polite⟩ | snack that accompanies drinks |

| | | |
|---|---|---|
| Bartender | **6 Otsumami wa nani ga ii deshoo ka.** | What would you like as a snack? (lit. What would be a good snack?) |

| | | |
|---|---|---|
| | **piinattsu** | peanuts |
| Yamaguchi | **7 Piinattsu wa suki ja arimasen ka.** | Don't you like peanuts? |
| | **daisuki/na/** | very pleasing, favorite |
| Kelly | **8 Iie, daisuki desu. Piinattsu o tanomimashoo.** | Yes (lit. no), I like them very much. Let's order peanuts. |
| Bartender | **9** *(serving peanuts)* **Doozo.** | Please. |
| | *(the manager, a woman, comes to the bar)* | |
| Woman Manager | **10 Yamaguchi-san, irasshaimase.** | Welcome! Mr. Yamaguchi. |
| | **mama** | (nickname for woman manager of a bar, cabaret, etc.) |
| | **uchi no kaisha** | our company |
| Yamaguchi | **11 Aa, mama, shibaraku (deshita). Kochira, uchi no kaisha no Kerii-san.** | Oh, mama, it's been a long time. This is Mr. Kelly of our company. |
| Woman Manager | **12 Kerii-san desu ka. Yoku irasshaimashita.** | Mr. Kelly? You are welcome here. |
| | **nakanaka** | very, quite |
| | **baa** | bar |
| | **kiniirimasu** | to be pleased |
| Kelly | **13 Nakanaka ii baa desu nee. Kiniirimashita yo.** | This is a very nice bar. I like it very much. |
| | **osoreirimasu** | thank you very much |
| | **subarashii** | wonderful, splendid |
| Woman Manager | **14 Osoreirimasu. Kerii-san no Nihongo mo subarashii desu nee.** | Thank you very much. And your Japanese is splendid. |

| | | |
|---|---|---|
| | **madamada** | not yet |
| | **kite kara** | after coming |
| | **yoku narimasu** | to become better, to improve |
| Kelly | 15 **Iie, madamada desu. Nihon e kite kara dandan yoku natte imasu ga...** | No, not yet. After coming to Japan, it's gradually improving, but... |

*(they talk for a while)*

| | | |
|---|---|---|
| | **yukkuri** | slowly |
| | **doozo goyukkuri** | please take your time |
| Woman Manager | 16 **De wa, doozo goyukkuri.** *(she leaves)* | Well, please take your time. |
| | **sorosoro** | now, soon |
| | **kaerimasu** | to return |
| | **kaikee** | bill, check |
| Yamaguchi | 17 **Jaa, sorosoro kaerimashoo.** *(to the bartender)* **Kaikee o.** | Well, shall we go home now? Check, please. |
| | **haraimasu** | to pay |
| | **gochisoo** | very enjoyable meal |
| | **gochisoo ni narimasu** | to be treated |
| Kelly | 18 **Yamaguchi-san, konban wa boku ga haraimasu yo, senjitsu mo gochisoo ni narimashita kara...** | Mr. Yamaguchi, I'll treat (lit. pay) this evening, because you treated the other day. |
| Yamaguchi | 19 **Dame, dame. Koko wa boku no baa desu yo.** | Oh, no. This is my bar. |
| | **warikan** | equal split (of the expenses) |
| | **warikan ni shimasu** | to split the bill |
| Kelly | 20 **Jaa, warikan ni shite kudasai.** | Well, (at least, let's) split the bill. |
| Yamaguchi | 21 **Jaa, soo shimashoo.** | OK, let's do so. |
| Bartender | 22 **Rokusen-en desu.** | (That'll be) 6,000 yen. |

| | | |
|---|---|---|
| | **kane/okane** 〈polite〉 | money |
| Yamaguchi | 23 **Jaa, kore o.** *(hands over the money)* **Kerii-san, okane wa ato de moraimasu kara...** | Here you are. Mr. Kelly, I'll collect from you later. (lit. I'll receive (your) money later.) |
| Bartender | 24 **Arigatoo gozaimashita.** | Thank you very much. |

## ADDITIONAL VOCABULARY

| | | |
|---|---|---|
| 1 | **oodoburu** | hors d'oeuvre(s) |
| | **A: Kono oodoburu wa oishii desu nee.** | These hors d'oeuvres are delicious! |
| | **hitotsu** | one unit |
| | **hutatsu** | two units |
| | **mittsu** | three units |
| | **yottsu** | four units |
| | **itsutsu** | five units |
| | **muttsu** | six units |
| | **nanatsu** | seven units |
| | **yattsu** | eight units |
| | **kokonotsu** | nine units |
| | **too** | ten units |
| | **moo hitotsu** | one more (unit) |
| | **B: Jaa, moo hitotsu tanomimashoo.** | Then, let's order one more. |
| 2 | **biyahooru** | beer hall |
| | **ikutsu** | how many units? |
| | **A: Ookii biyahooru desu nee! Teeburu ga ikutsu gurai arimasu ka.** | This is a (really) big beer hall! About how many tables are there? |
| | **B: Saa, nanajuu gurai deshoo.** | Well, I guess there are about 70. |

**3** **hima/ohima** <polite>/**na**/ — free time

| | |
|---|---|
| **A: Konban ohima desu ka.** | Are you free tonight? |

**betsu ni**/+ negative/ — not especially

| | |
|---|---|
| **B: Betsu ni yotee wa arimasen ga...** | I've nothing special to do.<br>(lit. I've no special plans.) |

**tsukiaimasu** — to go out (drinking)
**gochisoo-shimasu** — to treat someone to drinks or a meal

| | |
|---|---|
| **A: Jaa, chotto, tsukiatte kudasai.**<br>**Gochisoo-shimasu kara...** | Well, please go out with me.<br>My treat. (lit. Please go out with me for a while, because I'll treat.) |

**4** *(At the cashier's booth in a restaurant)*

**ryooshuusho** — receipt

| | |
|---|---|
| **A: Ryooshuusho, onegai-shimasu.** | Please (give me) a receipt. |

**namae/onamae** <polite> — name

| | |
|---|---|
| **B: Onamae wa doo nasaimasu ka.** | What name shall I use? |
| **A: Ajia Denki ni shite kudasai.** | Please use Asian Electric. |
| **B: Kashikomarimashita. Ajia Denki-sama desu ne. Shooshoo omachi kudasai.** | I understand. Asian Electric right? Just a moment please. |

**5** Additional bar terms

| | | | |
|---|---|---|---|
| **nomimono** | drinks | **poteto-chippu** | potato chips |
| **sutoreeto** | neat, straight | **sarami** | salami |
| **wain** | wine | **hamu** | ham |
| **kakuteru** | cocktail | **oshinko (o)** | Japanese-style pickled vegetables |
| **sohuto-dorinku** | soft drink | **chippu** | tip |
| **zeekin** | tax | **hosutesu** | hostess |
| **baaten** | bartender | **kyabaree** | cabaret |
| **naito-kurabu** | night club | | |

| | | | |
|---|---|---|---|
| **nomiya** | Japanese pub | **sunakku** | a small bar |
| **tabako** | cigarette, tobacco | **matchi** | match |
| **haizara** | ashtray | **raitaa** | lighter |
| **gurasu** | glass | **koppu** | cup |

## GRAMMATICAL NOTES

**1** Gerund + **KARA**

A verb gerund + **kara** is used as an adverbial phrase and means 'after doing ...' or 'since doing ...'

Examples: **Mainichi uchi e kaette *kara*, nihongo o benkyoo-shimasu.**
"I study Japanese everyday after returning home."
**Nihon e kite *kara*, koohoo no shigoto o shite imasu.**
"Since I came to Japan I've been working in P.R."

This combination is sometimes followed by the particle **no** to modify a following noun:
**Nihon e kite *kara no* shigoto**
'the job (I've been doing) since arriving in Japan.'

Note that a gerund + **kara** means 'after,' while a verb + **kara**, introduced in Unit 7, means 'because.'

Compare: **Nihon e kite *kara*, nihongo o benkyoo-shite imasu.**
"After coming to Japan, I've been studying Japanese."
**Nihon e kimashita *kara*, nihongo o benkyoo-shite imasu.**
"Because I came to Japan, I'm studying Japanese."

**2** Adverbial form of adjective + **NARIMASU**

**Yoku** is the adverbial form or -**ku** form of the adjective **ii** (or **yoi**). When it occurs with **narimasu** 'to become', it means 'to improve' or 'become better.'

To use this adverbial form, substitute -**ku** for the final -**i** of the adjective.

Examples:

| | Adverbial form | | |
|---|---|---|---|
| **akai** 'red' | **akaku** | **akaku narimasu** | 'to become red' |
| **hurui** 'old' | **huruku** | **huruku narimasu** | 'to become older' |
| **ookii** 'big' | **ookiku** | **ookiku narimasu** | 'to become bigger' |
| **takai** 'expensive' | **takaku** | **takaku narimasu** | 'to become more expensive' |

Note also a noun + **ni narimasu** introduced in Unit 12.

**3** Replying to a negative question (use of **HAI** and **IIE**)

**Hai** or **ee** means 'what you just said is correct.' So when answering affirmative questions, it corresponds to the English 'yes.' But when replying to negative questions, it confirms the negative and corresponds to the English 'no.'

**Iie** means 'what you just said is wrong.' In replying to affirmative questions it has the same meaning as the English 'no.' But for negative questions, it corresponds to the

English 'yes' and contradicts the negative inference.

| | | | |
|---|---|---|---|
| Examples: | Affirmative question: | **Shimasu ka.** | "Do you do (it)?" |
| | | ***Hai,* shimasu.** | "Yes, I do." |
| | | ***Iie,* shimasen.** | "No, I do not." |
| | Negative question: | **Shimasen ka.** | "Don't you do (it)?" |
| | | ***Hai,* shimasen.** | "You're right. I do not." |
| | | ***Iie,* shimasu.** | "You're wrong. I do." |

**4** **MOO** and **MADA**

**Moo** + an affirmative means 'already,' while **mada** + a negative means 'not yet.' Therefore, **mada** is often used for the negative reply to a **moo** question, and **moo** often occurs as the negative answer to a **mada** question.

| | | |
|---|---|---|
| Examples: | **Chiba-san ni *moo* aimashita ka.** | "Did you already meet Mr. Chiba?" |
| | **Hai, *moo* aimashita.** | "Yes, I already met (him)." |
| | **Iie, *mada* aimasen.** | "No, I didn't meet (him) yet." |

**Chiba-san ni *mada* aimasen ka.** "Haven't you met Mr. Chiba yet?"
**Hai, *mada* aimasen.** "You're right. I haven't met (him) yet."
**Iie, *moo* aimashita.** "You're wrong. I've already met (him)."

**5** Numerals of Japanese origin

In addition to numerals of Chinese origin (e.g. **ichi**, **ni**, **san**, etc.), there are also a set of numerals from 1 through 10 that developed in Japan. **Hitotsu** 'one unit' introduced in the ADDITIONAL VOCABULARY consists of **hito**, Japanese numeral 'one' + the counter **tsu**. This combination can be used for counting things in general.
These Japanese originated numerals are:

| | | | |
|---|---|---|---|
| **hito-** | 1 | **mu-** | 6 |
| **huta-** | 2 | **nana-** | 7 |
| **mi-** | 3 | **ya-** | 8 |
| **yo-** | 4 | **kokono-** | 9 |
| **itsu-** | 5 | **too*** | 10 |

**Too** '10' never occurs with the counter -**tsu**. However it is used with the counter -**ka**, to form **too-ka** for '10 days or the 10th.'
For counting units beyond 10, Chinese numerals without -**tsu** are used.

**6** Question words + **MO** + negative

A question word + **mo** + negative means 'not any…'.

| | | |
|---|---|---|
| **nani** 'what?' | + **mo**/+ negative/ | 'nothing, not anything' |
| **dare** 'who?' | + **mo**/+ negative/ | 'no one, not anyone' |
| **doko** 'where?' | + **mo**/+ negative/ | 'nowhere, not anywhere' |
| **dore** 'which?' | + **mo**/+ negative/ | 'nothing, not anything' |

These combinations usually occur without following particles, such as **wa**, **ga** and **o**. But **ni** and **e** often occur between a question word and **mo**.

| | |
|---|---|
| **dare ni mo** | 'to nobody' |
| **doko e mo** | 'to nowhere' |
| **doko ni mo** | 'at or to nowhere' |

Note that **itsu mo** occuring with a negative and affirmative means 'always.'

**7 NASAIMASU**

**Nasaimasu** is a respectful/honorific equivalent of **shimasu**. It is never used to refer to the speaker.

Examples: **Doko de benkyoo-*nasaimashita* ka.** "Where did you study?"
**Shachoo wa konban paatii o *nasaimasu.***
"The president will have a party tonight."

**8** Inversion

Like English, inversions often occur in Japanese also. Sentence 17 in the MODEL CONVERSATION is one example.

Normal: **Senjitsu mo gochisoo ni narimashita kara, konban wa boku ga haraimasu.**
"Since you also treated the other day, I'll pay this evening."

Inverted: **Konban wa boku ga haraimasu, senjitsu mo gochisoo ni narimashita kara...**
"I'll pay this evening, because you also treated the other day."

**9** Bar terms

**OTSUMAMI** In Japanese bars, **otsumami** refers to light snacks that go with the drinks, such as peanuts, potato chips, salami, etc. Remember that in most bars, it is obligatory to order some **otsumami** or some other 'light food' called **otooshi,** regardless of whether you want it or not.
It may seem unreasonable, but it remains a Japanese custom.

**MAMA** **Mama** is derived from English and refers to a woman manager of a bar or other drinking establishment. Some are actual owners, but generally these women are hired managers.

## PRACTICE

**1** Response drill

Example: Teacher: **Nani ka chuumon-shimashita ka.** "Have you ordered something?"
Student: **Iie, nani mo chuumon-shimasen.** "No, I haven't ordered anything."

| | |
|---|---|
| **1) Nani ka irimasu ka.** | **Iie, nani mo irimasen.** |
| **2) Konban dare ka kimasu ka.** | **Iie, dare mo kimasen.** |
| **3) Ima doko ka ikimasu ka.** | **Iie, doko (e) mo ikimasen.*** |
| **4) Dochira ka kaimasu ka.** | **Iie, dochira mo kaimasen.** |
| **5) Dare ka ni aimashita ka.** | **Iie, dare (ni) mo aimasen.*** |
| **6) Doko ka de hataraite imasu ka.** | **Iie, doko de mo hataraite imasen.** |

---

*For conversation, use of the particles in parenthesis is recommended.

**2** Response drill (in reply to negative questions)

Examples: Teacher: **Kinoo ikimasen deshita ka./ee/**or/**iie/**
"Didn't you go yesterday?"/yes/or/no/
**Ee, ikimasen deshita.** "You're right. I didn't go." *or*
**Iie, ikimashita.** "You're wrong. I went."

| | |
|---|---|
| **1) Biiru o nomimasen ka./iie/** | **Iie, nomimasu.** |
| **2) Buchoo o mimasen deshita ka./ee/** | **Ee, mimasen deshita.** |
| **3) Okane o haraimasen deshita ka./iie/** | **Iie, haraimashita.** |
| **4) Warikan ni shimasen deshita ka./iie/** | **Iie, warikan ni shimashita.** |
| **5) Otsumami o tanomimasen ka./iie/** | **Iie, tanomimasu.** |
| **6) Kono baa wa kiniirimasen ka./ee/** | **Ee, kiniirimasen.** |
| **7) Ebi-hurai wa suki ja arimasen ka./ee/** | **Ee, suki ja arimasen.** |
| **8) Ima hima ja arimasen ka./iie/** | **Iie, hima desu.** |
| **9) Ryooshuusho o moraimasen deshita ka. /iie/** | **Iie, moraimashita.** |
| **10) Anata wa sashimi o tabemasen ka./ee/** | **Ee, tabemasen.** |

After becoming familiar with the above drill, repeat it with the/**ee**/and/**iie**/responses reversed.

**3** Response drill

Example: Teacher: **Moo nani ka chuumon-shimashita ka./ee/**or/**iie/**
"Did you already order something?"/yes/or/no/
Student: **Ee, moo chuumon-shimashita.** "Yes, I already ordered." *or*
**Iie, mada chuumon-shimasen.** "No, I didn't order yet."

| | |
|---|---|
| **1) Nakano-san wa moo kaerimashita ka. /iie/** | **Iie, mada kaerimasen.** |
| **2) Moo nani ka tanomimashita ka./ee/** | **Ee, moo tanomimashita.** |
| **3) Moo Kyooto e ikimashita ka./iie/** | **Iie, mada ikimasen.** |
| **4) Moo okanjoo o haraimashita ka./iie/** | **Iie, mada haraimasen.** |
| **5) Tanaka-san ni moo denwa-shimashita ka./ee/** | **Ee, moo denwa-shimashita.** |
| **6) Moo washoku o tabete mimashita ka. /ee/** | **Ee, moo tabete mimashita.** |
| **7) Moo Shinkansen ni norimashita ka./iie/** | **Iie, mada norimasen.** |
| **8) Moo nihongo ga wakarimasu ka./iie/** | **Iie, mada wakarimasen.** |
| **9) Hikooki wa moo tsukimashita ka./ee/** | **Ee, moo tsukimashita.** |
| **10) Moo okusan ni tegami o kakimashita ka. /iie/** | **Iie, mada kakimasen.** |

After becoming familiar with the above drill, repeat it with the /**ee**/ and /**iie**/ responses reversed.

**4** Response drill

Example: Teacher: **Mada nani mo chuumon-shimasen ka./ee/**or/**iie/**
"Didn't you order anything yet?"/yes/or/no/
Student: **Ee, mada chuumon-shimasen.** "Yes.* I didn't order."
**Iie, moo chuumon-shimashita.** "No.* I already ordered."

*Remember the proper use of/**ee**/and/**iie**/in replying to negative questions.

| | |
|---|---|
| **1) Mada Kyooto e ikimasen ka./ee/** | **Ee, mada ikimasen.** |
| **2) Buchoo wa mada irasshaimasen ka./iie/** | **Iie, moo irasshaimashita.** |
| **3) Mada Nakamura-san ni aimasen ka./iie/** | **Iie, moo aimashita.** |
| **4) Mada Tookyoo no michi wa wakarimasen ka./ee/** | **Ee, mada wakarimasen.** |
| **5) Mada onaka ga sukimasen ka./iie/** | **Iie, moo onaka ga sukimashita.** |
| **6) Nihon no biiru o mada nomimasen ka. /ee/** | **Ee, mada nomimasen.** |
| **7) Mada hookokusho o kakimasen ka./iie/** | **Iie, moo kakimashita.** |
| **8) Kerii-san wa mada dekakemasen ka. /iie/** | **Iie, moo dekakemashita.** |
| **9) Shijoo ni tsuite mada shirabemasen ka./ee/** | **Ee, mada shirabemasen.** |
| **10) Sukiyaki wa mada tabemasen ka./iie/** | **Iie, moo tabemashita.** |

After becoming familiar with the above drill, repeat it with the/**ee**/and/**iie**/responses reversed.

**5** Usage drill

Basic pattern: **Tabako ga hitotsu arimasu.** "There is one (pack of) cigarettes."

| | |
|---|---|
| **matchi** | **hutatsu** |
| **haizara** | **mittsu** |
| **raitaa** | **yottsu** |
| **gurasu** | **itsutsu** |
| **koppu** | **muttsu** |
| **booshi** | **nanatsu** |
| **kyabinetto** | **yattsu** |
| **taipuraitaa** | **kokonotsu** |
| **koojoo** | **too** |
| **shiten** | **juuichi** |
| **heya** | **juuni** |

**6** Transformation drill

Example: Teacher: **Koko no ryoori wa takai desu.**
"Meals here are expensive."
Student: **Koko no ryoori wa takaku narimashita.**
"Meals here became expensive."

| | |
|---|---|
| **1) Kono waapuro wa hurui desu.** | **Kono waapuro wa huruku narimashita.** |
| **2) Kono goro keeki wa ii desu.** | **Kono goro keeki wa yoku narimashita.** |

| | |
|---|---|
| **3) Shigoto ga totemo isogashii desu.** | **Shigoto ga totemo isogashiku narimashita.** |
| **4) Kono koojoo wa ookii desu.** | **Kono koojoo wa ookiku narimashita.** |
| **5) Kerii-san no nihongo wa subarashii desu.** | **Kerii-san no nihongo wa subarashiku narimashita.** |
| **6) Wagasha no seehin wa yasui desu.** | **Wagasha no seehin wa yasuku narimashita.** |

**7** Transformation drill

Example: Teacher: **Nihon e kimashita.** "I came to Japan."
**Nihongo ga yoku natte imasu.** "My Japanese is improving."
Student: **Nihon e kite kara, nihongo ga yoku natte imasu.**
"After coming to Japan, my Japanese is improving."

| | |
|---|---|
| **1) Waapuro o kaimasu.<br>Waapuro o benkyoo-shimasu.** | **Waapuro o katte kara, (waapuro o) benkyoo-shimasu.** |
| **2) Uchi e kaerimashita.<br>Ano tegami o yomimashita.** | **Uchi e kaette kara, ano tegami o yomimashita.** |
| **3) Chiba-san ni aimasu.<br>Sore ni tsuite kikimasu.** | **Chiba-san ni atte kara, sore ni tsuite kikimasu.** |
| **4) Biiru o nomimasu.<br>Mizuwari o nomimashoo.** | **Biiru o nonde kara, mizuwari o nomimashoo.** |
| **5) Shiryoo o shirabemashita.<br>Hookokusho o kakimashita.** | **Shiryoo o shirabete kara, hookokusho o kakimashita.** |
| **6) Kanjoo o haraimashita.<br>Sono ryooriya o demashita.** | **Kanjoo o haratte kara, sono ryooriya o demashita.** |
| **7) Oosaka ni tsukimasu.<br>Buraun-san ni denwa-shimasu.** | **Oosaka ni tsuite kara, Buraun-san ni denwa-shimasu.** |
| **8) Daigaku o demashita.<br>Sugu kono kaisha ni hairimashita.** | **Daigaku o dete kara, sugu kono kaisha ni hairimashita.** |
| **9) Shinkansen ni norimasu.<br>Osake o nomimashoo.** | **Shinkansen ni notte kara, osake o nomimashoo.** |
| **10) Buchoo ni hanashimashita.<br>Kono shigoto o shimashita.** | **Buchoo ni hanashite kara, kono shigoto o shimashita.** |

**8** Transformation drill

Example: Teacher: **Totemo takakatta desu kara, are wa kaimasen deshita.**
"Because it was very expensive, I didn't buy that."
Student: **Are wa kaimasen deshita, totemo takakatta desu kara.**
"I didn't buy that, because it was very expensive."

| | |
|---|---|
| **1) Daisuki desu kara, yoku biiru o nomimasu.** | **Yoku biiru o nomimasu, daisuki desu kara.** |
| **2) Chuumon-shimashita kara, tsumami wa sugu kimasu.** | **Tsumami wa sugu kimasu, chuumon-shimashita kara.** |
| **3) Kiniirimashita kara, mata kimasu.** | **Mata kimasu, kiniirimashita kara.** |

| | |
|---|---|
| 4) **Wakarimasen deshita kara, buchoo ni kikimashita.** | **Buchoo ni kikimashita, wakarimasen deshita kara.** |
| 5) **Go-ji made ni kaerimasu kara, matte ite kudasai.** | **Matte ite kudasai, go-ji made ni kaerimasu kara.** |
| 6) **Warikan ni shimashita kara, takaku arimasen deshita.** | **Takaku arimasen deshita, warikan ni shimashita kara.** |

**9** Level drill

Example: Teacher: **Otsumami wa nan ni shimasu ka.**
"What (kind of) snack will you have?"
Student: **Otsumami wa nan ni nasaimasu ka.**
"What (kind of) snack will you have?"

| | |
|---|---|
| 1) **Nakano-san ni denwa-shimashita ka.** | **Nakano-san ni denwa-nasaimashita ka.** |
| 2) **Buchoo wa biiru o chuumon-shimashita.** | **Buchoo wa biiru o chuumon-nasaimashita.** |
| 3) **Kongetsu ryokoo-shimasu ka.** | **Kongetsu ryokoo-nasaimasu ka.** |
| 4) **Shachoo wa kono shiryoo o sankoo ni shimasu.** | **Shachoo wa kono shiryoo o sankoo ni nasaimasu.** |
| 5) **Kerii-san wa koohoo no shigoto o shite imasu.** | **Kerii-san wa koohoo no shigoto o nasatte imasu.** |
| 6) **Doi-san wa Haabaado de benkyoo-shimashita.** | **Doi-san wa Haabaado de benkyoo-nasaimashita.** |

## EXERCISES

**1** Fill in the blanks with numerals that best describe your situation:

1) **Watakushi no uchi ni wa haizara ga (       ) arimasu.**
2) **Wagasha wa shiten ga (       ) arimasu.**
3) **Jimusho ni tsukue ga (       ) arimasu.**
4) **Uchi wa heya ga (       ) arimasu.**
5) **Kaisha ni wa denwa ga (       ) arimasu.**
6) **Ima made ni raitaa o (       ) gurai kaimashita.**
7) **Uchi ni koppu wa (       ) gurai arimasu.**
8) **Mainichi kudamono o (       ) gurai tabemasu.**

**2** Translate the following sentences into Japanese:

1) Mr. Kelly ordered bourbon on the rocks and peanuts.
2) Japanese business conditions are probably getting better.
3) After I meet Mr. Nakamura, I'll go to JETRO.
4) About how many universities are there in Tokyo?

5) Mr. Yamaguchi often treats me, so I'll treat (him) this evening.
6) Did you already eat *tempura*? No, not yet.
7) Who paid the bill yesterday? General Manager Doi paid (it).
8) I like the wine in this restaurant very much. Yes, it's very delicious!
9) Mr. Tanaka usually doesn't go out with company colleagues.
10) Please come back to the office, after (you) receive the data from Mr. Chiba.

## FOR REFERENCE

### 〔MODEL CONVERSATION〕

| | | |
|---|---|---|
| Yamaguchi | **Osoku narimashita. Moo nani ka chuumon-shimashita ka.** | 遅く なりました。 もう 何 か 注文しました か。 |
| Kelly | **Iie, mada nani mo tanomimasen.** | いいえ、まだ なに も 頼みません。 |
| Bartender | **Nan ni nasaimasu ka.** | 何 に なさいます か。 |
| Yamaguchi | **Boku wa mizu-wari.** | ぼく は 水割り。 |
| Kelly | **Baabon no on-za-rokku, onegai-shimasu.** | バーボン の オン・ザ・ロック、お願いします。 |
| Bartender | **Otsumami wa nani ga ii deshoo ka.** | おつまみ は 何 が いい でしょう か。 |
| Yamaguchi | **Piinattsu wa suki ja arimasen ka.** | ピーナッツ は 好き じゃ ありません か。 |
| Kelly | **Iie, daisuki desu. Piinattsu o tanomimashoo.** | いいえ、大好き です。 ピーナッツ を 頼みましょう。 |
| Bartender | **Doozo.** | どうぞ。 |
| Woman Manager | **Yamaguchi-san, irasshaimase.** | 山口さん、いらっしゃいませ。 |
| Yamaguchi | **Aa, mama, shibaraku (deshita). Kochira, uchi no kaisha no Kerii-san.** | ああ、ママ、しばらく (でした)。 こちら、うち の 会社 の ケリーさん。 |
| Woman Manager | **Kerii-san desu ka. Yoku irasshaimashita.** | ケリーさん です か。 よく いらっしゃいました。 |
| Kelly | **Nakanaka ii baa desu nee. Kiniirimashita yo.** | なかなか いい バー です ねえ。 気に入りました よ。 |
| Woman Manager | **Osoreirimasu. Kerii-san no Nihongo mo subarashii desu nee.** | おそれいります。 ケリーさん の 日本語 も すばらしい です ねえ。 |
| Kelly | **Iie, madamada desu. Nihon e kite kara dandan yoku natte imasu ga...** | いいえ、まだまだ です。 日本 へ 来て から だんだん よく なって います が… |
| Woman Manager | **De wa, doozo goyukkuri.** | で は、どうぞ ごゆっくり。 |
| Yamaguchi | **Jaa, sorosoro kaerimashoo.** | じゃあ、そろそろ 帰りましょう。 |

| | | |
|---|---|---|
| | **Kaikee o.** | 会計 を。 |
| Kelly | **Yamaguchi-san, konban wa boku ga haraimasu yo, senjitsu mo gochisoo ni narimashita kara...** | 山口さん、今晩 は ぼく が 払います よ、 先日 も ごちそう に なりました から… |
| Yamaguchi | **Dame, dame. Koko wa boku no baa desu yo.** | だめ、だめ。 ここ は ぼく の バー です よ。 |
| Kelly | **Jaa, warikan ni shite kudasai.** | じゃあ、割り勘 に して ください。 |
| Yamaguchi | **Jaa, soo shimashoo.** | じゃあ、そう しましょう。 |
| Bartender | **Rokusen-en desu.** | 六千円 です。 |
| Yamaguchi | **Jaa, kore o.** | じゃあ、これ を。 |
| | **Kerii-san, okane wa ato de moraimasu kara...** | ケリーさん、お金 は あと で もらいます から… |
| Bartender | **Arigatoo gozaimashita.** | ありがとう ございました。 |

**〔ADDITIONAL VOCABULARY〕**

**1** **A: Kono oodoburu wa oishii desu nee.**
**B: Jaa, moo hitotsu tanomimashoo.**

この オードブル は おいしい です ねえ。
じゃあ、もう ひとつ 頼みましょう。

**2** **A: Ookii biyahooru desu nee! Teeburu ga ikutsu gurai arimasu ka.**
**B: Saa, nanajuu gurai deshoo.**

大きい ビヤホール です ねえ！テーブル が いくつ ぐらい あります か。
さあ、七十 ぐらい でしょう。

**3** **A: Konban ohima desu ka.**
**B: Betsu ni yotee wa arimasen ga...**
**A: Jaa, chotto, tsukiatte kudasai. Gochisoo-shimasu kara...**

今晩 お暇 です か。
別 に 予定 は ありません が…
じゃあ、ちょっと、つきあって ください。ごちそうします から…

**4** **A: Ryooshuusho, onegai-shimasu.**
**B: Onamae wa doo nasaimasu ka.**
**A: Ajia Denki ni shite kudasai.**
**B: Kashikomarimashita. Ajia Denki-sama desu ne. Shooshoo omachi kudasai.**

領収書、お願いします。
お名前 は どう なさいます か。
アジア 電機 に して ください。
かしこまりました。
アジア 電機さま です ね。
少々 お待ち ください。

**5**

| | |
|---|---|
| **nomimono** | 飲み物 |
| **sutoreeto** | ストレート |
| **wain** | ワイン |
| **kakuteru** | カクテル |
| **sohuto-dorinku** | ソフトドリンク |
| **zeekin** | 税金 |
| **baaten** | バーテン |
| **naito-kurabu** | ナイトクラブ |
| **nomiya** | のみや |
| **tabako** | 煙草 |
| **haizara** | 灰皿 |
| **gurasu** | グラス |
| **poteto-chippu** | ポテトチップ |
| **sarami** | サラミ |
| **hamu** | ハム |
| **oshinko (o)** | おしんこ(う) |
| **chippu** | チップ |
| **hosutesu** | ホステス |
| **kyabaree** | キャバレー |
| **sunakku** | スナック |
| **matchi** | マッチ |
| **raitaa** | ライター |
| **koppu** | コップ |

## BUSINESS COLUMN

## NIGHTCLUBBING

One of the many joys of living in Japan is the opportunity to do business the Japanese way.

It starts at the end of the working day, when men and women head for bars and eateries. In the convivial atmosphere of food, drink, and friendly companionship, people let their hair down, and that's when business gets done.

Foreigners—sometimes to their peril—discover that sales or any other contracts are seldom consummated on the first call. Consensus must be built in the potential customer's firm before any deals are cut.

And that consensus building takes place during entertainment. Time and time again, important relationships are built and nurtured over food and drink, with a friendly hostess or two nearby to keep the conversation light and the spirits flowing. Problems and ideas can be aired freely without anyone having to feel that their time is being encroached upon or that an answer is expected. This give and take goes back to work the next day, as consensus building continues in light of the new information.

The kinds of venues available are simply mindboggling; an ordinary mortal couldn't sample even one percent of everything that is available. There are *sushi* bars, where business can be as light or as delicate as the day's catch.

*Akachoochin*, or red lantern restaurants (as often as not barely holes in the wall), cater to a more raucous clientele. Kababs cooked over a brazier and dunked in sauce keep the conversation flowing. These places are wonderful on a cold night, and are a great place to take either boss or business client.

You can't claim that you've been out, however, until you've experienced a *karaoke* bar. *Karaoke* means, basically, 'empty orchestra,' and describes (sort of) the background music to a popular song—either Japanese or Western. You sing the song itself into a microphone. It's a great way to have fun with a colleague or a client.

Finally there are the numerous cafes, where the young 'salarymen' (and women) hang out. These are great places to obtain basic nutrition enroute to the *karaoke* establishments.

Furthermore, certain nightclubs cater to specific levels of clientele. Company presidents gather at clubs habituated by other presidents. A department or section chief wouldn't be caught dead there. Similarly, a corporate president wouldn't be seen alive or dead in a bar catering to salesmen, department heads or secretaries. The casual eye rarely sees the difference, but Japanese know.

One salesman I know attempted to solicit advertising from an executive of a huge Japanese multinational corporation. They met at a club, where costs, deadlines, printing problems and a host of other issues came up. In a friendly way, over exquisite Japanese cuisine and copious quantities of *sake*, they could both let it all hang out.

And the multinational bought that ad, because the salesman did the right thing: he spent more than one evening building a relationship of trust and frankness, when he really wanted to be home with his loved ones.

**by Terry D. Ragan**
(Deputy Editor, the Journal of the American Chamber of Commerce in Japan)

## REVIEW SECTION III (UNIT 11-15)

**1** Complete the following sentences using the correct particles:

1) **Oosaka kara nan (　　) kimashita ka.**
"How (lit. By what means) did you come from Osaka?"
2) **Shinbashi (　　) densha (　　) orite, chikatetsu (　　) norikaemasu.**
"I'll get off the train at Shinbashi and transfer to the subway".
3) **Kono michi (　　) itte, tsugi no kado (　　) hidari e magatte kudasai.**
"Please go along this street and turn to the right at the next corner."
4) **Nakamura-san no shookai (　　) ukagaimashita.**
"I came here through Mr. Nakamura's introduction."
5) **Chiba-san ga anata (　　) yoroshiku (　　) itte imashita.**
"Mr. Chiba wishes to be remembered to you."
6) **Tsugi no ryokoo wa doko (　　) shimashoo ka.**
"Where shall we decide to go for our next trip?"
7) **Washoku (　　) yooshoku (　　) dochira (　　) suki desu ka.**
"Which do you like, Japanese meals or Western meals?"
8) **Nodo (　　) kawakimashita kara, kono hen (　　) biiru de mo nomimashoo.**
"I'm thirsty, so let's drink draft beer or something."
9) **Kono hon wa Chiba-san (　　) moraimashita ga, taihen sankoo (　　) narimashita.**
"I received this book from Mr. Chiba and it has become a valuable reference."
10) **Nani (　　) gozaimasen ga, doozo goyukkuri.**
"It's really nothing but please relax and take your time."

**2** Complete the following sentences.

1) **Kinoo yori kyoo no hoo ga (　　) desu.**
"Today is hotter than yesterday."
2) **Shikago yori Nyuuyooku no hoo ga (　　) desu.**
"New York is bigger than Chicago."
3) **Tenisu yori (　　) no hoo ga omoshiroi desu.**
"X is more interesting than tennis."
4) **(　　) yori Tookyoo no hoo ga suki desu.**
"I like Tokyo better than X."
5) **Taipuraitaa yori waapuro no hoo ga (　　) desu.**
"A word processor is easier (lit. more convenient) than a typewriter."
6) **Sukiyaki yori (　　) no hoo ga oishii desu.**
"X tastes better than sukiyaki."

**3** Level drill (ordinary to respectful/modest/polite)

Example: Teacher: **Watakushi wa Tanaka desu.** "I'm Tanaka."
Student: **Watakushi wa Tanaka de gozaimasu.** "I'm Tanaka."

| | |
|---|---|
| 1) **Shachoo wa jimusho ni imasu.** | **Shachoo wa jimusho ni irasshaimasu.** |
| 2) **Ashita mata kimasu.** | **Ashita mata ukagaimasu.** |
| 3) **Oosaka e ikimasu ka.** | **Oosaka e irasshaimasu ka.** |
| 4) **Gogo wa uchi ni imasu.** | **Gogo wa uchi ni orimasu.** |
| 5) **Nakamura-san wa sugu kimasu.** | **Nakamura-san wa sugu irasshaimasu.** |

| | |
|---|---|
| 6) **Buchoo wa ryokoo-shimasu ka.** | **Buchoo wa ryokoo-nasaimasu ka.** |
| 7) **Sore wa buchoo no kuruma desu.** | **Sore wa buchoo no kuruma de gozaimasu.** |
| 8) **Kinoo Yokohama e ikimashita.** | **Kinoo Yokohama e mairimashita.** |
| 9) **Buchoo wa kyoo jimusho e kimasen.** | **Buchoo wa kyoo jimusho e irasshaimasen.** |
| 10) **Koko ni denwa ga arimasu ka.** | **Koko ni denwa ga gozaimasu ka.** |
| 11) **Chiba-san wa paatii ni kimasen deshita.** | **Chiba-san wa paatii ni irasshaimasen deshita.** |
| 12) **Nakano-san wa koko ni imasu.** | **Nakano-san wa koko ni irasshaimasu.** |
| 13) **Anata wa daigaku de nani o benkyoo-shimashita ka.** | **Anata wa daigaku de nani o benkyoo nasaimashita ka.** |
| 14) **Roku-ji ni otaku e ikimasu.** | **Roku-ji ni otaku e ukagaimasu.** |

**4** Transformation drill (ordinary to respectful)

Example: Teacher: **Matte kudasai.** "Please wait."
Student: **Omachi kudasai.**"Please wait."

| | |
|---|---|
| 1) **Kono kusuri o nonde kudasai.** | **Kono kusuri o onomi kudasai.** |
| 2) **Kono shorui o yonde kudasai.** | **Kono shorui o oyomi kudasai.** |
| 3) **Sugu dekakete kudasai.** | **Sugu odekake kudasai.** |
| 4) **Denwa-bangoo o kaite kudasai.** | **Denwa-bangoo o okaki kudasai.** |
| 5) **Shachoo ni atte kudasai.** | **Shachoo ni oai kudasai.** |
| 6) **Shibuya de norikaete kudasai.** | **Shibuya de onorikae kudasai.** |
| 7) **Juu-ji made ni kaette kudasai.** | **Juu-ji made ni okaeri kudasai.** |
| 8) **Yokohama-eki de orite kudasai.** | **Yokohama-eki de oori kudasai.** |
| 9) **Buchoo ni kiite kudasai.** | **Buchoo ni okiki kudasai.** |
| 10) **Shinkansen ni notte kudasai.** | **Shinkansen ni onori kudasai.** |

**5** Response drill

Example: Teacher: **Nani o kaite imasu ka./yushutsu, hookoku/**
"What are you writing?" /export, report/
Student: **Yushutsu ni tsuite no hookoku o kaite imasu.**
"I'm writing a report concerning exports."

| | |
|---|---|
| 1) **Nani o yonde imasu ka. /Nihon no shijoo, hon/** | **Nihon no shijoo ni tsuite no hon o yonde imasu.** |
| 2) **Nani o mite imasu ka. /ginkoo, shiryoo/** | **Ginkoo ni tsuite no shiryoo o mite imasu.** |
| 3) **Nani o shirabete imasu ka. /yunyuu, hooritsu/** | **Yunyuu ni tsuite no hooritsu o shirabete imasu.** |
| 4) **Nani o kaimashita ka. /Amerika no rekishi, hon/** | **Amerika no rekishi ni tsuite no hon o kaimashita.** |
| 5) **Chiba-san kara nani o moraimashita ka./Nihon no shijoo, deeta/** | **Nihon no shijoo ni tsuite no deeta o moraimashita.** |

# UNIT 16

*AT THE BANK*

銀行

ぎんこう

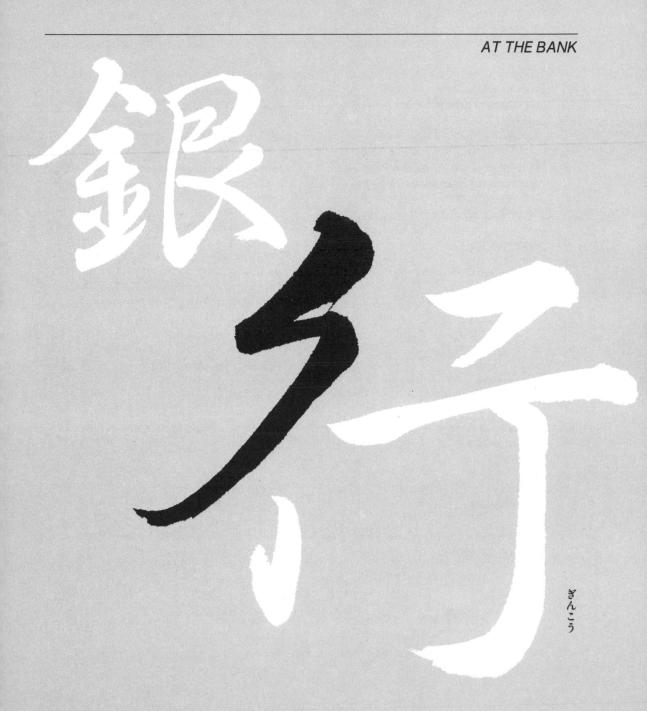

## MODEL CONVERSATION

## SITUATION

*Kelly has lunch with Hiromi Aoki, a woman who works with him in the P.R. Department. He asks her how to go about opening a bank account and she offers to help him. Together they go to a neighborhood bank.*

| | |
|---|---|
| **yokin** | deposit |
| **yokin-shimasu** | to deposit (money) |
| **yokin-shitai n desu** | to want to deposit (money) |
| **tetsuzuki** | procedure |
| **muzukashii** | difficult, complicated |

Kelly **1 Ginkoo ni yokin-shitai n desu ga, tetsuzuki wa muzukashii desu ka.** — I want to open a bank account, (lit. I want to deposit money in a bank) is it a complicated procedure?

| | |
|---|---|
| **kantan/na/** | easy, simple |
| **issho ni** | together, with |
| **itte agemasu** | to go for you |

Aoki **2 Iie, tetsuzuki wa kantan desu ga, issho ni itte agemashoo ka.** — No, the procedure is easy, shall I go with you (lit. for you)?

| | |
|---|---|
| **sore wa doomo** | it's kind of you, thank you |
| **tetsudaimasu** | to help, assist |
| **tetsudatte kuremasu** | to help (the speaker) |

Kelly **3 Sore wa doomo. Jaa, tetsudatte kuremasu ka.** — Thank you. Will you help me?

| | |
|---|---|
| **ii desu yo** | it's OK, fine |
| **han** *or* **hankoo** | personal seal |

Aoki **4 Ee, ii desu yo. Tokoro de, Kerii-san, hankoo ga arimasu ka.** — Yes, I'll be happy to. (lit. it's fine) By the way, Mr. Kelly, do you have a seal?

| | |
|---|---|
| **tsukurimasu** | to make, produce |
| **tsukutte moraimasu** | to have (something) made |

| | | |
|---|---|---|
| Kelly | **5 Ee, arimasu. Senjitsu tsukutte moraimashita.** | Yes, I do. I had (one) made the other day. |
| Aoki | **6 Soo desu ka. Jaa, ikimashoo.** | Is that so? Well, let's go. |

*(at the bank window)*

| | |
|---|---|
| **kooza** | an account |
| **hirakimasu** | to open |
| **hirakitai n desu** | to want to open |

| | | |
|---|---|---|
| Kelly | **7 Kooza o hirakitai n desu ga...** | I'd like to open an account, but... |

| | |
|---|---|
| **hutsuu** | ordinary |
| **hutsuu-yokin (kooza)** | savings account |

| | | |
|---|---|---|
| Clerk | **8 Hutsuu-yokin deshoo ka.** | Will it be a savings account? |
| Kelly | **9 Ee, soo desu.** | Yes, that's right. |

| | |
|---|---|
| **kaado** | card, form |
| **juusho** | address |

| | | |
|---|---|---|
| Clerk | **10 De wa, kono kaado ni onamae to juusho o onegai-shimasu.** | Well, please (write) your name and address on this card. |

*(Kelly and Aoki go to a courtesy desk)*

| | |
|---|---|
| **katakana** | square form of Japanese syllabary used especially for foreign words |
| **hiragana** | cursive form of Japanese syllabary |
| **kanji** | Chinese characters |

| | | |
|---|---|---|
| Aoki | **11 Kerii-san, koko ni katakana de namae o kaite, sono shita ni kanji de juusho o kaite kudasai.** | Mr. Kelly, please write your name here in *katakana* and your address below it in Chinese characters. |

| | | |
|---|---|---|
| Kelly | **12 Kore de ii desu ka.** | Is this all right? |
| | **daijoobu** /**na**/ | safe, surely, OK |
| Aoki | **13 Ee, daijoobu desu yo.** | Yes, it's OK. |
| | *(they return to the window)* | |
| | **dekimasu** | to complete, finish |
| Kelly | **14 Dekimashita yo.** | I finished it. |
| | **oikura** 〈polite〉<br>**nyuukin-shimasu/nasaimasu** 〈respectful〉 | how much?<br>to pay, deposit |
| Clerk | **15 Kyoo wa oikura nyuukin-nasaimasu ka.** | How much will you deposit today? |
| Kelly | **16 Goman-en desu.** | 50,000 yen. |
| | **inkan** | seal |
| Clerk | **17 Arigatoo gozaimasu. De wa okane to inkan o doozo.** *(Kelly hands them to the clerk)* **Shooshoo omachi kudasai.** | Thank you very much. Then, may I please have the money and your seal.<br>Just a moment please. |
| | **tsuuchoo** | bankbook, savings passbook |
| Clerk | **18 Omatase-shimashita.**<br>**Kore ga tsuuchoo desu.**<br>**Arigatoo gozaimasu.** | Thank you for waiting.<br>Here is your bankbook.<br>Thank you very much. |
| Kelly | **19 Yaa, doomo.**<br>**Aoki-san, doomo arigatoo gozaimashita.** | Oh, thanks.<br>Ms. Aoki, thank you very much. |

## ADDITIONAL VOCABULARY

| | |
|---|---|
| 1 kyasshu-kaado | cash card for a particular bank |
| tsukutte moraitai n desu | to want to have something made |
| **A: Kyasshu-kaado o tsukutte moraitai n desu ga...** | I'd like you to issue (lit. make) me a cash card, but... |
| watakushidomo | we, our company |
| yokin-kooza | savings account |
| **B: Watakushidomo ni yokin-kooza ga gozaimasu ne.** | You have a savings account with our bank, don't you? |
| **A: Ee, arimasu yo.** | Yes, I have. |
| shorui | form, document |
| **B: De wa, kono shorui ni okaki kudasai.** | All right then, please fill (lit. write) out this form. |
| 2 teeki-yokin | time deposit |
| riritsu | interest rate |
| **A: Ima teeki (-yokin) no riritsu wa dono gurai desu ka.** | How much is the current interest rate for time deposits? |
| nen | year, annually |
| paasento | percent |
| san-ten-nana | 3.7 |
| **B: Nen san-ten-nana paasent gurai desu yo.** | (The annual rate) is about 3.7%. |
| sagarimasu | to decrease, drop |
| **A: Zuibun sagarimashita nee.** | It's dropped a lot, hasn't it? |
| desu kara | therefore, that's why |
| kabu | stocks, shares |

| | |
|---|---|
| **B: Desu kara, ima wa kabu no hoo ga omoshiroi desu yo.** | That's why stocks are so interesting right now. |

| | |
|---|---|
| **demo** | but, however |
| **abunai** | dangerous, risky |

| | |
|---|---|
| **A: Demo, kabu wa abunai deshoo?** | But stocks are risky, aren't they? |

| | |
|---|---|
| **anzen/na/** | safe |
| **rishi** | interest (on the deposit) |
| **tsumaranai** | uninteresting, unattractive, worthless |

| | |
|---|---|
| **B: Teeki wa anzen desu ga, rishi ga yasui desu kara, tsumaranai desu yo.** | Time deposits are safe, but because interest rates are low (lit. cheap), they are unattractive. |

3

| | |
|---|---|
| **gasu** | gas |
| **ryookin** | charge, rate, fee |
| **shiharai** | payment |
| **mendoo/na/** | troublesome, problematic |

| | |
|---|---|
| **A: Denki ya gasu no ryookin no shiharai wa mendoo desu nee.** | Paying electricity and gas bills are (really) a problem! |

| | |
|---|---|
| **jidoo-hurikomi** | automatic bank deposit |
| **mondai ga arimasu** | there is a problem |
| **mondai (wa) arimasen** | there is no problem |

| | |
|---|---|
| **B: Uchi wa ginkoo no jidoo-hurikomi ni shite imasu kara, mondai arimasen yo.** | We use automatic bank deposits, so there's no problem. |

| | |
|---|---|
| **sassoku** | at once, immediately, right now |
| **soodan-shimasu** | to consult |

| | |
|---|---|
| **A: Soo desu ka. Sore wa ii desu nee. Boku mo sassoku ginkoo ni soodan-shimashoo.** | Is that so? That's very good! I'll consult with my bank right away. |

4

| | |
|---|---|
| **kogitte** | check |
| **azukemasu** | to deposit, leave (something) with |
| **oroshite kimasu** | to withdraw and return |

| | |
|---|---|
| **A: Ginkoo e itte, kono kogitte o azukete, sore kara kono tsuuchoo kara juuman-en oroshite kite kudasai.** | Go to the bank, deposit this check and then withdraw 100,000 yen from this account (lit. bankbook) and return. |

**genkin** — cash, money
**zenbu** — all
**ichiman-en satsu** — 10,000 yen bill

| | |
|---|---|
| **B: Kashikomarimashita. Genkin wa zenbu ichiman-en satsu desu ka.** | Certainly. (Do you want) all the money in 10,000 yen bills? |

| | |
|---|---|
| **A: Ee, soo desu.** | Yes, that's right. |

5 **tekisuto** — textbook

| | |
|---|---|
| **A: Kono tekisuto wa muzukashii desu nee.** | This textbook is very difficult! |

**kyookasho** — textbook
**yasashii** — easy, simple

| | |
|---|---|
| **B: Soo desu ka. Kono kyookasho wa yasashii desu yo.** | Is that so? This one is simple. |

6 Additional bank terms

| | | | |
|---|---|---|---|
| **tooza-yokin** | checking account | **tegata** | promissory note |
| **yuushi** | loan, financing | **roon** | loan |
| **husai** | debt | **shakkin** | borrowed money |
| **tanpo** | security, mortgage | **saiken** | credit, claim |
| **hyaku-en kooka** *or* **hyaku-en-dama** | 100 yen coin | **sen-en satsu** | 1,000 yen bill |

## GRAMMATICAL NOTES

1 -**TAI** form

-**Tai** 'to want to' or 'would like to' replaces **masu** following a verb stem and usually is followed by **desu** or **n desu**:

**aimasu** 'to meet' — **ai*tai n desu*** 'to want to meet'

| | |
|---|---|
| **kaimasu** 'to buy' | **kai*tai n desu*** 'to want to buy' |
| **mimasu** 'to see' | **mi*tai n desu*** 'to want to see' |
| **nomimasu** 'to drink' | **nomi*tai n desu*** 'to want to drink' |
| **tabemasu** 'to eat' | **tabe*tai n desu*** 'to want to eat' |

A special grammatical feature of the -**tai** form is when a transitive verb stem -**tai** + **n desu** is used as a predicate directly after an object, the object is indicated by the particle **ga**.

Compare: **Biiru o nomimasu.** "I'll drink beer."
**Biiru *ga* nomi*tai n desu*.** "I want to drink beer."

In this -**tai** sentence, the subject wanting to do something would be followed by the particle **wa**. The basic pattern for -**tai** sentences is:

| Subject | Objective | -**TAI** predicate |
|---|---|---|
| **Watakushi wa** | **sono hon *ga*** | **yomi*tai (n) desu.*** |
| | I want to read that book. | |

Particle **o** may also occur after an object, i.g. **Biiru o nomitai n desu.** This happens when an adverbial phrase or a number-counter combination occurs between the object and -**tai** predicate.

Compare: **Watakushi wa koohii ga nomitai n desu.** "I want to drink coffee."
**Watakushi wa koohii *o ip-pai* nomitai n desu.**
"I want to drink a cup of coffee."
**Kono hon ga yomitakatta n desu.** "( I ) wanted to read this book."
**Kono hon *o kinoo* yomitakatta n desu.**
"( I ) wanted to read this book yesterday."

The -**tai** form itself is a type of adjective and has the following inflections:

| | | |
|---|---|---|
| Non-past affirmative: | **shitai (n) desu** | "want to do" |
| Non-past negative: | **shitaku arimasen** | "not want to do" |
| Past affirmative: | **shitakatta (n) desu** | "wanted to do" |
| Past negative: | **shitaku arimasen deshita** | "not wanted to do" |
| Gerund affirmative: | **shitakute** | "wanting to do" |
| Gerund negative: | **shitakunakute** | "not wanting to do" |

**2** Gerund + **AGEMASU/KUREMASU/MORAIMASU**

**1) AGEMASU** 'to give someone something'

A verb gerund + **agemasu** means 'to do something for someone'. In this pattern, the person doing the action is the subject. The person who benefits from the action is indicated by the particle **ni**, when the following predicate has an object and the particle **o**, when the following predicate has no object.

| Person doing the action | Person who benefits | Action taken |
|---|---|---|
| **Watakushi wa/ga** | **Kerii-san *ni*** | **michi o oshiete *agemashita.*** |

| | | |
|---|---|---|
| I showed Mr. Kelly the way (for him). | | |
| **Watakushi wa** | **Kerii-san o** | **tetsudaimashita.** |
| I helped Mr. Kelly (for him). | | |

Examples: **Aoki-san ni kono hon *o* misete *agemasu.***
"I'll show Miss Aoki this book."
**Sono tegami *o* kaite *agemashoo ka.***
"Shall I write that letter for you?"
**Kerii-san *o* annai-shite *agete kudasai.***
"Please show Mr. Kelly (around the company)."

Remember with this pattern, the speaker is never the person who benefits from the action.

2) **KUREMASU** 'something received by the speaker or members of the speaker's group'
A verb gerund + **kuremasu** means that someone does something to/for the speaker or members of the speaker's group. When used in question form, the person being questioned is usually the beneficiary.

Examples: **Chiba-san ga shiryoo o misete *kuremashita.***
"Mr. Chiba showed me the data."
**Kerii-san ga kanai ni eego o oshiete *kuremasu.***
"Mr. Kelly'll teach my wife English."
**Dare ga sono tegami o kaite *kuremashita ka.***
"Who wrote the letter for you?"

3) **MORAIMASU** 'to recieve something from someone'
A verb gerund + **moraimasu** means 'to have something done by someone.' In this pattern, the person who benefits is indicated as the subject and the person providing the service is indicated by the particle **ni.**

| Person who benefits | Person performing service | Action taken |
|---|---|---|
| **Kerii-san wa/ga** | **Nakano-san *ni*** | **nihongo o oshiete *moraimasu*** |
| Mr. Kelly is going to have Mr. Nakano teach him Japanese. | | |

Examples: **Boku wa sono shigoto o tomodachi ni tetsudatte *moraimashita.***
"I had my friend help me with that work."
**Anata wa dare *ni* ryoori o tanonde *moraimashita ka.***
"Who ordered the food for you? (lit. Whom did you have order the food?)"
**Ryooshuusho o kaite *moraimashoo ka.***
"Shall I have a receipt written?"

A verb gerund + **moraitai n desu ga...** is often used as an indirect request.

Compare: **Chotto oshiete *moraitai n desu ga*...**
"I'd like to have you teach me a little, but..."
**Chotto oshiete kudasai.** "Please teach me a little."

**3** How to read groups of numbers with decimal points
The word in Japanese for decimal point is **shoosuuten.** However, when reading groups of numbers that include decimal points the word **ten** is used and the numbers following the decimal are pronounced individually using Chinese derived numerals.

3.2 **san-*ten*-ni**
7.68 **nana-*ten*-roku-hachi**
69.05 **rokujuukyuu-*ten*-zero-go(o)***
156.26 **hyaku gojuuroku-*ten*-ni( i )-roku***

*As explained in Unit 6, the pronunciation for 2 and 5 is slightly longer, when used independently as in the above examples.

**4** Gerund + **KURU**
A gerund + **kuru** literally means 'to do something and return.' This combination can also mean to 'go and do something (and return).'
Examples: **Ima Chiba-san ni atte *kimasu*.** "I'll go and see Mr. Chiba now."
**Kinoo kore o katte *kimashita*.** "I went to buy this yesterday."
**Ginkoo de okane o oroshite *kite* kudasai.**
"Please go to the bank and withdraw the money."

## PRACTICE

**1** Transformation drill
Example: Teacher: **Yokin-shimasu.** "I'll deposit (money in a bank)."
Student: **Yokin-shitai n desu.** "I want to deposit (money in a bank)."

| | |
|---|---|
| 1) **Chuumon-shimasu.** | **Chuumon-shitai n desu.** |
| 2) **Benkyoo-shimasu.** | **Benkyoo-shitai n desu.** |
| 3) **Tetsudaimasu.** | **Tetsudaitai n desu.** |
| 4) **Ikimasu.** | **Ikitai n desu.** |
| 5) **Kaimasu.** | **Kaitai n desu.** |
| 6) **Kimasu.** | **Kitai n desu.** |
| 7) **Moraimasu.** | **Moraitai n desu.** |
| 8) **Oshiemasu.** | **Oshietai n desu.** |
| 9) **Denwa o kakemasu.** | **Denwa o kaketai n desu.** |
| 10) **Matte imasu.** | **Matte itai n desu.** |

**2** Response drill
Example: Teacher: **Ano ginkoo ni kooza o hirakimasu ka.**

"Are you going to open an account with that bank?"
Student: **Ee, hirakitai n desu.** "Yes, I'd like to open (an account)."

| | |
|---|---|
| **1) Kyoo tegami o kakimasu ka.** | **Ee, kakitai n desu.** |
| **2) Ima okane o haraimasu ka.** | **Ee, haraitai n desu.** |
| **3) Buchoo ni aimasu ka.** | **Ee, aitai n desu.** |
| **4) Biiru o nomimasu ka.** | **Ee, nomitai n desu.** |
| **5) Sugu okane o oroshimasu ka.** | **Ee, oroshitai n desu.** |
| **6) Yuubinkyoku ni okane o azukemasu ka.** | **Ee, azuketai n desu.** |
| **7) Gogo dekakemasu ka.** | **Ee, dekaketai n desu.** |
| **8) Kono shiryoo o shirabemasu ka.** | **Ee, shirabetai n desu.** |
| **9) Ano kuruma o urimasu ka.** | **Ee, uritai n desu.** |
| **10) Sono hon o yomimasu ka.** | **Ee, yomitai n desu.** |

**3** Response drill
Example: Teacher: **Kooza o hirakimasu ka.** "Are you going to open an account?"
Student: **Iie, hirakitaku arimasen.** "No, I don't want to (open)."

(Use the sentences from Drill **2** )

**4** Transformation drill
Example: Teacher: **Watakushi ga tetsudaimasu yo.** "I'll help."
Student: **Watakushi ga tetsudatte agemasu yo.** "I'll help you."

| | |
|---|---|
| **1) Watakushi ga ikimasu yo.** | **Watakushi ga itte agemasu yo.** |
| **2) Ku-ji made ni kimasu yo.** | **Ku-ji made ni kite agemasu yo.** |
| **3) Shachoo ni hanashimasu yo.** | **Shachoo ni hanashite agemasu yo.** |
| **4) Ima chizu o kakimasu yo.** | **Ima chizu o kaite agemasu yo.** |
| **5) Sono shiryoo o shirabemasu yo.** | **Sono shiryoo o shirabete agemasu yo.** |
| **6) Watakushi ga eego o oshiemasu yo.** | **Watakushi ga eego o oshiete agemasu yo.** |

**5** Transformation drill
Example: Teacher: **Aoki-san ga tetsudaimasu.** "Ms. Aoki will help."
Student: **Aoki-san ga tetsudatte kuremasu.** "Ms. Aoki will help me."

| | |
|---|---|
| **1) Kachoo ga annai-shimasu.** | **Kachoo ga annai-shite kuremasu.** |
| **2) Anata ga shirabemasu ka.** | **Anata ga shirabete kuremasu ka.** |
| **3) Doi-san ga shookai-shimashita.** | **Doi-san ga shookai-shite kuremashita.** |
| **4) Chiba-san ga michi o oshiemasu.** | **Chiba-san ga michi o oshiete kuremasu.** |
| **5) Ryoori o chuumon-shimashita ka.** | **Ryoori o chuumon-shite kuremashita ka.** |
| **6) Buchoo ga kanjoo o haraimasu.** | **Buchoo ga kanjoo o haratte kuremasu.** |

**6** Transformation drill
Example: Teacher: **Aoki-san ga tetsudatte kuremasu.** "Ms. Aoki will help me."
Student: **Aoki-san ni tetsudatte moraimasu.** "I'll have Ms. Aoki help me."

| | |
|---|---|
| 1) **Doi-san ga annai-shite kuremashita.** | **Doi-san ni annai-shite moraimashita.** |
| 2) **Chiba-san ga kanji o oshiete kuremasu.** | **Chiba-san ni kanji o oshiete moraimasu.** |
| 3) **Aoki-san ga ryoori o tsukutte kuremashita.** | **Aoki-san ni ryoori o tsukutte moraimashita.** |
| 4) **Kachoo ga issho ni itte kuremashita.** | **Kachoo ni issho ni itte moraimashita.** |
| 5) **Nakano-san ga okane o azukete kuremasu.** | **Nakano-san ni okane o azukete moraimasu.** |
| 6) **Buchoo ga hookoku o yonde kuremasu.** | **Buchoo ni hookoku o yonde moraimasu.** |

**7** Response drill

Example: Teacher: **Tetsudatte kuremasu ka.** "Will you help me?"
Student: **Ee, tetsudatte agemasu yo.** "Yes, I'll help you."

| | |
|---|---|
| 1) **Chotto matte kuremasu ka.** | **Ee, matte agemasu yo.** |
| 2) **Ashita mo kite kuremasu ka.** | **Ee, kite agemasu yo.** |
| 3) **Hookoku o kaite kuremasu ka.** | **Ee, kaite agemasu yo.** |
| 4) **Denki-ryookin o haratte kuremasu ka.** | **Ee, haratte agemasu yo.** |
| 5) **Suupu o chuumon-shite kuremasu ka.** | **Ee, chuumon-shite agemasu yo.** |
| 6) **Kyoo nyuukin-shite kuremasu ka.** | **Ee, nyuukin-shite agemasu yo.** |

**8** Response drill

Example: Teacher: **Dare ni tetsudatte moraimashita ka./Aoki-san/**
"Who did you have help you?"/Ms. Aoki/
Student: **Aoki-san ga tetsudatte kuremashita.** "Ms. Aoki helped me."

| | |
|---|---|
| 1) **Dare ni katakana o oshiete moraimasu ka. /Yamaguchi-san/** | **Yamaguchi-san ga oshiete kuremasu.** |
| 2) **Dare ni ginkoo ni itte moraimasu ka. /Tanaka-san/** | **Tanaka-san ga itte kuremasu.** |
| 3) **Dare ni hookoku o kaite moraimashita ka. /Kerii-san/** | **Kerii-san ga kaite kuremashita.** |
| 4) **Dare ni denwa o kakete moraimasu ka. /Nakano-san/** | **Nakano-san ga kakete kuremasu.** |
| 5) **Dare ni jimusho ni ite moraimasu ka. /Doi-san/** | **Doi-san ga ite kuremasu.** |
| 6) **Dare ni ryookin o haratte moraimasu ka. /Chiba-san/** | **Chiba-san ga haratte kuremasu.** |

**9** Usage drill

Practice reading the following numbers in Japanese:

| | | | |
|---|---|---|---|
| 2.5 | 20.5 | 2.05 | 2.005 |
| 7.34 | 9.99 | 6.15 | 0.67 |
| 53.87 | 3.28 percent | 5.54 percent | 4.62 |

**10** Transformation drill

Example: Teacher: **Ginkoo ni okane o azukemasu.**
"I'll deposit the money in the bank."

Student: **Ginkoo ni okane o azukete kimasu.**
"I'll go and deposit money in the bank."

| | |
|---|---|
| **1) Buchoo no iken o kikimasu.** | **Buchoo no iken o kiite kimasu.** |
| **2) Tookyoo no chizu o kaimasu.** | **Tookyoo no chizu o katte kimasu.** |
| **3) Chotto koohii o nomimasu.** | **Chotto koohii o nonde kimasu.** |
| **4) Kyoo Chiba-san ni aimasu.** | **Kyoo Chiba-san ni atte kimasu.** |
| **5) Gasu no ryookin o haraimasu.** | **Gasu no ryookin o haratte kimasu.** |
| **6) Yushutsu no deeta o shirabemasu.** | **Yushutsu no deeta o shirabete kimasu.** |

**11** Response drill
Example: Teacher: **Kono kabu wa abunai desu ka.** "Is this stock risky?"
Student: **Ee, abunai kabu desu yo.** "Yes, it's risky stock."

| | |
|---|---|
| **1) Kono kabu wa anzen desu ka.** | **Ee, anzen na kabu desu yo.** |
| **2) Sono hon wa omoshiroi desu ka.** | **Ee, omoshiroi hon desu yo.** |
| **3) Sono hon wa muzukashii desu ka.** | **Ee, muzukashii hon desu yo.** |
| **4) Sono hon wa yasashii desu ka.** | **Ee, yasashii hon desu yo.** |
| **5) Ano shigoto wa tsumaranai desu ka.** | **Ee, tsumaranai shigoto desu yo.** |
| **6) Ano shigoto wa mendoo desu ka.** | **Ee, mendoo na shigoto desu yo.** |
| **7) Kono byooin wa dame desu ka.** | **Ee, dame na byooin desu yo.** |
| **8) Kono byooin wa subarashii desu ka.** | **Ee, subarashii byooin desu yo.** |

## EXERCISE

**1** Fill in the blanks with the word(s) that best describe your situation.

1) **Watakushi wa (          )-ginkoo ni kooza ga arimasu.**
2) **(          )-nen (          )-gatsu goro kooza o hirakimashita.**
3) **Sono ginkoo ni wa tooza-yokin no kooza wa/mo (          )** ⟨have/have not⟩
4) **Sono ginkoo no kyasshu-kaado ga (          ).** ⟨have/have not⟩
5) **Sono ginkoo de wa inkan ga (          ).** ⟨need/do not need⟩
6) **Konogoro hutsuu-yokin no rishi wa (          ) paasento gurai de, teeki-yokin no rishi wa (          ) paasento gurai desu.**
7) (your country) **de anzen na kabu wa** (company) **no desu.**
8) **Ima** (company) **no kabu ga omoshiroi deshoo.**

**2** Translate the following sentences into Japanese:

1) Mr. Brown had a personal seal made last week.
2) Mr. Nakano will teach me import procedures.
3) I wrote a map of Ginza for Mr. Kelly.
4) Mr. Chiba uses Yokohama Bank's automatic deposit, so paying gas and electricity bills is no problem.
5) I want to deposit 100,000 yen in the Bank of Tokyo.

6) Both my seal and bankbook are on that table over there.
7) I'd like to have Ms. Aoki fill in this form.
8) Shall I help you? No thank you. I can do (it).
9) General Manager Doi bought a new word-processor for me.
10) The yearly interest rate for time deposits in Japan is about 4.2 percent.
11) What is the safest stock in Japan? I'd like to have someone tell (teach) me about it.
12) I don't want to buy stocks because they are usually risky.
13) Did you pay (it) by (lit. by means of) check? No. I paid (it) with cash.
14) How much of a loan do you have with that bank? It's about 500,000 yen.
15) About how much is that interest rate? Its annual rate is 12.45%.

## FOR REFERENCE

### 〔MODEL CONVERSATION〕

| | | |
|---|---|---|
| Kelly | **Ginkoo ni yokin-shitai n desu ga, tetsuzuki wa muzukashii desu ka.** | 銀行 に 預金 したい ん です が、 手続き は 難しい です か。 |
| Aoki | **Iie, tetsuzuki wa kantan desu ga, issho ni itte agemashoo ka.** | いいえ、 手続き は 簡単 です が、一緒 に 行って あげましょう か。 |
| Kelly | **Sore wa doomo. Jaa, tetsudatte kuremasu ka.** | それ は どうも。 じゃあ、 手伝って くれます か。 |
| Aoki | **Ee, ii desu yo. Tokoro de, Kerii-san, hankoo ga arimasu ka.** | ええ、いいです よ。 ところ で、 ケリーさん、はんこう が あります か。 |
| Kelly | **Ee, arimasu. Senjitsu tsukutte moraimashita.** | ええ、あります。 先日 作って もらいました。 |
| Aoki | **Soo desu ka. Jaa, ikimashoo.** | そうです か。じゃあ、行きましょう。 |
| Kelly | **Kooza o hirakitai n desu ga...** | 口座 を 開きたい ん です が… |
| Clerk | **Hutsuu-yokin deshoo ka.** | 普通預金 でしょう か。 |
| Kelly | **Ee, soo desu.** | ええ、そう です。 |
| Clerk | **De wa, kono kaado ni onamae to juusho o onegai-shimasu.** | で は、この カード に お名前 と 住所 を お願いします。 |
| Aoki | **Kerii-san, koko ni katakana de namae o kaite, sono shita ni kanji de juusho o kaite kudasai.** | ケリーさん、ここ に カタカナ で 名前 を 書いて、その 下 に 漢字 で 住所 を 書いて ください。 |
| Kelly | **Kore de ii desu ka.** | これで いい です か。 |
| Aoki | **Ee, daijoobu desu yo.** | ええ、大丈夫 です よ。 |
| Kelly | **Dekimashita yo.** | できました よ。 |
| Clerk | **Kyoo wa oikura nyuukin-nasaimasu ka.** | 今日 は おいくら 入金なさいます か。 |
| Kelly | **Goman-en desu.** | 五万円 です。 |
| Clerk | **Arigatoo gozaimasu. De wa okane to inkan o doozo. Shooshoo omachi kudasai.** | ありがとう ございます。で は お金 と 印鑑 を どうぞ。 少々 お待ち ください。 |

| | | |
|---|---|---|
| Clerk | **Omatase-shimashita. Kore ga tsuuchoo desu. Arigatoo gozaimasu.** | お待たせしました。これ が 通帳 です。ありがとう ございます。 |
| Kelly | **Yaa, doomo. Aoki-san, doomo arigatoo gozaimashita.** | やあ、どうも。 青木さん、 どうも ありがとう ございました。 |

**〔ADDITIONAL VOCABULARY〕**

**1** **A: Kyasshu-kaado o tsukutte moraitai n desu ga...**
キャッシュ・カード を 作って もらいたい ん です が…
**B: Watakushidomo ni yokin-kooza ga gozaimasu ne.**
わたくしども に 預金口座 が ございます ね。
**A: Ee, arimasu yo.**
ええ、あります よ。
**B: De wa, kono shorui ni okaki kudasai.**
で は、この 書類 に お書き ください。

**2** **A: Ima teeki (-yokin) no riritsu wa dono gurai desu ka.**
いま 定期(預金)の 利率 は どの ぐらい です か。
**B: Nen san-ten-nana paasent gurai desu yo.**
年 3.7 パーセント ぐらい です よ。
**A: Zuibun sagarimashita nee.**
ずいぶん 下がりました ねえ。
**B: Desu kara, ima wa kabu no hoo ga omoshiroi desu yo.**
です から、今 は 株 の ほう が おもしろい です よ。
**A: Demo, kabu wa abunai deshoo?**
でも、株 は 危ない でしょう?
**B: Teeki wa anzen desu ga, rishi ga yasui desu kara, tsumaranai desu yo.**
定期 は 安全 です が、利子 が 安い です から、 つまらない です よ。

**3** **A: Denki ya gasu no ryookin no shiharai wa mendoo desu nee.**
電気 や ガス の 料金 の 支払い は 面倒 です ねえ。
**B: Uchi wa ginkoo no jidoo-hurikomi ni shite imasu kara, mondai arimasen yo.**
うち は 銀行 の 自動振り込み に して います から、問題 ありません よ。
**A: Soo desu ka. Sore wa ii desu nee. Boku mo sassoku ginkoo ni soodan-shimashoo.**
そう です か。 それは いい です ねえ。 ぼく も さっそく 銀行 に 相談 しましょう。

**4** **A: Ginkoo e itte, kono kogitte o azukete, sore kara kono tsuuchoo kara juuman-en oroshite kite kudasai.**
銀行 へ 行って、この 小切手 を 預けて、それ から この 通帳 から 十万円 おろして きて ください。
**B: Kashikomarimashita. Genkin wa zenbu ichiman-en satsu desu ka.**
かしこまりました。 現金 は 全部 一万円 札 です か。
**A: Ee, soo desu.**
ええ、そう です。

**5** **A: Kono tekisuto wa muzukashii desu nee.**
この テキスト は むずかしい です ねえ。
**B: Soo desu ka. Kono kyookasho wa yasashii desu yo.**
そう です か。 この 教科書 は やさしい です よ。

**6**

| | | | |
|---|---|---|---|
| **tooza-yokin** | 当座預金 | **tegata** | 手形 |
| **yuushi** | 融資 | **roon** | ローン |
| **husai** | 負債 | **shakkin** | 借金 |
| **tanpo** | 担保 | **saiken** | 債権 |
| **hyaku-en kooka** *or* | 百円硬貨 | **sen-en satsu** | 千円札 |
| **hyaku-en-dama** | 百円玉 | | |

## BUSINESS COLUMN

## LIFETIME EMPLOYMENT

Lifetime employment, one of the distinctive features of the Japanese employment system, hasn't been around for a lifetime yet. It took root in the twenty years after World War Ⅱ, as Japan picked up the pieces and embarked on a course of dramatic recovery and high growth.

Also known more optimistically as 'career-long employment,' the lifetime employment system was the response to a lack of skilled labor. Companies didn't want to lose people they had gone to the trouble of training, so they guaranteed them job security and periodic promotions in return for a career-long commitment to the firm. And just to make sure that workers didn't head for greener pastures once they'd learned the ropes, managers structured the reward system so that it paid employees to stick around.

Career-long employment goes hand-in-hand with the seniority system. Pay and promotion are based on age and length of service, and countless other factors, such as arriving on time and keeping one's nose out of trouble. Starting salaries are often low, and employees are encouraged to wait in line to enjoy the financial benefits that regular promotion brings. The system is the same for both blue and white-collar workers, though the latter proceed upward at a faster pace.

Moving through life with the same company has several advantages. Promotions and pay rises correspond with changes in one's status in the outside world—from bachelor, to spouse, to parent—and may even dictate them. The security of lifetime employment adds stability to one's position in society, and, at its best, cements close ties of loyalty to the company extending far beyond money and rank. The company takes a paternal interest in its full-time employees, and makes available to them such perks as cheap housing and recreational facilities. Seniors take a personal interest in their juniors, and cultivate them for higher posts.

But lifetime employment isn't for everyone. For a start, the practice is much more common among large corporations than small. Second, female employees are rarely considered as candidates for lifetime service. Third, as 'lifers' sit pretty during a recession, temporary workers and subcontracted labor must shoulder the full force of the cutbacks.

A recession is not necessarily any fun for those with job security, either. In an era of rapid growth, the company expands and new positions of responsibility open up. Not everybody can get right to the top (in what company can they?) but there are plenty of promotions to hand round. In times of recession, such as at present, there is less of the cake to pass round. Younger members of the staff see the writing on the wall, and don't want to wait around to read the rest of the script. Switching jobs is no longer unheard of, and disgruntled employees, where they can, keep their eyes open for other opportunities.

But for the brightest and the best, lifetime employment can bring its due rewards, while for the also-rans it provides security if not satisfaction.

**by Jonathan Lloyde-Owen**
(Senior Editor, PHP Intersect)

# UNIT 17

*MEETING*

会議

かいぎ

## MODEL CONVERSATION

## SITUATION

*Kelly and Yamaguchi are on their way to a P. R. Department staff meeting.*

**kakaru *(kakarimasu)*** — to take (time)

Kelly **1 Yamaguchi-san, kyoo no kaigi wa dono gurai kakaru deshoo ka.** — Mr. Yamaguchi, how long (do you think) today's meeting will take?

**daiji/na/** — important
**kanari** — considerably, fairly
**da *(desu)*** — ⟨informal copula⟩
**omou *(omoimasu)*** — to think

Yamaguchi **2 Saa, daiji na kaigi da kara, kanari jikan ga kakaru to omoimasu yo.** — Well, (this) is an important meeting, so I think it'll take a considerable (amount of) time.

Kelly **3 Soo desu ka.** — Is that so?

**kono mae** — last time, before this
**kono mae no kaigi** — the previous meeting
**hajimaru *(hajimarimasu)*** — to start, begin, commence
**tsuzuku *(tsuzukimasu)*** — to continue

Yamaguchi **4 Kono mae no kaigi wa san-ji ni hajimatte, ku-ji sugi made tsuzukimashita yo.** — The previous meeting started at three and continued until after nine.

**to** — with
**tomodachi to** — with my friend

Kelly **5 Kyoo wa tomodachi to roku-ji ni yakusoku ga arimasu ga...** — Today, I have an appointment with my friend at six.

**owaru *(owarimasu)*** — to finish, be over, come to an end

Yamaguchi **6 Demo roku-ji mae ni wa owaranai to omoimasu yo.** — But I think (it) will not be over before six.

| | | |
|---|---|---|
| | **torikesu *(torikeshimasu)*** | to cancel |
| | **hoo ga ii** | is better (to do) |
| Kelly | **7 Jaa, ima denwa-shite, yakusoku o torikeshita hoo ga ii desu ne.** | Well, I had better telephone and cancel the appointment now. |
| | **sono hoo ga ii** | it's better do it |
| Yamaguchi | **8 Sono hoo ga ii desu yo.** | That would be best. |
| | **denwa-shite kuru *(kimasu)*** | to go and telephone |
| Kelly | **9 Ja, chotto denwa-shite kimasu.** | Well, I'll go and telephone. |

*(in the conference room, after the meeting)*

| | | |
|---|---|---|
| | **tsukareru *(tsukaremasu)*** | to be tired |
| Yamaguchi | **10 Kerii-san, tsukaremashita ka.** | Mr. Kelly, are you tired? (lit. Did you get tired?) |
| Kelly | **11 Ee, chotto.** | Yes, a little. |
| | **doo omou *(omoimasu)*** | what do you think? |
| Yamaguchi | **12 Kyoo no kaigi, doo omoimashita ka.** | What did you think about today's meeting? |
| | **nagai** | long |
| Kelly | **13 Soo desu nee. Nagai kaigi deshita nee.** | Let me see. (It) was a long meeting! |
| | **iron na** | various |
| | **iken** | opinion, views |
| Yamaguchi | **14 Ee, iron na iken ga arimasu kara nee.** | Yes, there are various opinions, so… |
| | **wakaru *(wakarimasu)*** | to understand, know |
| | **node** | because, so |
| | **totemo** | very, quite |

Kelly **15 Tonikaku, minasan no iken ga wakatta node, totemo yokatta to omoimasu.** — Anyway, I learned everyone's opinion, so (that's) very good, I think.

| | |
|---|---|
| **keredo** | although |
| **konsensasu** | consensus (from the English, consensus) |
| **dekiru *(dekimasu)*** | to complete, finish |
| **konsensasu ga dekiru** | to agree, come to an agreement |

Yamaguchi **16 Jikan wa kakatta keredo, konsensasu ga dekita kara...** — Although it took time, we could reach an agreement, so...

| | |
|---|---|
| **seekoo** | success |

Kelly **17 Kaigi wa seekoo deshita ne.** — The meeting was a success, wasn't it?

| | |
|---|---|
| **sono toori da *(desu)*** | that's right |

Yamaguchi **18 Sono toori desu yo.** — That's right!

## ADDITIONAL VOCABULARY

**1**

| | |
|---|---|
| **hajimeru *(hajimemasu)*** | to begin (it), start (it) |
| **kaigishitsu** | conference room |

**A: Kaigi o hajimemasu node, kaigishitsu ni kite kudasai.** — Please come to the conference room, the meeting (is going) to start.

| | |
|---|---|
| **gidai** | topics of discussion, agenda |

**B: Kyoo no gidai wa nan desu ka.** — What is today's agenda?

| | |
|---|---|
| **choosa** | survey, investigation |
| **shijoo-choosa** | market research |

| | |
|---|---|
| **A: Shijoo-choosa no mondai desu yo.** | Problems (concerning) market research. |
| **B: Jikan wa dono gurai kakaru deshoo ka.** | About how long will it take? |
| **A: San-jikan gurai kakaru to omoimasu yo.** | I think it will take about three hours. |

2 shusseki-suru *(shimasu)* — to attend, be present at

| | |
|---|---|
| **A: Kinoo no kaigi ni shusseki-shimashita ka.** | Did you attend yesterday's meeting? |

kesseki-suru *(shimasu)* — to be absent
byooki da *(desu)* — to be sick

| | |
|---|---|
| **B: Iie, kesseki-shimashita, kinoo wa byooki datta kara...** | No I didn't, I was sick yesterday. (lit. No, I was absent because I was sick yesterday.) |

3 keekaku — plan

| | |
|---|---|
| **A: Buchoo no atarashii keekaku, doo omoimasu ka.** | What do you think of the general manager's new plan? |

sansee — agreement, support

| | |
|---|---|
| **B: Boku wa buchoo no keekaku ni sansee desu. Anata wa?** | I agree with it (lit. the general manager's plan). How about you? |

hantai — opposition
to (wa) omowanai *(omoimasen)* — don't think

| | |
|---|---|
| **A: Watakushi wa kono keekaku ni hantai desu. Ii keekaku to wa omoimasen yo.** | I'm opposed to it (lit. this plan). I don't think it's a good plan. |

4 shippai — failure

| | |
|---|---|
| **A: Shijoo-choosa wa shippai deshita ka.** | Was the market research unsuccessful? |

| | |
|---|---|
| **soo omou *(omoimasu)*** | I think so |
| **soo (wa) omowanai *(omoimasen)*** | I don't think so |
| **mijikai** | short |

| | |
|---|---|
| **B: Watakushi wa soo wa omoimasen ga, jikan ga mijikakatta kara..⋯** | I don't think so, but there wasn't much time... |

## GRAMMATICAL NOTES

**1** Informal verbs

Up until now verbs have been introduced in their formal or **masu** form. In this unit we will study informal verbs which are sometimes used as predicate verbs for informal situations.

| | | |
|---|---|---|
| Examples: | **Kyoo no kaigi, jikan ga kakaru?** | "Will today's meeting take time?" |
| | **Ee, kanari kakaru yo.** | "Yes, (it'll) take considerable time." |

However, informal verbs are mainly used as a constituent element within the sentence.

| | | |
|---|---|---|
| Examples: | **Jikan ga kakaru to omoimasu.** | "I think it takes time." |
| | **Torikeshita hoo ga ii desu.** | "You had better cancel." |
| | **Minasan no iken ga wakatta node...** | "Because I understood their opinions..." |
| | **Jikan wa kakatta keredo...** | "It took a time, but..." |

Informal verbs are not used as predicate verbs in the above examples. The predicate verb for each of these sentences is formal, which makes the sentence itself formal for use in appropriate situations. The non-past affirmative of the informal verb is known as the 'citation form' and is listed as such in dictionaries.

There are four groups of informal verbs:

Class I verbs (or **RU** verbs)

This class ends in -**ru**, which corresponds to -**masu** in formal usage.

| | | |
|---|---|---|
| Examples: | **deki*ru*** 'to complete, can do' | **deki*masu*** |
| | **hajime*ru*** 'to start' | **hajime*masu*** |

Class II verbs (or **U** verbs)

This class ends in-**u**, which corresponds to -**imasu** in formal usage.

| | | |
|---|---|---|
| Examples: | **kakar*u*** 'to take (time)' | **kakar*imasu*** |
| | **tsuzuk*u*** 'to continue' | **tsuzuk*imasu*** |

Note that all informal verbs ending in -**ru** are not necessarily Class I verbs. For example, **kakaru** ending in -**ru** is a Class II verb. **U** occurs after one of the eight consonants, **b**, **g**, **k**, **m**, **n**, **r**, **s**, or **ts** or one of the four vowels, **a**, **i**, **o**, or **u**.

Class III verbs (or **ARU** verbs)
This class ends in -**aru**, which corresponds to -**aimasu** in formal usage.
All verbs in this class are polite verbs.
Examples: **irassh*aru*** 'to be, go or come' **irassh*aimasu***
**nas*aru*** 'to do' **nas*aimasu***

Irregular verbs
This group includes only two verbs.
**kuru** 'to come' **kimasu**
**suru** 'to do' **shimasu**
In following units, new verbs will be introduced in the informal form with an indication of the group, / I /,/ II /or/ III /, in which they belong. Two of these verbs were introduced in earlier units.

The past form for informal verbs is made by replacing the final/-**e**/of the gerund with -**a**. Thus, **mite** 'seeing' becomes **mit*a*** 'saw'.

Informal negative from informal non-past affirmative:

Class I verbs (or **RU** verbs): Replace the final -**ru** with -**nai.**
Example: **deki*ru*** 'to complete, can do' **deki*nai***

Class II verbs (or **U** verbs): Replace the final -**u** with -**anai**.
Example: **kakar*u*** 'to take (time)' **kakar*anai***
However, when a Class II verb ends in a vowel -**u**, replace the final -**u** with -**wanai**.
Thus, ka***u*** 'to buy' **ka*wanai***

Class III verbs (or **ARU** verbs): Replace the final -**aru** with -**aranai.**
Example: **irassh*aru*** 'to be, go or come' **irassh*aranai***

Irregular verbs:
**kuru** 'to come' **konai**
**suru** 'to do' **shinai**

The past negative ends in -**nakatta**, like negative endings for adjectives.

Informal Verb Inflection Chart

| Class | Formal | Affirmative | | Negative | |
|---|---|---|---|---|---|
| | (meaning) | Non-past | Past | Non-past | Past |
| I | **age*masu*** 'to give' | **age*ru*** | **aget*a*** | **age*nai*** | **age*nakatta*** |
| | **dekake*masu*** 'to go out' | **dekake*ru*** | **dekaket*a*** | **dekake*nai*** | **dekake*nakatta*** |

| | | | | | |
|---|---|---|---|---|---|
| | **hue*masu*** 'to increase' | **hue*ru*** | **hue*ta*** | **hue*nai*** | **hue*nakatta*** |
| II | **ari*masu*** 'to be, have' | **aru** | **atta** | **nai**** | ***nakatta**** |
| | **i*imasu*** 'to say' | **iu** | **itta** | **i*wanai*** | **i*wanakatta*** |
| | **hanash*imasu*** 'to tell' | **hanasu** | **hanashi*ta*** | **hanas*anai*** | **hanas*anakatta*** |
| | **kak*imasu*** 'to write' | **kaku** | **kaita** | **kak*anai*** | **kak*anakatta*** |
| | ***aimasu*** 'to meet' | **au** | **atta** | **a*wanai*** | **a*wanakatta*** |
| III | **ir*asshaimasu*** 'to be,come' | **irassh*aru*** | **irassha*tta*** | **irassh*aranai*** | **irassh*aranakatta*** |
| Irregular | **ki*masu*** 'to come' | **ku*ru*** | **ki*ta*** | **ko*nai*** | **ko*nakatta*** |
| | **shimasu** 'to do' | **su*ru*** | **shi*ta*** | **shi*nai*** | **shi*nakatta*** |

*The verb **aru** 'to be, have' has no negative form. **Nai** 'there is not, does not exist' is used for the non-past negative and **nakatta** for the past negative.

WARNING: The informal verb inflections introduced here are not easy to master. Therefore, it isn't necessary to learn these all at one time. It is recommended instead to gradually familiarize yourself with them as you progress.

**2** Informal copula

The informal copula is **da** and the formal is **desu**. Like informal verbs, **da** occurs at the end of a sentence as a predicate in informal speech. It also occurs as a predicate for a quotation in formal speech.

**Kaigi wa ni-ji kara *da*.** "The meeting is from two." ⟨informal⟩
**Dame *da* to iimashita.** "(He) said it's no good." ⟨formal⟩
**Ano hito wa Tanaka-san *da* to omoimasu.** "I think he is Mr. Tanaka." ⟨formal⟩

Remember that when the main predicate at the end of the sentence is formal, the sentence also becomes formal, even if an informal verb, copula or adjective is used as a constituent element. For example, **Dame da** is an informal sentence, but when it is used as a constituent element followed by the main predicate in formal form **(to) omoimasu** "I think (that)", the sentence also becomes formal.

Inflection for the Informal Copula

| Non-past Affirmative | Past Affirmative | Non-past Negative | Past Negative |
|---|---|---|---|
| **da** | **datta** | **ja nai** | **ja nakatta** |

**3** Informal adjectives

In formal speech, an adjective is always followed by a copula, but for informal speech, the adjective is used alone.

**Sore wa ii desu yo.** "It's good!" 〈formal〉
**Sore (wa) ii yo.** "It's good!" 〈informal〉

**4** **TO OMOU**

A sentence + **to omou** means 'to think that ...' The predicate of the preceding phrase usually ends in an informal verb, adjective or copula.

Examples: **Chiba-san ga kuru *to omoimasu*.** "I think Mr. Chiba will come."
**Kono hon wa omoshiroi *to omoimasu*.** "I think this book is interesting."
**Kerii wa genki da *to omoimasu*.** "I think Kelly is well."

When this is used in the negative form, the particle **wa** occurs between **to** and **omowanai.**

**Kaigi ga go-ji made ni owaru *to wa omoimasen*.**
"I don't think the meeting will end by five."

**Doo omoimasu ka** "what do you think?" is often used to ask someone's opinion.

Examples: **Buchoo no keekaku o *doo omoimasu ka*.**
"What do you think about the general manager's plan?"
**Kono hon wa *doo omoimasu ka*.**
"As for this book, what do you think?"

**5** More about **HOO GA II**

An informal past verb + **hoo ga ii** is used to suggest something should be done and is equivalent to the English, '...had better do...'

Examples: **Kore wa sugu buchoo ni hookoku-shita *hoo ga ii* desu yo.**
"You had better report this to the general manager right now."
**Moo juu-ji da kara, ashita itta *hoo ga ii* to omoimasu.**
"I think you had better go tomorrow, because it's already 10 o'clock."

For a negative suggestion, the preceding verb is usually an informal negative in the non-past.

**Ima ikanai *hoo ga ii* desu.** "It's better not to go now."

This combination is also used to invite a suggestion.

Examples: **Yakusoku o torikeshita *hoo ga ii* desu ka.**
"Should I cancel the appointment?
(lit. Had I better cancel the appointment?)"
**Ima kawanai *hoo ga ii* desu ka.** "Would it be better not to buy (it) now?"

## 6 NODE

A phrase ending with an informal predicate + **node** is used to indicate the reason for whatever follows.

Examples: **Takakatta *node*, kaimasen deshita.** "It was expensive, so I didn't buy it."
**Yoku hataraita *node*, tsukaremashita.** "I worked hard, so I was tired."
**Kono jisho wa dame na* *node*, atarashii no o kaitai n desu.**
"This dictionary is no good, so I'd like to buy a new one."
**Kaigi ga seekoo datta* *node*, totemo yokatta desu.**
"The meeting was successful, so it was very good."

*When a non-past copula precedes **node**, **da** becomes **na**.
However, the past copula **datta** never changes.

## 7 KEREDO

A sentence + **keredo** is used to refer to 'although' or 'even though.' with the preceding phrase usually ending in an informal predicate. **Keredo** is sometimes pronounced **kedo** in less formal speech.

Examples: **Denwa-shita *keredo,* Chiba-san wa jimusho ni imasen deshita.**
"Although I telephoned, Mr. Chiba wasn't at the office."
**Kono kuruma wa chiisai *keredo*, totemo takai n desu yo.**
"This car is small, but it's very expensive."
**Washoku wa suki da *kedo*, osashimi wa kirai da.**
"Although I like Japanese foods, I don't like *sashimi*."

## 8 Usage notes

1) **KAKARU** 'to take (time)' can also refer to cost or expense.

Examples: **Kono keekaku wa nanajuu-man-en gurai *kakarimasu*.**
"This plan will cost us 700,000 yen."
**Ryokoo wa dono gurai *kakarimashita* ka.**
"About how much did you need for your trip?"

2) Many Japanese nouns can be changed into verbs by adding the verb **SURU**.
For example, **shusseki-suru** is a compound verb consisting of the noun **shusseki** 'attendance' + **suru** 'to do' and means 'to attend.'
Some nouns introduced in this unit also become verbs when used with **suru**.

| | |
|---|---|
| **seekoo** 'success' | **seekoo-suru** 'to succeed' |
| **shippai** 'failure' | **shippai-suru** 'to fail' |
| **sansee** 'approval, support' | **sansee-suru** 'to agree, support' |
| **hantai** 'opposition' | **hantai-suru** 'to oppose' |

Hereafter all nouns which can be used as compound verbs will be introduced with (-**suru**).

Example: **benkyoo (-suru)** 'study (to learn)'

## 9 More about particle TO

In addition to 'and' introduced in Unit 4, **to** also means 'with':
**Tomodachi *to* yakusoku ga arimasu.**
"I have an appointment with my friend."

**Sore ni tsuite kachoo *to* hanashimashita.**
"I talked about that with the manager."

## PRACTICE

Note that drills in this unit are mainly for practicing inflections of informal verbs. While you may find these usages initially difficult, it is recommended that you carefully study these drills to familiarize yourself with the various forms of informal verbs.

**1** Response drill (Class I verbs: informal affirmative to informal negative)
Example: Teacher: **Taberu to omoimasu ka.** "Do you think (he) will eat (it)?"
Student: **Iie, *tabenai* to omoimasu.** "No, I think (he) will not eat (it)."

| | |
|---|---|
| **1) Dekakeru to omoimasu ka.** | **Iie, *dekakenai* to omoimasu.** |
| **2) Dekiru to omoimasu ka.** | **Iie, *dekinai* to omoimasu.** |
| **3) Denwa o kakeru to omoimasu ka.** | **Iie, *kakenai* to omoimasu.** |
| **4) Hookoku o miru to omoimasu ka.** | **Iie, *minai* to omoimasu.** |
| **5) Tegami o miseru to omoimasu ka.** | **Iie, *misenai* to omoimasu.** |
| **6) Rekishi o oshieru to omoimasu ka.** | **Iie, *oshienai* to omoimasu.** |
| **7) Shiryoo o kureru to omoimasu ka.** | **Iie, *kurenai* to omoimasu.** |
| **8) Koko de norikaeru to omoimasu ka.** | **Iie, *norikaenai* to omoimasu.** |
| **9) Tsugi no eki de oriru to omoimasu ka.** | **Iie, *orinai* to omoimasu.** |
| **10) Kyoo shiraberu to omoimasu ka.** | **Iie, *shirabenai* to omoimasu.** |

**2** Response drill (Class I verbs: formal to informal)
Example: Teacher: **Washoku o tabemasu ka.**
"Does (he) eat Japanese foods?"
Student: **Ee, *taberu* to omoimasu.** "Yes, I think (he) eats Japanese foods."

| | |
|---|---|
| **1) Kyoo dekakemasu ka.** | **Ee, *dekakeru* to omoimasu.** |
| **2) Sugu dekimasu ka.** | **Ee, *dekiru* to omoimasu.** |
| **3) Denwa o kakemasu ka.** | **Ee, *kakeru* to omoimasu.** |
| **4) Kono hookoku o mimasu ka.** | **Ee, *miru* to omoimasu.** |
| **5) Shiryoo o misemasu ka.** | **Ee, *miseru* to omoimasu.** |
| **6) Eego o oshiemasu ka.** | **Ee, *oshieru* to omoimasu.** |
| **7) Ano jisho o kuremasu ka.** | **Ee, *kureru* to omoimasu.** |
| **8) Chikatetsu ni norikaemasu ka.** | **Ee, *norikaeru* to omoimasu.** |
| **9) Kono eki de orimasu ka.** | **Ee, *oriru* to omoimasu.** |
| **10) Deeta o shirabemasu ka.** | **Ee, *shiraberu* to omoimasu.** |

**3** Response drill (Class I verbs: formal past to informal past)

Example: Teacher: **Buraun-san wa osushi o tabemashita ka.**
"Did Mr. Brown eat *sushi?*"
Student: **Ee, *tabeta* to omoimasu.** "Yes, I think (he) ate (it)."

| | |
|---|---|
| **1) Kerii-san wa kinoo dekakemashita ka.** | **Ee, *dekaketa* to omoimasu.** |
| **2) Hookoku wa dekimashita ka.** | **Ee, *dekita* to omoimasu.** |
| **3) Moo denwa o kakemashita ka.** | **Ee, *kaketa* to omoimasu.** |
| **4) Doi-san wa kore o mimashita ka.** | **Ee, *mita* to omoimasu.** |
| **5) Buchoo ni deeta o misemashita ka.** | **Ee, *miseta* to omoimasu.** |
| **6) Kerii-san wa kinoo eego o oshiemashita ka.** | **Ee, *oshieta* to omoimasu.** |
| **7) Aoki-san ga tetsudatte kuremashita ka.** | **Ee, *tetsudatte kureta* to omoimasu.** |
| **8) Basu ni norikaemashita ka.** | **Ee, *norikaeta* to omoimasu.** |
| **9) Tookyoo-eki de orimashita ka.** | **Ee, *orita* to omoimasu.** |
| **10) Shiryoo o shirabemashita ka.** | **Ee, *shirabeta* to omoimasu.** |

**4** Response drill (Class II verbs: informal affirmative to informal negative)

Example: Teacher: **Jikan ga kakaru to omoimasu ka.** "Do you think it takes time?"
Student: **Iie, *kakaranai* to omoimasu.** "No, I think it doesn't take time."

| | |
|---|---|
| **1) Ano hito wa kono kaisha ni hairu to omoimasu ka.** | **Iie, *hairanai* to omoimasu.** |
| **2) Yunyuu ga hueru to omoimasu ka.** | **Iie, *huenai* to omoimasu.** |
| **3) Buchoo wa Oosaka e iku to omoimasu ka.** | **Iie, *ikanai* to omoimasu.** |
| **4) Waapuro o kau to omoimasu ka.** | **Iie, *kawanai* to omoimasu.** |
| **5) Kore wa sankoo ni naru to omoimasu ka.** | **Iie, *(sankoo ni) naranai* to omoimasu.** |
| **6) Doi-san wa osake o nomu to omoimasu ka.** | **Iie, *nomanai* to omoimasu.** |
| **7) Ano hito wa matte iru to omoimasu ka.** | **Iie, *matte inai* to omoimasu.** |
| **8) Shachoo wa Kerii-san mo yobu to omoimasu ka.** | **Iie, *yobanai* to omoimasu.** |
| **9) Konna hon o yomu to omoimasu ka.** | **Iie, *yomanai* to omoimasu.** |
| **10) Tanaka-san wa yakusoku o torikesu to omoimasu ka.** | **Iie, *torikesanai* to omoimasu.** |

**5** Response drill (Class II verbs: formal to informal)

Example: Teacher: **Kaigi wa jikan ga kakarimasu ka.**
"Will the meeting take time?"
Student: **Ee, (jikan ga) *kakaru* to omoimasu.**
"Yes, it will take time."

| | |
|---|---|
| **1) Ano hito wa kaisha ni hairimasu ka.** | **Ee, *hairu* to omoimasu.** |
| **2) Yunyuu ga huemasu ka.** | **Ee, *hueru* to omoimasu.** |
| **3) Buchoo wa Oosaka e ikimasu ka.** | **Ee, *iku* to omoimasu.** |
| **4) Shachoo wa waapuro o kaimasu ka.** | **Ee, *kau* to omoimasu.** |
| **5) Kore wa sankoo ni narimasu ka.** | **Ee, *sankoo ni naru* to omoimasu.** |

6) **Doi-san wa osake o nomimasu ka.** — **Ee, *nomu* to omoimasu.**
7) **Ano hito wa matte imasu ka.** — **Ee, *matte iru* to omoimasu.**
8) **Kerii-san mo yobimasu ka.** — **Ee, *yobu* to omoimasu.**
9) **Konna hon o yomimasu ka.** — **Ee, *yomu* to omoimasu.**
10) **Nakano-san wa yakusoku o torikeshimasu ka.** — **Ee, *torikesu* to omoimasu.**

**6** Response drill (Class II verbs: formal past to informal past)

Example: Teacher: **Kaigi wa jikan ga kakarimashita ka.**
"Did the meeting take time?"
Student: **Ee, jikan ga *kakatta* to omoimasu.**
"Yes, I think it took time."

1) **Aoki-san wa ano kaisha ni hairimashita ka.** — **Ee, *haitta* to omoimasu.**
2) **Aishii no yunyuu wa huemashita ka.** — **Ee, *hueta* to omoimasu.**
3) **Kerii-san wa Kyooto e ikimashita ka.** — **Ee, *itta* to omoimasu.**
4) **Buchoo wa waapuro o kaimashita ka.** — **Ee, *katta* to omoimasu.**
5) **Ano shiryoo wa sankoo ni narimashita ka.** — **Ee, *(sankoo ni) natta* to omoimasu.**
6) **Kinoo Doi-san wa osake o nomimashita ka.** — **Ee, *nonda* to omoimasu.**
7) **Ano hito wa matte imashita ka.** — **Ee, *matte ita* to omoimasu.**
8) **Shachoo wa Kerii-san mo yobimashita ka.** — **Ee, *yonda* to omoimasu.**
9) **Kachoo wa shiryoo o yomimashita ka.** — **Ee, *yonda* to omoimasu.**
10) **Moo yakusoku o torikeshimashita ka.** — **Ee, *torikeshita* to omoimasu.**

**7** Response drill (Class III verbs and irregular verbs: informal affirmative to informal negative)

Example: Teacher: **Buchoo ga sansee-suru to omoimasu ka.**
"Do you think the general manager will support (it)?"
Student: **Iie, *sansee-shinai* to omoimasu.**
"No, I think he won't support (it)."

1) **Kyoo Nakamura-san ga kuru to omoimasu ka.** — **Iie, *konai* to omoimasu.**
2) **Shachoo wa jimusho ni irassharu to omoimasu ka.** — **Iie, *irassharanai* to omoimasu.**
3) **Hookoku wa buchoo ga nasaru to omoimasu ka.** — **Iie, *nasaranai* to omoimasu.**
4) **Kerii-san wa konban nihongo o benkyoo-suru to omoimasu ka.** — **Iie, *benkyoo-shinai* to omoimasu.**
5) **Aoki-san ga kippu o katte kuru to omoimasu ka.** — **Iie, *katte konai* to omoimasu.**

**8** Response drill (Class III verbs and irregular verbs: formal to informal)

Example: Teacher: **Buchoo wa sansee-shimasu ka.**

"Will the general manager support (it)?"
Student: **Ee, *sansee-suru* to omoimasu.**
"Yes, I think he will support (it)."

| | |
|---|---|
| **1) Kyoo Nakamura-san wa kimasu ka.** | **Ee, *kuru* to omoimasu.** |
| **2) Shachoo wa jimusho ni irasshaimasu ka.** | **Ee, *irassharu* to omoimasu.** |
| **3) Hookoku wa buchoo ga nasaimasu ka.** | **Ee, *nasaru* to omoimasu.** |
| **4) Kerii-san wa konban nihongo o benkyoo-shimasu ka.** | **Ee, *benkyoo-suru* to omoimasu.** |
| **5) Aoki-san ga kippu o katte kimasu ka.** | **Ee, *katte kuru* to omoimasu.** |

**9** Response drill (Class III verbs and irregular verbs: formal past to informal past)
Example: Teacher: **Buchoo wa sansee-shimashita ka.**
"Did the general manager support (it)?"
Student: **Ee, *sansee-shita* to omoimasu.**
"Yes, I think he supported (it)."

| | |
|---|---|
| **1) Kyoo Nakamura-san ga kimashita ka.** | **Ee, *kita* to omoimasu.** |
| **2) Shachoo wa jimusho ni irasshaimashita ka.** | **Ee, *irasshatta* to omoimasu.** |
| **3) Hookoku wa buchoo ga nasaimashita ka.** | **Ee, *nasatta* to omoimasu.** |
| **4) Kerii-san wa kinoo nihongo o benkyoo-shimashita ka.** | **Ee, *benkyoo-shita* to omoimasu.** |
| **5) Aoki-san ga kippu o katte kimashita ka.** | **Ee, *katte kita* to omoimasu.** |

**10** Response drill
Example: Teacher: **Yakusoku o torikeshimashoo ka.** "Shall I cancel the appointment?"
Student: **Ee, torikeshita hoo ga ii desu.** "Yes, you had better cancel it."

| | |
|---|---|
| **1) Ima kaigi o hajimemashoo ka.** | **Ee, hajimeta hoo ga ii desu.** |
| **2) Sugu Jetoro e ikimashoo ka.** | **Ee, itta hoo ga ii desu.** |
| **3) Minasan no iken o kikimashoo ka.** | **Ee, kiita hoo ga ii desu.** |
| **4) Ano kaigi ni shusseki-shimashoo ka.** | **Ee, shusseki-shita hoo ga ii desu.** |
| **5) Biiru o motto chuumon-shimashoo ka.** | **Ee, chuumon-shita hoo ga ii desu.** |
| **6) Ashita shachoo ni aimashoo ka.** | **Ee, atta hoo ga ii desu.** |
| **7) Chikatetsu ni norikaemashoo ka.** | **Ee, norikaeta hoo ga ii desu.** |
| **8) Kono okane o ginkoo ni azukemashoo ka.** | **Ee, azuketa hoo ga ii desu.** |
| **9) Ima hookoku o kakimashoo ka.** | **Ee, kaita hoo ga ii desu.** |
| **10) Kore o buchoo ni misemashoo ka.** | **Ee, miseta hoo ga ii desu.** |

**11** Response drill (formal copula to informal copula)
Example: Teacher: **Kyoo wa daiji na kaigi desu ka./ee/**
"Is today's meeting an important one?"/yes/
Student: **Ee, daiji na kaigi da to omoimasu.**
"Yes, I think it's an important meeting."

1) Kaigi wa shippai deshita ka./ee/ Ee, shippai datta to omoimasu.
2) Tanaka-san wa eegyoobu desu ka./iie/ Iie, eegyoobu ja nai to omoimasu.
3) Kaigi wa san-ji kara desu ka./ee/ Ee, san-ji kara da to omoimasu.
4) Kono kooza wa hutsuu-yokin desu ka./iie/ Iie, hutsuu-yokin ja nai to omoimasu.
5) Ano biru wa byooin deshita ka./iie/ Iie, byooin ja nakatta to omoimasu.

**12** Transformation drill

Example: Teacher: **Totemo takakatta n desu. Kaimasen deshita.**
"It was very expensive." "I didn't buy it."
Student: **Totemo takakatta node, kaimasen deshita.**
"It was very expensive, so I didn't buy it."

1) Konsensasu ga dekimashita. Kaigi wa seekoo deshita. — Konsensasu ga dekita node, kaigi wa seekoo deshita.
2) Nagai kaigi deshita. Chotto tsukaremashita. — Nagai kaigi datta node, chotto tsukaremashita.
3) Okane ga irimasu. Gogo ginkoo e itte kimasu. — Okane ga iru node, gogo ginkoo e itte kimasu.
4) Kyoo no kaigi wa daiji desu. Jikan ga kakaru to omoimasu. — Kyoo no kaigi wa daiji na node, jikan ga kakaru to omoimasu.
5) Chiba-san ga tetsudatte kuremashita. Mondai wa arimasen deshita. — Chiba-san ga tetsudatte kureta node, mondai wa arimasen deshita.
6) Washoku ga suki desu. Ryooriya e yoku ikimasu. — Washoku ga suki na node, ryooriya e yoku ikimasu.
7) Senjitsu gochisoo ni narimashita. Konban wa boku ga haraimasu. — Senjitsu gochisoo ni natta node, konban wa boku ga haraimasu.
8) Buchoo ga hantai desu. Kono keekaku wa dekinai to omoimasu. — Buchoo ga hantai na node, kono keekaku wa dekinai to omoimasu.

**13** Transformation drill

Example: Teacher: **Totemo takakatta desu. Kaimashita.**
"It was very expensive." "I bought it."
Student: **Totemo takakatta keredo, kaimashita.**
"Although it was very expensive, I bought it."

1) Chiba-san ni denwa-shimashita. Jimusho ni imasen deshita. — Chiba-san ni denwa-shita keredo, jimusho ni imasen deshita.
2) Uchi wa Shinjuku desu. Otaku wa dochira desu ka. — Uchi wa Shinjuku da keredo, otaku wa dochira desu ka.
3) Kinoo no kaigi wa seekoo deshita. Totemo tsukaremashita. — Kinoo no kaigi wa seekoo datta keredo, totemo tsukaremashita.
4) Kaigi ni wa buchoo wa kesseki-shimashita. Kachoo ga shusseki-shimashita. — Kaigi ni wa buchoo wa kesseki-shita keredo, kachoo ga shusseki-shimashita.
5) Nakamura-san no iken o kikimashita. Yoku wakarimasen deshita. — Nakamura-san no iken o kiita keredo, yoku wakarimasen deshita.
6) Ano resutoran no ryoori wa oishikatta n desu. Totemo takakatta n desu. — Ano resutoran no ryoori wa oishikatta n da keredo, totemo takakatta n desn.

## EXERCISES

**1** Guessing game: Read the following sentences, find the informal verb and convert it into the formal **masu** form.

**1) Kaigi wa go-ji made tsuzuita to iimashita.**
**2) Ano hito wa yoku hataraku keredo...**
**3) Aoki-san ga tetsudau to omoimasu.**
**4) Kanji de kaita node, wakarimasen deshita.**
**5) Kerii-san wa kyoo ginkoo de okane o orosu to iimashita.**
**6) Buraun-san no nihongo wa dandan yoku naru to omoimasu.**
**7) Kanjoo wa boku ga haratta keredo, yasukatta n desu.**
**8) Shujin wa kyoo roku-ji ni kaeru tte iimashita ga...**
**9) Sumisu-san wa osashimi wa tabenai to omoimasu.**
**10) Chiba-san wa atarashii shiryoo o ageru tte iimashita.**

**2** Translate the following sentences into Japanese:

1) I think the president will not attend the meeting.
2) Today I'm very tired, so I'll come home right away.
3) You had better go to JETRO and check market research data.
4) I don't think the manager opposes the general manager's plan.
5) Mr. Kelly told me that he'll ask Mr. Yamaguchi's opinion.
6) Although I like *sukiyaki* very much, I don't want to eat *sukiyaki* at that restaurant.
7) The president said that this plan will cost about 700,000 yen.
8) I think you had better start the meeting after Mr. Tanaka arrives (lit. after Mr. Tanaka comes).
9) It's better not to cancel the appointment with your friend.
10) Although I was late, Ms. Aoki was waiting for me.

## FOR REFERENCE

### 〔MODEL CONVERSATION〕

| | | |
|---|---|---|
| Kelly | **Yamaguchi-san, kyoo no kaigi wa dono gurai kakaru deshoo ka.** | 山口さん、今日 の 会議 は どの ぐらい かかる でしょう か。 |
| Yamaguchi | **Saa, daiji na kaigi da kara, kanari jikan ga kakaru to omoimasu yo.** | さあ、大事 な 会議 だ から、かなり 時間 が かかる と 思います よ。 |
| Kelly | **Soo desu ka.** | そう です か。 |
| Yamaguchi | **Kono mae no kaigi wa san-ji ni hajimatte, ku-ji sugi made tsuzukimashita yo.** | この 前 の 会議 は 三時 に 始まって、九時 すぎ まで 続きました よ。 |

| | | |
|---|---|---|
| Kelly | **Kyoo wa tomodachi to roku-ji ni yakusoku ga arimasu ga...** | 今日 は 友達 と 六時 に 約束 が あります が… |
| Yamaguchi | **Demo roku-ji mae ni wa owaranai to omoimasu yo.** | でも 六時 前 に は 終わらない と 思います よ。 |
| Kelly | **Jaa, ima denwa-shite, yakusoku o torikeshita hoo ga ii desu ne.** | じゃあ、今 電話して、約束 を 取り消した ほう が いい です ね。 |
| Yamaguchi | **Sono hoo ga ii desu yo.** | その ほう が いい です よ。 |
| Kelly | **Ja, chotto denwa-shite kimasu.** | じゃ、ちょっと 電話して きます。 |
| Yamaguchi | **Kerii-san, tsukaremashita ka.** | ケリーさん、疲れました か。 |
| Kelly | **Ee, chotto.** | ええ、ちょっと。 |
| Yamaguchi | **Kyoo no kaigi, doo omoimashita ka.** | 今日 の 会議 どう 思いました か。 |
| Kelly | **Soo desu nee. Nagai kaigi deshita nee.** | そう です ねえ。 長い 会議 でした ねえ。 |
| Yamaguchi | **Ee, iron na iken ga arimasu kara nee.** | ええ、いろん な 意見 が あります から ねえ。 |
| Kelly | **Tonikaku, minasan no iken ga wakatta node, totemo yokkatta to omoimasu.** | とにかく、みなさん の 意見 が わかった ので、とても 良かった と 思います。 |
| Yamaguchi | **Jikan wa kakatta keredo, konsensasu ga dekita kara...** | 時間 は かかった けれど、コンセンサス が できた から… |
| Kelly | **Kaigi wa seekoo deshita ne.** | 会議 は 成功 でした ね。 |
| Yamaguchi | **Sono toori desu yo.** | その とおり です よ。 |

**〔ADDITIONAL VOCABULARY〕**

**1** **A: Kaigi o hajimemasu node, kaigishitsu ni kite kudasai.** 会議 を 始めます ので、会議室 に 来て ください。
**B: Kyoo no gidai wa nan desu ka.** 今日 の 議題 は 何 です か。
**A: Shijoo-choosa no mondai desu yo.** 市場調査 の 問題 です よ。
**B: Jikan wa dono gurai kakaru deshoo ka.** 時間 は どの ぐらい かかる でしょう か。
**A: San-jikan gurai kakaru to omoimasu yo.** 三時間 ぐらい かかる と 思います よ。

**2** **A: Kinoo no kagi ni shusseki-shimashita ka.** 昨日 の 会議 に 出席しました か。
**B: Iie, kesseki-shimashita, kinoo wa byooki datta kara...** いいえ、欠席しました。 昨日 は 病気 だった から…

**3** **A: Buchoo no atarashii keekaku, doo omoimasu ka.** 部長 の 新しい 計画、どう 思います か。
**B: Boku wa buchoo no keekaku ni sansee desu. Anata wa?** ぼく は 部長 の 計画 に 賛成 です。 あなた は?
**A: Watakushi wa kono keekaku ni hantai desu. Ii keekaku to wa omoimasen yo.** わたくし は この 計画 に 反対 です。 いい 計画 と は 思いません よ。

**4** **A: Shijoo-choosa wa shippai deshita ka.** 市場調査 は 失敗 でした か。
**B: Watakushi wa soo wa omoimasen ga, jikan ga mijikakatta kara...** わたくし は そう は 思いません が、時間 が 短かった から…

## BUSINESS COLUMN

# THE MEETING AS A RITUAL

For many Japanese—as well as foreigners employed by Japanese firms—the worst part of the working day has got to be the morning meeting, a time when an entire division (the entire firm if it's small enough) gets together for pep talks and exercises.

This tradition starts in grade school, when children gather on the playground to be reminded of school rules, their responsibilities as Japanese citizens, and just about anything else the principal wants to talk about that day. And then one of the coaches (but it can be any adult) leads the school in a few calisthenics to get the blood running for the day's academic rigor. And it has always been that way: Men and women retired from the working life still stretch their muscles in the morning, in tune with what they have been doing since they were children.

Sales organizations in Japan find a special value in the morning meeting, when every one can sing the company song, participate in rousing pep talks, and do a few muscle stretches in preparation for making calls. Almost no one enjoys these gatherings, but the results tell the story: When they hit the streets, they're tigers. Customers find it hard to resist these highly motivated go-getters.

One Japanese restaurant chain has a great way to motivate its cooks, waiters, and busboys. Before the restaurants open for meals, everyone gathers in the dining room. They say a prayer, they sing, and they practice (with feeling) welcoming customers and saying 'thank you.' That diners love the food and the extra special service is no sham; they return again and again to these truly delightful eating establishments.

The role of women during morning meetings has changed in the past several years. Typically, they were to observe and stay in the background—as silently as possible, thank you. When 'Team Demi' (scissors, stapler, ruler, and cellophane tape dispenser—all compact enough to fit into a plastic box not much larger than a pack of cigarettes) hit the all- time consumer best-seller list, no one knew that the idea was put forth at a morning meeting—by a woman.

Perhaps the closest equivalent to the morning meeting that Americans experience is in the military. Virtually all of the services have a morning 'formation', when everyone lines up for the day's orders. Nobody liked that, either, but everyone came away with clear objectives: Here's what has to be done, and here's what we're going to do. The element of teamwork was clear to all. For those of us who lived that kind of life, and work in Japan today, it's not hard to relate to the Japanese morning meeting.

Looked at in its most positive light, foreigners would be well served to reflect on the effect these morning motivators have had on the Japanese economy. After all of the complaining, the fact remains that Japanese commerce is the envy of the world. Maybe now it's a little easier to figure out why.

**by Terry D. Ragan**

# UNIT 18

*COMPLETING A VOUCHER*

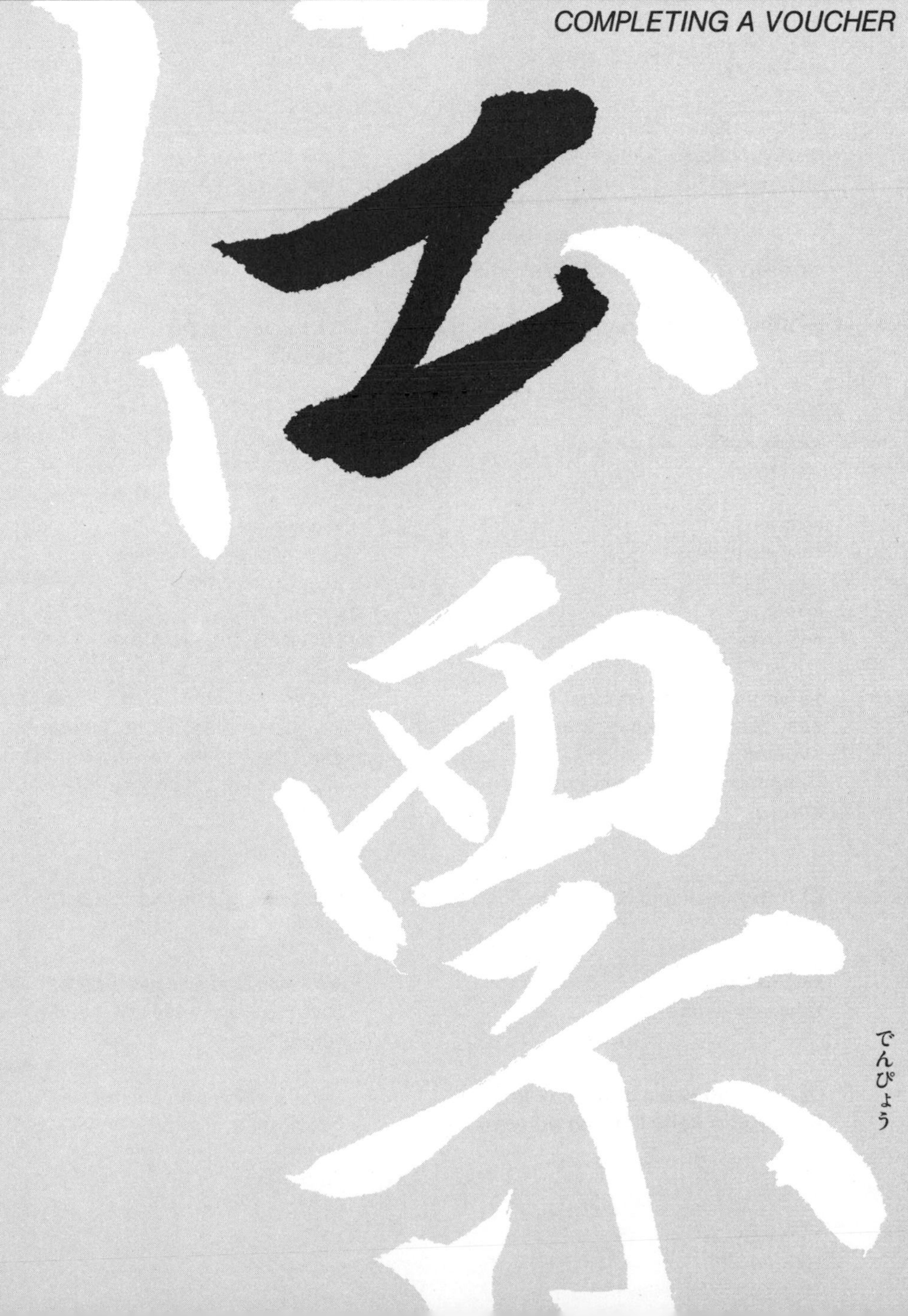


でんぴょう

## MODEL CONVERSATION

## SITUATION

*Kelly receives a bill for photographs used in a recent P.R. leaflet and asks the chief clerk, Ishikawa, how to handle it.*

| | | |
|---|---|---|
| | **San Kookoku** | Sun Advertising Co. |
| | **seekyuusho** | bill |
| Kelly | **1 Kakarichoo, San Kookoku kara seekyuusho ga kimashita ga, doo shimashoo ka.** | Chief clerk, (lit. Mr. Ishikawa), I received a bill from (lit. a bill came from) Sun Advertising. How should I handle it? |
| | **shashin** | photograph, picture |
| Ishikawa | **2 Kono mae no shashin no ryookin desu ne.** | It's the fee for the recent photos (we used), isn't it? |
| Kelly | **3 Ee, kore desu. Doozo.** | Yes, here it is. |
| | **denpyoo** | voucher |
| | **denpyoo o kaku** | fill out (lit. write) a voucher |
| | **dasu**/ II / | to send, hand over |
| | **tokoro** | place |
| | **Aoki-san no tokoro** | Ms. Aoki's desk (lit. place) |
| Ishikawa | **4 Niman gosen-en desu ne.<br>Jaa, denpyoo o kaite, keeribu ni dashite kudasai.<br>Denpyoo wa Aoki-san no tokoro ni aru kara...** | 25,000 yen, right? Well, please fill out a voucher and send it to General Accounting. Ms. Aoki has the vouchers at her desk (lit. there are vouchers at Ms. Aoki's place). |
| Kelly | **5 Kono seekyuusho wa doo shimasu ka.** | What should I do with the bill? |
| | **koto ga aru** | 〈experience of doing something〉 |
| | **kaita koto ga aru** | have (you) ever written (lit. had the experience of writing) |
| Ishikawa | **6 Sore mo issho ni dashite kudasai.<br>Denpyoo o kaita koto ga arimasu ka.** | Send it along with (the voucher).<br>Have you ever written a voucher (before)? |

| | | |
|---|---|---|
| | **koto wa nai** | never have had (the experience) |
| | **yaru/ II /** | to do |
| Kelly | **7 Iie, kaita koto wa arimasen ga, yatte mimasu.** | No, I've never written (one), but I'll (give it a) try. |
| | **dekinakattara** | if you can't do it |
| Ishikawa | **8 Dekinakattara, oshiete agemasu yo.** | If you can't do it, I'll show you (how). |
| Kelly | **9 Ee, onegai-shimasu.** | Yes, please. |

*(Kelly gets a voucher from Ms. Aoki and fills it out)*

| | | |
|---|---|---|
| | **daijoobu dattara** | if it's all right |
| Kelly | **10 Aoki-san, dekimashita ga, chotto mite kudasai. Daijoobu dattara, kakarichoo ni dashimasu kara...** | Ms. Aoki, I finished (filling it out), please check it. If it's OK, I'll send (it) to the chief clerk... |
| | **osu/ II /** | to push, impress |
| | **tsugi ni** | next, and then |
| | **han o morau** | to have a seal placed on something |
| Aoki | **11 Ee, ii desu yo.** *(Aoki checks it)* **Daijoobu desu. Demo, koko ni anata no han o oshite, tsugi ni kakarichoo to kachoo no han o moratte kudasai.** | Sure, I'll be glad to. This is OK, But, please put (lit. impress) your seal on it and then (lit. next) have the chief clerk and manager put their seals on it (also). |

*(Kelly takes the voucher to Ishikawa's desk)*

| | | |
|---|---|---|
| Kelly | **12 Kakarichoo, denpyoo ga dekimashita.** | Mr. Ishikawa, I filled out the voucher (lit. The voucher has been completed). |
| | **ookee da** | it's OK |
| | **itadaku** | to receive 〈humble〉 |
| | **mite itadaku** 〈respectful〉 | to have someone see |
| | **kyoka (-suru)** | approval, permission |
| | **morattara** | if you receive, when you receive |

| | | |
|---|---|---|
| | **mawasu**/II / | to send |
| Ishikawa | **13** *(after looking it over)* **Hai, ookee desu. Jaa, kachoo ni mite itadaite, kyoka o morattara, keeribu ni mawashite kudasai.** | Yes, it's OK. So, have the manager look at it and if he OKs it, send it to General Accounting. |
| Kelly | **14 Wakarimashita. Doomo arigatoo gozaimashita.** | I see. Thank you very much. |

## ADDITIONAL VOCABULARY

**1**

| | |
|---|---|
| **chuumonsho** | order form |
| **nan-mai** | how many sheets? |
| **okuru**/II / | to send |
| **A: Chuumonsho wa nan-mai okurimasu ka.** | How many order forms shall I send? |
| **ichi-mai** | one sheet |
| **ni-mai** | two sheets |
| **san-mai** | three sheets |
| **kopii** | copy |
| **B: San-mai desu yo. Sore kara kopii o ichi-mai Aoki-san ni agete kudasai.** | Three sheets. And please give a copy to Ms. Aoki. |

**2**

| | |
|---|---|
| **todokeru**/ I / | to deliver |
| **A: Kono seekyuusho o Ajia Denki ni todokete kudasai.** | Please deliver this bill to Asian Electric. |
| **B: Hai, sugu ikimasu. Shiharai wa kyoo desu ka.** | All right, I'll go right now. Will they pay today? |
| **shiharaibi** | date of payment |
| **getsumatsu** | end of the month |
| **A: Iya, shiharaibi wa getsumatsu desu yo.** | No, the date of payment is the end of the month. |

3 **kookokuryoo** — advertising rates
**uketoru**/ II / — to receive

| | |
|---|---|
| **A: Ajia Denki kara kookokuryoo o uketotte kimashita.** | I received the ad rates from Asian Electric (lit. and returned). |

**nyuukin-denpyoo** — pay-in voucher

| | |
|---|---|
| **B: Jaa, sugu nyuukin-denpyoo o kaite kudasai.** | Well, please write a pay-in voucher right away. |

4 **shinamono/shina** — commodities, goods
**chuumon no shina** — ordered goods
**todoku**/ II / — to reach, arrive at destination

| | |
|---|---|
| **A: Amerika kara chuumon no shina ga todokimashita yo.** | The goods ordered from America have arrived. |

**tsutsumi** — package
**akeru**/ I / — to open
**noohinsho** — delivery statement
**motsu**/ II / — to have, hold, possess
**motte kuru** — to bring

| | |
|---|---|
| **B: Tsutsumi o akete, noohinsho o motte kite kudasai.** | Please open the package and bring me the delivery statement. |

**oku**/ II / — to put, lay down, keep

| | |
|---|---|
| **A: Shinamono wa doko ni okimashoo ka.** | Where shall I put (these) goods? |

**sooko** — storeroom, warehouse
**motte iku** — to take

| | |
|---|---|
| **B: Aa, sore wa sooko ni motte itte kudasai.** | Oh, please take them to the warehouse. |

5 Additional office terms

| | | | |
|---|---|---|---|
| **shukkin-denpyoo** | pay-out voucher | **choobo** | book, account book |
| **okurijoo** | invoice | **hassoo (-suru)** | shipping |

## GRAMMATICAL NOTES

**1** Conditional

Japanese verbs, adjectives and copula (**da**/**desu**) also have conditional forms that can express 'if' or 'when.' For this usage add -**ra** to the informal past form of the verb, adjective or copula.

| | Non-past (meaning) | Past | Conditional |
|---|---|---|---|
| Verb | **iku** 'to go' | **itta** | **itta*ra*** |
| Adjective | **takai** 'expensive' | **takakatta** | **takakatta*ra*** |
| Copula | **desu/da** 'to be' | **deshita/datta** | **deshita*ra*/datta*ra*** |

Examples: **Tanaka-san ni *attara*, yoroshiku itte kudasai.**
"If you meet Mr. Tanaka, please give him my regards."
**Seekyuusho ga *kitara*, sugu haraimasu yo.**
"If (or when) the bill comes, I'll pay (it) right away."
**Kinoo Jetoro e *ittara*, Nakamura-shachoo ga imashita.***
"When I went to JETRO yesterday, President Nakamura was there."
**Okane ga *attara*, kaimashita ga...**
"If I had the money, I would have bought it, but..."
***Takakattara*, kaimasen yo.**
"If it's expensive, I won't buy it."
**Ima isogashiku *nakattara*, chotto tetsudatte kudasai.**
"If you aren't busy right now, please give me a little help."
**Omoshiroi hon *dattara*, yomitai n desu ga...**
"If the book is interesting, I'd like to read it, but ..."

*The conditional is also used to indicate two actions that occur coincidentally and means 'when.' In this example, the speaker went to JETRO without expecting Mr. Nakamura to be there.

The conditional itself is tenseless and the predicate of the following main clause determines the tense of the entire sentence.

**2** **KOTO GA ARU**

The informal past of a verb plus **koto ga aru** is used to express experience in doing something.

Examples: **Kyooto e itta *koto ga arimasu.***
"I have been to Kyoto. (lit. I have had the experience of going to Kyoto.)"
**Sukiyaki o tabeta *koto ga arimasu.*** "I have eaten *sukiyaki.*"
**Eego o benkyoo-shita *koto ga arimasu ka.*** "Have you ever studied English?"

The negative is the informal past of a verb + **koto wa (ga) nai** and means to never have had the experience of doing something.

**Amerika e itta *koto wa arimasen.*** "I've never been to America."
**Doi-san ni atta *koto wa arimasen ka.*** "Haven't you ever met Mr. Doi?"

When the informal non-past precedes **koto ga aru** it usually means something has been experienced at certain times.

Examples: **Kuruma de kaisha e iku *koto ga arimasu.***
"There are times when I go to the company by car."
**Kuruma de kaisha e iku *koto wa arimasen.***
"I never to go to the company by car."

**3** Gerund + **ITADAKU**

A gerund + the respectful verb **itadaku** is the polite equivalent of gerund + **morau** (see Unit 16, GRAMMATICAL NOTE **2**) and expresses respect for the person carrying out the action.

Examples: **Kono hookoku wa buchoo ni yonde *itadakimashita.***
"I had the general manager read this report."
**Ashita mata kite *itadakitai* n desu ga...**
"I want you to come again tomorrow, but..."
**Kachoo ni chuumonsho o todokete *itadakimashita.***
"I had the manager deliver the order form."
**Dare ni tetsudatte *itadakimashoo ka.*** "Who shall I have help me?"

Note that in this pattern, the agent of the action is indicated by the particle **ni**.

**4** **MOTTE IKU** vs. **MOTTE KURU**

**Motte** is the gerund of **motsu** 'to have, hold, own.' **Motte iku** literally means 'to hold something and go with it.' This is used for taking something from one place to another. **Motte kuru** means to bring something to the location of conversation.
Remember, this usage can only refer to inanimate objects.

Examples: **Kore o sooko ni *motte ikimasu.*** "I'll take this to the warehouse."
**Dare ga sore o *motte kimashita ka.*** "Who brought that to this place?"
**Sono kaban o boku no kuruma made *motte itte* kudasai.**
"Please take that bag to (lit. as far as) my car."
**Ima denpyoo o *motte kimashoo ka.*** "Shall I bring the slip now?"

Note: **Motte irassharu** is the respectful equivalent of both **motte iku** and **motte kuru**. **Motte mairu** is the humble form for **motte iku** and **motte kuru**.

**5** -**MAI**

The counter -**mai** combined with Chinese derived numerals is used for counting thin, flat objects, such as paper, bills, plates, rugs, etc.
Numbers from 1 to 10 are:

| | | | |
|---|---|---|---|
| **ichi-mai** | '1 thin, flat unit' | **shichi-mai** | '7 thin, flat units' |
| **ni-mai** | '2 thin, flat units' | *or* **nana-mai** | |
| **san-mai** | '3 thin, flat units' | **hachi-mai** | '8 thin, flat units' |
| **yon-mai** | '4 thin, flat units' | **kyuu-mai** | '9 thin, flat units' |
| **go-mai** | '5 thin, flat units' | **juu-mai** | '10 thin, flat units' |
| **roku-mai** | '6 thin, flat units' | **nan-mai** | 'how many thin, flat units?" |

In Japanese all counters are used as adverbs without any particle.

Compare: **Denpyoo o kudasai.** "Please give me a voucher (or vouchers)."
**Denpyoo o *ichi-mai* kudasai.** "Please give me one voucher."

**Biiru o nomimashita.** "I drank beer."
**Biiru o *ip-pon* nomimashita.** "I drank a bottle of beer."

## PRACTICE

**1** Usage drill
Basic pattern: **Kono denpyoo o keeribu ni mawashite kudasai.**
"Please send this voucher to the General Accounting Dept."

| | |
|---|---|
| **seekyuusho** | **buchoo** |
| **chuumonsho** | **eegyoobu** |
| **nyuukin-denpyoo** | **kachoo** |
| **noohinsho** | **sooko** |
| **shorui** | **soomubu** |
| **okurijoo** | **seezoobu** |

**2** Usage drill
Basic pattern: **Denpyoo o ichi-mai kudasai.** "Please give me a voucher."

| | |
|---|---|
| **shukkin-denpyoo** | **ni-mai** |
| **kaado** | **san-mai** |
| **sen-en satsu** | **yon-mai** |
| **noohinsho** | **go-mai** |
| **pan** | **roku-mai** |
| **shashin** | **nana-mai** |
| **meeshi** | **hachi-mai** |
| **kono seetaa** | **kyuu-mai** |
| **konna kami** | **juu-mai** |

**3** Response drill
Example: Teacher: **Denpyoo o kaita koto ga arimasu ka./Ee**/or/**Iie**/
"Have you ever filled out (lit. written) a voucher?"/Yes/or/No/
Student: **Ee, kaita koto ga arimasu.** "Yes, I have (lit. written)." *or* **Iie, kaita koto wa arimasen.** "No, I never have (lit. written)."

| | |
|---|---|
| **1) Shachoo ni atta koto ga arimasu ka./Ee/** | **Ee, atta koto ga arimasu.** |
| **2) Koojoo e itta koto ga arimasu ka./Iie/** | **Iie, itta koto wa arimasen.** |
| **3) Osake o nonda koto ga arimasu ka./Ee/** | **Ee, nonda koto ga arimasu.** |
| **4) Shinkansen ni notta koto ga arimasu ka. /Iie/** | **Iie, notta koto wa arimasen.** |

5) **Eego o benkyoo-shita koto ga arimasu ka./Ee/** — **Ee, benkyoo-shita koto ga arimasu.**
6) **Kono hon o yonda koto ga arimasu ka./Iie/** — **Iie, yonda koto wa arimasen.**

**4** Transformation drill

Example: Teacher: **Mae ni Kyooto e ikimashita.** "I went to Kyoto before."
Student: **Kyooto e itta koto ga arimasu.** "I've been to Kyoto."

1) **Mae ni osashimi o tabemashita.** — **Osashimi o tabeta koto ga arimasu.**
2) **Mae ni buchoo no iken o kikimashita.** — **Buchoo no iken o kiita koto ga arimasu.**
3) **Mae ni sono deeta o shirabemashita.** — **Sono deeta o shirabeta koto ga arimasu.**
4) **Mae ni sono kaigi ni shusseki-shimashita.** — **Sono kaigi ni shusseki-shita koto ga arimasu.**
5) **Mae ni shukkin-denpyoo o todokemashita.** — **Shukkin-denpyoo o todoketa koto ga arimasu.**
6) **Mae ni eegyoo no shigoto o shimashita.** — **Eegyoo no shigoto o shita koto ga arimasu.**

**5** Transformation drill

Example: Teacher: **Mada kanji o benkyoo-shimasen.** "I haven't studied *kanji* yet."
Student: **Kanji o benkyoo-shita koto wa arimasen.** "I've never studied *kanji*."

1) **Mada koohoo no shigoto o shimasen.** — **Koohoo no shigoto o shita koto wa arimasen.**
2) **Mada Nihon no ginkoo ni okane o azukemasen.** — **Nihon no ginkoo ni okane o azuketa koto wa arimasen.**
3) **Mada hankoo o tsukutte moraimasen.** — **Hankoo o tsukutte moratta koto wa arimasen.**
4) **Mada seekyuusho o uketorimasen.** — **Seekyuusho o uketotta koto wa arimasen.**
5) **Mada keeribu no hookoku o yomimasen.** — **Keeribu no hookoku o yonda koto wa arimasen.**
6) **Mada buchoo wa uchi e irasshaimasen.** — **Buchoo wa uchi e irasshatta koto wa arimasen.**

**6** Transformation drill

Example: Teacher: **Wakarimasen.** "I don't understand."
**Chiba-san ni kikimasu.** "I'll ask Mr. Chiba."
Student: **Wakaranakattara, Chiba-san ni kikimasu.**
"If I don't understand, I'll ask Mr. Chiba."

1) **Okane ga arimasu.**
**Ii kuruma o kaimasu.** — **Okane ga attara, ii kuruma o kaimasu.**
2) **Kachoo no kyoka o moraimasu.**
**Sugu Jetoro e itte kimasu.** — **Kachoo no kyoka o morattara, sugu Jetoro e itte kimasu.**

| | |
|---|---|
| 3) **Nedan ga takai desu. Chuumon-shimasen yo.** | **Nedan ga takakattara, chuumon-shimasen yo.** |
| 4) **Seekyuusho ga arimasen. Shiharai wa dekimasen.** | **Seekyuusho ga nakattara, shiharai wa dekimasen.** |
| 5) **Buchoo ga hantai desu. Shachoo mo sansee-shimasen.** | **Buchoo ga hantai dattara, shachoo mo sansee-shimasen.** |
| 6) **Kaigi ga seekoo-shimasu. Kanpai-shimashoo.** | **Kaigi ga seekoo-shitara, kanpai-shimashoo.** |
| 7) **Kono hon ga omoshiroku arimasen. Hoka no hon o yomimasu.** | **Kono hon ga omoshiroku nakattara, hoka no hon o yomimasu.** |
| 8) **Shinamono ga todokimasu. Sugu okane o haraimasu yo.** | **Shinamono ga todoitara, sugu okane o haraimasu yo.** |

**7** Response drill

Example: Teacher: **Dare ga mite kuremashita ka./kachoo/**
"Who checked (this) for you?"/the manager/
Student: **Kachoo ni mite itadakimashita.**
"I had the manager check (it)."

| | |
|---|---|
| 1) **Dare ga nihongo o oshiete kuremasu ka./Nakano-san/** | **Nakano-san ni oshiete itadakimasu.** |
| 2) **Dare ga denpyoo o kaite kuremashita ka./kakarichoo/** | **Kakarichoo ni kaite itadakimashita.** |
| 3) **Dare ga shiryoo o shirabete kuremasu ka./Chiba-san/** | **Chiba-san ni shirabete itadakimasu.** |
| 4) **Dare ga kanjoo o haratte kuremashita ka./buchoo/** | **Buchoo ni haratte itadakimashita.** |
| 5) **Dare ga tetsudatte kuremasu ka. /Aoki-san/** | **Aoki-san ni tetsudatte itadakimasu.** |
| 6) **Dare ga hookoku o yonde kuremasu ka. /shachoo/** | **Shachoo ni yonde itadakimasu.** |

**8** Response drill

Example: Teacher: **Kore o doko ni okimashoo ka./tonari no heya/**
"Where shall I put this?"/the next room/
Student: **Tonari no heya ni motte itte kudasai.**
"Please take (it) to the next room."

| | |
|---|---|
| 1) **Kono hon o doko ni okimashoo ka. /oosetsushitsu/** | **Oosetsushitsu ni motte itte kudasai.** |
| 2) **Ano tsutsumi wa doko ni okimashoo ka. /sooko/** | **Sooko ni motte itte kudasai.** |
| 3) **Sono shorui wa doko ni okimashoo ka. /shachooshitsu/** | **Shachooshitsu ni motte itte kudasai.** |
| 4) **Kono ryooshuusho wa doko e okimashoo ka. /keeribu/** | **Keeribu e motte itte kudasai.** |

| | |
|---|---|
| **5) Ano tsukue wa doko ni okimashoo ka. /yakuin-shokudoo/** | **Yakuin-shokudoo ni motte itte kudasai.** |

**9** Response drill

Example: Teacher: **Otetsudai-shimashoo ka./Tookyoo no chizu/**
"May I help you?"/map of Tokyo/

Student: **Ee, Tookyoo no chizu motte kite kudasai.**
"Yes. Please bring me a map of Tokyo."

| | |
|---|---|
| **1) Otetsudai-shimashoo ka. /nyuukin-denpyoo/** | **Ee, nyuukin-denpyoo o motte kite kudasai.** |
| **2) Otetsudai-shimashoo ka. /denwachoo/** | **Ee, denwachoo o motte kite kudasai.** |
| **3) Otetsudai-shimashoo ka. /kami to enpitsu/** | **Ee, kami to enpitsu o motte kite kudasai.** |
| **4) Otetsudai-shimashoo ka. /keeribu no choobo/** | **Ee, keeribu no choobo o motte kite kudasai.** |
| **5) Otetsudai-shimashoo ka. /yushutsu no shiryoo/** | **Ee, yushutsu no shiryoo o motte kite kudasai.** |

## EXERCISE

Translate the following sentences into Japanese:

1) If Mr. Tanaka of the General Accounting Dept. comes, please give him this voucher.
2) I have studied French and German.
3) If you haven't received the manager's OK, I can't pay you (the money).
4) Mr. Kelly hasn't been to Asakusa yet, so Ms. Aoki will take him (to Asakusa) next Sunday.
5) When I went to the Japanese-style restaurant in Akasaka yesterday, General Manager Doi was there.
6) Shall I send this voucher to the Sales and Marketing Dept?
7) Who put this package on the president's desk? I did, that arrived from Korea today.
8) Have you ever put your seal on a voucher? No, I never have (put my seal).
9) How many sheets of paper do you need? Please give me five sheets.
10) If I'm busy tomorrow too, I won't attend the meeting in Yokohama.

## FOR REFERENCE

〔MODEL CONVERSATION〕

| | | |
|---|---|---|
| Kelly | **Kakarichoo, San-kookoku kara seekyuusho ga kimashita ga, doo shimashoo ka.** | 係長、サン広告 から 請求書 が きました が、どう しましょう か。 |
| Ishikawa | **Kono mae no shashin no ryookin desu ne.** | この 前 の 写真 の 料金 です ね。 |
| Kelly | **Ee, kore desu. Doozo.** | ええ、これ です。 どうぞ。 |
| Ishikawa | **Niman gosen-en desu ne. Jaa, denpyoo o kaite, keeribu ni dashite kudasai. Denpyoo wa Aoki-san no tokoro ni aru kara...** | 二万 五千円 です ね。じゃあ、伝票 を 書いて、経理部 に 出して ください。伝票 は 青木さん の ところ に ある から… |
| Kelly | **Kono seekyuusho wa doo shimasu ka.** | この 請求書 は どう します か。 |
| Ishikawa | **Sore mo issho ni dashite kudasai. Denpyoo o kaita koto ga arimasu ka.** | それ も 一緒 に 出して ください。伝票 を 書いた こと が あります か。 |
| Kelly | **Iie, kaita koto wa arimasen ga, yatte mimasu.** | いいえ、書いた こと は ありません が、やって みます。 |
| Ishikawa | **Dekinakattara, oshiete agemasu yo.** | できなかったら、教えて あげます よ。 |
| Kelly | **Ee, onegai-shimasu.** | ええ、お願いします。 |
| Kelly | **Aoki-san, dekimashita ga, chotto mite kudasai. Daijoobu dattara, kakarichoo ni dashimasu kara...** | 青木さん、できました が、ちょっと 見て ください。 だいじょうぶ だったら、係長 に 出します から… |
| Aoki | **Ee, ii desu yo. Daijoobu desu. Demo, koko ni anata no han o oshite, tsugi ni kakarichoo to kachoo no han o moratte kudasai.** | ええ、いい です よ。 だいじょうぶ です。でも、ここ に あなた の 判 を おして、次 に 係長 と 課長 の 判 を もらって ください。 |
| Kelly | **Kakarichoo, denpyoo ga dekimashita.** | 係長、伝票 が できました。 |
| Ishikawa | **Hai, ookee desu. Jaa, kachoo ni mite itadaite, kyoka o morattara, keeribu ni mawashite kudasai.** | はい、 オーケー です。 じゃあ、課長 に 見て いただいて、許可 を もらったら、経理部 に まわして ください。 |
| Kelly | **Wakarimashita. Doomo arigatoo gozaimashita.** | わかりました。 どうも ありがとう ございました。 |

〔ADDITIONAL VOCABULARY〕

**1** **A: Chuumonsho wa nan-mai okurimasu ka.** 注文書 は 何枚 送ります か。

| | |
|---|---|
| **B: San-mai desu yo. Sore kara kopii o ichi-mai Aoki-san ni agete kudasai.** | 三枚 です よ。 それ から コピー を 一枚 青木さん に あげて ください。 |
| **2 A: Kono seekyuusho o Ajia Denki ni todokete kudasai.** | この 請求書 を アジア 電機 に 届けて ください。 |
| **B: Hai, sugu ikimasu. Shiharai wa kyoo desu ka.** | はい、すぐ 行きます。 支払い は 今日 です か。 |
| **A: Iya, shiharaibi wa getsumatsu desu yo.** | いや、支払い日 は 月末 です よ。 |
| **3 A: Ajia Denki kara kookokuryoo o uketotte kimashita.** | アジア 電機 から 広告料 を 受け取って きました。 |
| **B: Jaa, sugu nyuukin-denpyoo o kaite kudasai.** | じゃあ、すぐ 入金伝票 を 書いて ください。 |
| **4 A: Amerika kara chuumon no shina ga todokimashita yo.** | アメリカ から 注文 の 品 が 届きました よ。 |
| **B: Tsutsumi o akete, noohinsho o motte kite kudasai.** | 包み を 開けて、納品書 を 持って きて ください。 |
| **A: Shinamono wa doko ni okimashoo ka.** | 品物 は どこ に 置きましょう か。 |
| **B: Aa, sore wa sooko ni motte itte kudasai.** | ああ、それ は 倉庫 に 持って いって ください。 |

**5**

| | | | |
|---|---|---|---|
| **shukkin-denpyoo** | 出金伝票 | **choobo** | 帳簿 |
| **okurijoo** | 送り状 | **hassoo (suru)** | 発送(する) |

## BUSINESS COLUMM

## PERSEVERANCE

*Isshookenmee* is a superlative that has been variously translated as 'taking it all the way,' 'going for it,' and 'for one's life,' as in, "He ran for his life."

However it is translated, the concept embodied by this deceptively simple term is important to the Japanese way of thinking. Examples of *isshookenmee*, in light that is both positive and negative, abound.

A customer was once awaiting a time-consuming transaction when he decided to use the phone in the bank lobby. He asked the teller for change. She courteously requested that he hold on just a moment, then returned with an application form, in triplicate, to report the client's name, age, sex, address, and date of birth, all of which he would also have to legitimize, in triplicate, by his signature or family stamp. The teller was merely following basic procedure to the 'T'. This is bureaucratic *isshookenmee*.

In 1912, the Emperor Meiji ended his earthly career. A certain General Nogi, known as a severe traditionalist, was, it seems, deeply affected by the Mikado's passing. On that same day, on the *tatami* floor of his home, the general led a group of his followers and his own wife in ritual suicide. This is *isshookenmee* loyalty.

The attribute of *isshookenmee* here is pervasive. There are, however, less acute cases of this extremism. A small-time supplier of machine parts, for example, received a long distance call from his contractor company. The last order he had filled was a few pieces short. Immediately after hanging up the phone, the president of this suburban cottage-industry placed a box of the wanting goods on the passenger seat of his family sedan, and proceeded to drive directly to the contractor's factory, that is, for eight hours straight, in order to make a swift delivery. This is *isshookenmee* service, one of the qualities which have made Japan a great economic power.

The underpinnings of *isshookenmee* are *gaman-suru* and *ganbaru*. Patience and endurance are expressed by *gaman*. Take a walk even in some of the less challenging mountains of Japan. You will inevitably pass hikers laden with boots, packs and equipment worthy of a glacial expedition. The heavy alpine get-up, ostentatious as it may be, is not for looks. The burdened amateur trekker is out to overcome his own limits, and once he has reached the peak, he will experience a peculiar satisfaction. This is *gaman-suru*.

*Ganbaru* is go-getting, the active version of *gaman-suru*. It has the sense of seeing something, a single project or a life's dream, to the finish, an affirmative 'never say die!' In the heat of confrontation in a *sumoo* bout, even the robe-clad referee can be heard screaming at the combatants. He is just vociferously nudging them to *ganbaru*.

One way for the foreigner to *ganbaru* in Japan is simply by tackling the recalcitrant language. Japan's 99.7% literacy rate, second only to the that of the U.S.S.R., means that about any Japanese you meet over the age of fifteen will have gone through the gruelling process of learning thousands of *kanji*. Evidence of your personal *isshookenmee* will no doubt be the subject of constant admiration.

**by Daniel Masler**
(Free-lance journalist and columnist for the Tokyo Journal)

# UNIT 19

*DATE FOR THE MOVIES*

映画

えいが

## MODEL CONVERSATION

## SITUATION

*In gratitude for the many kindnesses Ms. Aoki has shown Kelly since he arrived at Asian Electric, he wants to do something for her in return. One day as he returns to the office after collecting data for a P.R. article, he meets Aoki at a subway station and asks her out to a movie.*

| | | |
|---|---|---|
| | **okaeri** 〈polite〉 | going home |
| Kelly | **1 Aa, Aoki-san, ima okaeri desu ka.** | Oh, Ms. Aoki! Are you going home now? |
| | **shuzai** | collecting data, researching |
| Aoki | **2 Ee, soo desu.**<br>**Shuzai wa doo deshita ka.** | Yes, that's right.<br>How did the research go? |
| | **umai**<br>**umaku iku**<br>**seeri-suru** | good, skillful<br>to go well<br>to arrange, put in order, sort out |
| Kelly | **3 Umaku ikimashita yo. Ima kara kaisha e kaette, shiryoo o seeri-shimasu.** | It went well. I'm going back to the office now and put it all together. |
| Aoki | **4 Soo desu ka. Gokuroosama desu.** | Is that so? You're really working hard.<br>(lit. thank you for all your trouble.) |
| | **asu** | tomorrow |
| Kelly | **5 Tokoro de, Aoki-san, asu no nichiyoobi yotee ga arimasu ka.** | Anyway, Ms. Aoki, do you have any plans for Sunday, tomorrow? |
| Aoki | **6 Iie, betsu ni.** | No, nothing special. |
| | **jitsu wa**<br>**eega**<br>**mi ni iku**<br>**goissho ni** 〈polite〉 | to tell the truth, in fact<br>movie<br>to go to see<br>together, with |

| | | |
|---|---|---|
| Kelly | **7 Jitsu wa ashita eega o mi ni ikimasu ga, ohima deshitara, goissho ni (ikitai) to omoimashite...** | To tell the truth, I'm going to see a movie tomorrow. (And) if you're free, we can go together...(lit. I'm thinking I'd like to go together with you.) |
| Aoki | **8 Ii desu nee. Donna eega desu ka.** | That sounds great (lit. it's good). What kind of movie is it? |
| | **'Koorasu-rain'** | 'Chorus Line' |
| | **myuujikaru** | musical |
| | **myuujikaru-eega** | musical film |
| Kelly | **9 'Koorasu-rain' desu. Amerika no myuujikaru-eega desu ga, Aoki-san wa myuujikaru wa suki ja arimasen ka.** | It's 'Chorus Line,' an American musical. Ms. Aoki, don't you like musicals? |
| | **miyoo** | 〈informal tentative of **miru**〉 |
| | **miyoo to omou** | to think of seeing |
| Aoki | **10 Iie, daisuki desu. Watakushi mo miyoo to omotte imashita, ano eega.** | No, I like them very much. I've been thinking of about seeing that movie myself. |
| | **Miyukiza** | 〈movie theater in Hibiya〉 |
| | **za** | theater |
| Kelly | **11 Soo desu ka. Sore wa ii. Ja, ni-ji ni Miyukiza no mae de.** | Is that so? That's great. Well then (let's meet) in front of Miyukiza at two. |
| Aoki | **12 Ja, ashita. Sayoonara.** | OK, tomorrow then. Good-by. |
| Kelly | **13 Sayoonara.** | Good-by. |

*(the next day. Kelly is waiting for Aoki in front of the theater)*

| | | |
|---|---|---|
| | **gomennasai** | I'm sorry |
| Aoki | **14 Gomennasai. Osoku narimashita.** | I'm sorry. I'm (lit. was) late. |

| | | |
|---|---|---|
| Kelly | **15 Iya, daijoobu desu yo. Mada juugo-hun gurai aru kara...** | Oh, no. It's OK, we still have about 15 minutes. |
| | **yokatta** | to feel relieved |
| | **hashiru**/II/ | to run |
| | **hashitte kuru** | to come running |
| Aoki | **16 Aa, yokatta. Osoku natta to omotte, eki kara hashitte kimashita.** | Oh good, I thought I was late (so) I ran (all the way) from the station. |
| | **taihen/na/** | to be awful, be hard work |
| Kelly | **17 Sore wa taihen deshita nee. Ja, tonikaku hairimashoo.** | That's too bad! Well, anyway, shall we go in? |
| | *(after the movie)* | |
| Kelly | **18 Ii eega deshita nee.** | (That) was a good movie! |
| | **tanoshii** | pleasant, delightful |
| Aoki | **19 Ee, tanoshii eega deshita.** | Yes, it was a delightful film. |
| | **shokuji** | meal, dinner |
| | **shokuji o suru** | to have a meal |
| Kelly | **20 Kono hen de, shokuji o shimashoo ka.** | Let's have something to eat while we're here. (lit. Shall we have a meal in this neighborhood?) |
| Aoki | **21 Ee, doko e ikimashoo ka.** | OK, where shall we go? |
| | **chikai** | near |
| | **kono chikaku ni** | in this neighborhood |
| | **ikitsuke no mise** | my favorite shop |
| Kelly | **22 Osushi wa doo? Kono chikaku ni, ikitsuke no mise ga aru kara...** | How about *sushi*? I have a favorite shop in this neighborhood, so... |

| | | |
|---|---|---|
| Aoki | 23 **Ii desu nee. Ikimashoo.** | (That sounds) good. Shall we go? |

## ADDITIONAL VOCABULARY

1 **kesa** — this morning
**hayai** — early

| | |
|---|---|
| **A: Ohayoo gozaimasu. Kesa wa hayai desu nee.** | Good morning. (You're) early this morning! |

**chikoku-suru** — to come late
**hayaku kuru** — to come early

| | |
|---|---|
| **B: Iya, kinoo mo chikoku-shita node, kyoo wa hayaku kite mimashita.** | Oh, I was late yesterday, so today I tried to get in early. |

2 **tenki** — weather

| | |
|---|---|
| **A: Kyoo wa ii tenki desu nee.** | Today is a fine day! |

**ame** — rain
**huru**/ II / — to fall, (rain, snow)

| | |
|---|---|
| **B: Soo desu nee. Kinoo wa zuibun ame ga hurimashita ga...** | That's right. Yesterday, it rained hard but... (lit. very much rain fell). |

3 **yuki** — snow

| | |
|---|---|
| **A: Mada yuki ga hutte imasu ka.** | Is it still snowing? |

**yamu**/ II / — to stop (raining/snowing)
**kumoru**/ II // — to become cloudy
**hareru**/ I / — to clear up (weather)

| | |
|---|---|
| **B: Iie, moo yamimashita yo. Sukoshi mae made kumotte imashita ga, ima wa moo yoku harete imasu yo.** | No. It already stopped. It was cloudy up until a short while ago, but its clearing up now. |

| | |
|---|---|
| **4** **hidoi** | terrible |
| **kaze** | wind |
| **A: Hidoi kaze desu nee.** | It's a terrible wind! |
| **hontoo** | truth |
| **hontoo ni** | really, truly |
| **huku**/I/ | to blow |
| **B: Hontoo ni yoku kaze ga hukimasu nee.** | Really, it blows so hard (lit. very much). |
| **5** **sanpo-suru**/Irr/ | to take a walk |
| **A: Chotto sanpo-shimasen ka.** | Won't you take a walk (with me)? |
| **aruku**/II/ | to walk |
| **B: Ee, ii desu nee. Sukoshi arukimashoo.** | Sure, that sounds good. Let's take a short walk. (lit. It's good. Let's walk for a little while.) |
| **6** **kon'ya** | this night |
| **okuru**/II/ | to see (a person) home |
| **A: Kon'ya wa otaku made okurimasu yo.** | I'll see you home tonight. |
| **B: Soo desu ka. Jaa, onegai-shimasu.** | Really? Please do. |

**7** Additional terms

| | | | |
|---|---|---|---|
| **shibai/oshibai** | play, drama | **gekijoo** | theater |
| **kabuki** | kabuki drama | **Kabukiza** | the Kabuki Theater |
| **noo** | noh drama | **bunraku** | puppet show |
| **ongaku** | music | **ongakukai** | concert |
| **nyuujooken** | ticket | **nyuujooryoo** | admission fee |

## GRAMMATICAL NOTES

**1** Informal tentative of verbs
The **mashoo** form introduced in Unit 9 is the formal tentative verb form while the usage appearing in this unit is the informal tentative form (i.e. **miyoo**).
Both tentative forms mean 'let's do something' or 'I guess I'll do something.'
Using the informal tentative form:

Class I verbs (-**RU** verbs): Replace -**RU** with -**YOO**.
**Example:** **tabe*ru*** 'to eat' **tabe*yoo***

Class II verbs (-**U** verbs): Replace -**U** with -**OO**.
**Example:** **hanas*u*** 'to speak' **hanas*oo***

Irregular verbs:
**ku*ru*** 'to come' **ko*yoo***
**su*ru*** 'to do' **shi*yoo***

The informal tentative form often occurs with **to omou** 'I think' and means 'I think I'll probably do something.'
Examples: **Kyoo kabuki o mi ni ikoo *to omoimasu.***
"I think I'll probably go to see *kabuki* today."
**Atarashii kuruma o kaoo *to omotte imasu.***
"I'm thinking of buying a new car."
**Ashita ii tenki dattara, sanpo-shiyoo *to omoimasu.***
"If the weather is good tomorrow, I think I'll take a walk."

**2** Verb stem + **NI IKU**
The verb stem + **ni iku** means 'to go to do something.' This combination is often used to explain the reason for going somewhere.
The verb stem is the -**masu** form minus -**masu** (i.e. **mimasu** 'to see' - stem: **mi).**
Examples: **Kesa Chiba-san ni ai *ni ikimasu.*** "I'll go to see Mr. Chiba this morning.
**Ginza e kaban o kai *ni ikimashita.*** "I went to the Ginza to buy a bag."
**Ginkoo e okane o oroshi *ni itte kudasai.***
"Please go to the bank and withdraw the money."
The verb stem + **ni kuru** means 'to come to do something.'
Example: **Buraun-san wa kyoo eego o oshie *ni kimasu.***
"Mr. Brown will come to teach English today."

**3** Inversion
In Japanese, word order is flexible and the word or phrase to be emphasized usually appears at the beginning of the sentence. In sentence 10 of the MODEL CONVERSATION, Ms. Aoki says she wants to see the movie also with: "**Watakushi mo miyoo to omotte imashita.**" and then adds the object '**ano eega.**' This kind of inversion is typical of conversational Japanese.
Examples: **Kinoo kaimashita yo, atarashii kuruma.** "I bought a new car yesterday."
**Kyoo aimasu yo, Nakamura-san ni.** "I'll see Mr. Nakamura today."

**Motto irimasu yo, yushutsu no shiryoo ga.** "We need more data on exports."

**4** Gerund to indicate the means
Gerunds can be used to indicate the means of achieving the action expressed by the main verb.
Examples: **Koko made *hashitte* kimashita.** "I came here by running (or on the run)."
**Kaisha e *aruite* ikimasu.** "I go to the company on foot."
**Chizu o *misete* michi o oshiemashita.** "I taught him the way by showing him a map."
Compare: **Basu ni *notte* ikimasu.** 'to go by riding a bus'
**Basu de ikimasu**. 'to go by bus'
In this case the two actions indicated by the gerund and the main verb usually occur coincidentally.

**5** More about **GA**
The sentence particle **ga** is usually used to connect two opposing clauses and means 'but.' However, **ga** can also mean 'and.' The **ga** in sentence 7 of the MODEL CONVERSATION is an example of this usage.
Examples: **Sono sushiya wa watakushi mo itta koto ga arimasu *ga*, totemo ii mise desu.**
"I've been to that *sushi* shop and it's very good."
**Kinoo eega o mimashita *ga*, totemo tanoshii eega deshita.**
"I saw a movie yesterday and it was very good."

**6** Use of the adverbial form of adjectives
The adverbial form of an adjective was introduced in Unit 15 as 'Adverbial form + **narimasu**.' This form is often used by itself.
Examples: **Tanaka-san wa kyoo jimusho e *hayaku* kimashita.**
"Mr. Tanaka came to the office early today."
**Kinoo Chiba-san wa *osoku* kaerimashita.**
"Mr. Chiba came home late yesterday."

## PRACTICE

**1** Usage drill
Basic pattern: **Ohima deshitara, goissho ni eega ni ikimasen ka.**
"If you are free, won't you go to a movie with me."

| | |
|---|---|
| **ongakukai** | **shokuji** |
| **kabuki** | **sanpo** |
| **noo** | |

**2** Transformation drill

Example: Teacher: **Kyoo eega o mimasu.** "I'll see a movie today."
Student: **Kyoo eega o mi ni ikimasu.** "I'll go to see a movie today."

| | |
|---|---|
| **1) Ashita Tanaka-san ni aimasu.** | **Ashita Tanaka-san ni ai ni ikimasu.** |
| **2) Yushutsu no shiryoo o moraimasu.** | **Yushutsu no shiryoo o morai ni ikimasu.** |
| **3) Osushi o tabemasu.** | **Osushi o tabe ni ikimasu.** |
| **4) Okane o azukemashita.** | **Okane o azuke ni ikimashita.** |
| **5) Shibai no kippu o kaimasu.** | **Shibai no kippu o kai ni ikimasu.** |
| **6) Yokin o oroshimasu.** | **Yokin o oroshi ni ikimasu.** |
| **7) Buchoo no iken o kikimashita.** | **Buchoo no iken o kiki ni ikimashita.** |
| **8) Kinoo seekyuusho o todokemashita.** | **Kinoo seekyuusho o todoke ni ikimashita.** |

**3** Response drill

Example: Teacher: **Ano eega o mimasu ka.** "Will you see that movie?"
Student: **Ee, miyoo to omoimasu.** "Yes, I think I'll probably see it."

| | |
|---|---|
| **1) Kono kuruma o kaimasu ka.** | **Ee, kaoo to omoimasu.** |
| **2) Raishuu ryokoo-shimasu ka.** | **Ee, ryokoo-shiyoo to omoimasu.** |
| **3) Ryooshuusho o moraimasu ka.** | **Ee, moraoo to omoimasu.** |
| **4) Ima shiryoo o seeri-shimasu ka.** | **Ee, seeri-shiyoo to omoimasu.** |
| **5) Kono denpyoo o kachoo ni misemasu ka.** | **Ee, miseyoo to omoimasu.** |
| **6) Ashita mo shuzai ni ikimasu ka.** | **Ee, (shuzai ni) ikoo to omoimasu.** |
| **7) Kyoo ginkoo ni okane o azukemasu ka.** | **Ee, azukeyoo to omoimasu.** |
| **8) Honsha ni tegami o kakimasu ka.** | **Ee, kakoo to omoimasu.** |
| **9) Konban Aoki-san ni aimasu ka.** | **Ee, aoo to omoimasu.** |
| **10) Kyoo hayaku kaerimasu ka.** | **Ee, hayaku kaeroo to omoimasu.** |

**4** Transformation drill

Example: Teacher: **Watakushi mo mimashita, ano eega.** "I saw that movie too."
Student: **Watakushi mo ano eega o mimashita.** "I saw that movie too."

| | |
|---|---|
| **1) Ashita seeri-shimasu, kono shiryoo.** | **Ashita kono shiryoo o seeri-shimasu.** |
| **2) Chiba-san ga kuremashita, kono hon.** | **Chiba-san ga kono hon o kuremashita.** |
| **3) Konban aimasu yo, buchoo ni.** | **Konban buchoo ni aimasu yo.** |
| **4) Sugu haraimasu yo, kono kanjoo.** | **Sugu kono kanjoo o haraimasu yo.** |
| **5) Daisuki desu, anna shibai.** | **Anna shibai ga daisuki desu.** |
| **6) Kaita koto wa arimasen, konna denpyoo.** | **Konna denpyoo o kaita koto wa arimasen.** |
| **7) Oishii desu nee, koko no osushi wa.** | **Koko no osushi wa oishii desu nee.** |
| **8) Kyoo mo osoi desu nee, Tanaka-san wa.** | **Tanaka-san wa kyoo mo osoi desu nee.** |

**5** Transformation drill

Example: Teacher: **Eki kara kimashita./hashitte/** "I came from the station." /running/
Student: **Eki kara hashitte kimashita.** "I came running from the station."

| | |
|---|---|
| **1) Yuubinkyoku e ikimashita. /aruite/** | **Yuubinkyoku e aruite ikimashita.** |
| **2) Kyuushuu kara kimashita. /Shinkansen/** | **Kyuushuu kara Shinkansen ni notte kimashita.** *or* **Shinkansen ni notte Kyuushuu kara kimashita.** |
| **3) Shiryoo o seeri-shimasu. /waapuro o tsukatte/** | **Waapuro o tsukatte shiryoo o seeri-shimasu.** *or* **Shiryoo o waapuro o tsukatte seeri-shimasu.** |
| **4) Chiba-san no iken o kikimashita. /denwa o kakete/** | **Denwa o kakete Chiba-san no iken o kikimashita.** |

6 Response drill (negative answer)

Example: Teacher: **Ima ame ga hutte imasu ka.** "Is it raining now?"
Student: **Iie, (ame wa) hutte imasen.** "No, it isn't raining."

| | |
|---|---|
| **1) Ima harete imasu ka.** | **Iie, harete imasen.** |
| **2) Kyoo wa kaze ga hidoi desu ka.** | **Iie, (kaze wa) hidoku arimasen.** |
| **3) Kesa kumotte imashita ka.** | **Iie, kumotte imasen deshita.** |
| **4) Kyooto wa ii tenki deshita ka.** | **Iie, ii tenki ja arimasen deshita.** |
| **5) Yuki ga hutte imashita ka.** | **Iie, (yuki wa) hutte imasen deshita.** |
| **6) Mada kaze ga huite imasu ka.** | **Iie, moo (kaze wa) huite imasen.** |
| **7) Moo ame wa yamimashita ka.** | **Iie, mada (ame wa) yamimasen.** |
| **8) Kinoo ame ga hurimashita ka.** | **Iie, (kinoo ame wa) hurimasen deshita.** |

7 Response drill (for review)

Example: Teacher: **Myuujikaru wa suki ja arimasen ka./ee/** or/**iie/**
"Don't you like musicals?"/yes/or/no/
Student: **Ee, suki ja arimasen.** "Yes, you're right. I don't like (them)."
**Iie, suki desu.** "No, you're wrong. I like (them)."

| | |
|---|---|
| **1) Ano eega wa tanoshiku arimasen ka./ee/** | **Ee, tanoshiku arimasen.** |
| **2) Kono hen ni ikitsuke no mise wa arimasen ka./iie/** | **Iie, arimasu.** |
| **3) Shikago wa kaze ga hidoku arimasen ka. /iie/** | **Iie, (kaze ga) hidoi desu.** |
| **4) Kyoo shiryoo o seeri-shimasen ka./ee/** | **Ee, (shiryoo o seeri-) shimasen.** |
| **5) Kinoo yuki ga hurimasen deshita ka./iie/** | **Iie, (yuki ga) hurimashita.** |
| **6) Ima hima ja arimasen ka./iie/** | **Iie, hima desu.** |
| **7) Tanaka-san wa mainichi hayaku kimasen ka./ee/** | **Ee, hayaku kimasen.** |
| **8) Kinoo eega o mi ni ikimasen deshita ka. /iie/** | **Iie, (eega o mi ni) ikimashita.** |

## EXERCISES

**1** Complete the following sentences:
1) **Sukoshi mae made ame ga hutte imashita ga, ima wa ame wa moo (        ).**
2) **Kinoo wa ii tenki deshita ga, kyoo wa (        ).**
3) **Ame ga (        ) kara, kyoo wa sanpo-shimasen.**
4) **Kesa wa harete imashita ga, hiru goro kara yuki ga (        ).**
5) **Kono hen wa ni-gatsu ni wa kaze ga yoku (        ).**
6) **Kumotte imasu ga, ame wa (        ) to omoimasu.**

**2** Translate the following sentences into Japanese:
1) If you're free now, won't you go have something to eat with me?
2) Yesterday was Sunday, but I came to the office to check this data.
3) Mr. Doi's favorite Japanese-style restaurant is in front of the Kabuki Theater.
4) This morning Ms. Aoki thought she would be late, so she ran from the station to the company.
5) I think I'll put the data in order today.
6) Today is a fine day, so I think I'll take a walk.
7) I didn't go to see Mr. Chiba of JETRO yesterday, because of bad weather.
8) I've been thinking about asking the general manager's opinion, but...
9) It's already after eleven o'clock, so shall I see you home?
10) If it clears up tomorrow, I think I'll go to *Kamakura**.

*A famous, historical city in Kanagawa Prefecture.

## FOR REFERENCE

〔**MODEL CONVERSATION**〕

| | | |
|---|---|---|
| Kelly | **Aa, Aoki-san, ima okaeri desu ka.** | ああ、青木さん、いま お帰り です か。 |
| Aoki | **Ee, soo desu.** | ええ、そう です。 |
| | **Shuzai wa doo deshita ka.** | 取材 は どう でした か。 |
| Kelly | **Umaku ikimashita yo. Ima kara kaisha e kaette, shiryoo o seeri-shimasu.** | うまく いきました よ。 いま から 会社 へ 帰って、資料 を 整理します。 |
| Aoki | **Soo desu ka. Gokuroosama desu.** | そう です か。 ご苦労さま です。 |
| Kelly | **Tokoro de, Aoki-san, asu no nichiyoobi yotee ga arimasu ka.** | ところ で、青木さん、あす の 日曜日 予定 が あります か。 |
| Aoki | **Iie, betsu ni.** | いいえ、別 に。 |

| | | |
|---|---|---|
| Kelly | **Jitsu wa ashita eega o mi ni ikimasu ga, ohima deshitara, goissho ni (ikitai) to omoimashite...** | じつ は あした 映画 を 見 に 行きます が、おひま でしたら、ご一緒 に （行きたい） と 思いまして… |
| Aoki | **Ii desu nee. Donna eega desu ka.** | いい です ねえ。 どんな 映画 です か。 |
| Kelly | **'Koorasu-rain' desu. Amerika no myuujikaru-eega desu ga, Aoki-san wa myuujikaru wa suki ja arimasen ka.** | 「コーラス・ライン」です。 アメリカ の ミュージカル映画 です が、青木さん は ミュージカル は 好き じゃ ありません か。 |
| Aoki | **Iie, daisuki desu. Watakushi mo miyoo to omotte imashita, ano eega.** | いいえ、大好き です。 わたくし も 見よう と 思って いました、あの 映画。 |
| Kelly | **Soo desu ka. Sore wa ii. Ja, ni-ji ni Miyukiza no mae de.** | そう です か。 それ は いい。 じゃ、二時 に みゆき座 の 前 で。 |
| Aoki | **Ja, ashita. Sayoonara.** | じゃ、あした。 さようなら。 |
| Kelly | **Sayoonara.** | さようなら。 |
| Aoki | **Gomennasai. Osoku narimashita.** | ごめんなさい。 遅く なりました。 |
| Kelly | **Iya, daijoobu desu yo. Mada juugo-hun gurai aru kara...** | いや、だいじょうぶ です よ。 まだ 十五分 ぐらい ある から… |
| Aoki | **Aa, yokatta. Osoku natta to omotte, eki kara hashitte kimashita.** | ああ、よかった。 遅く なった と 思って、駅 から 走って きました。 |
| Kelly | **Sore wa taihen deshita nee. Ja, tonikaku hairimashoo.** | それ は たいへん でした ねえ。 じゃ、とにかく 入りましょう。 |
| Kelly | **Ii eega deshita nee.** | いい 映画 でした ねえ。 |
| Aoki | **Ee, tanoshii eega deshita.** | ええ、楽しい 映画 でした。 |
| Kelly | **Kono hen de, shokuji o shimashoo ka.** | この 辺 で、食事 を しましょう か。 |
| Aoki | **Ee, doko e ikimashoo ka.** | ええ、どこ へ 行きましょう か。 |
| Kelly | **Osushi wa doo? Kono chikaku ni, ikitsuke no mise ga aru kara...** | お寿司 は どう？この 近く に、行きつけ の 店 が ある から… |
| Aoki | **Ii desu nee. Ikimashoo.** | いい です ねえ。 行きましょう。 |

**〔ADDITIONAL VOCABULARY〕**

**1** **A: Ohayoo gozaimasu.**
**Kesa wa hayai desu nee.**
**B: Iya, kinoo mo chikoku-shita node,**
**kyoo wa hayaku kite mimashita.**

おはよう ございます。
今朝 は 早い です ねえ。
いや、きのう も 遅刻した ので、
きょう は 早く 来て みました。

**2** **A: Kyoo wa ii tenki desu nee.**
**B: Soo desu nee. Kinoo wa zuibun**
**ame ga hurimashita ga...**

きょう は いい 天気 です ねえ。
そう です ねえ。 きのう は ずいぶん
雨 が 降りました が…

**3** **A: Mada yuki ga hutte imasu ka.**
**B: Iie, moo yamimashita yo. Sukoshi mae**
**made kumotte imashita ga, ima wa**
**moo yoku harete imasu yo.**

まだ 雪 が 降って います か。
いいえ、もう やみました よ。 少し 前
まで 曇って いました が、今 は
もう よく 晴れて います よ。

**4** **A: Hidoi kaze desu nee.**
**B: Hontoo ni yoku kaze ga hukimasu nee.**

ひどい 風 です ねえ。
本当 に よく 風 が 吹きます ねえ。

**5** A: Chotto sanpo-shimasen ka.
B: Ee, ii desu nee. Sukoshi arukimashoo.

ちょっと 散歩しません か。
ええ、いい です ねえ。 少し 歩きましょう。

**6** A: Kon'ya wa otaku made okurimasu yo.
B: Soo desu ka. Jaa, onegaishimasu.

今夜 は お宅 まで 送ります よ。
そう です か。 じゃあ、お願いします。

**7**

| | | | |
|---|---|---|---|
| shibai/oshibai | 芝居/お芝居 | gekijoo | 劇場 |
| Kabuki | 歌舞伎 | Kabukiza | 歌舞伎座 |
| noo | 能 | bunraku | 文楽 |
| ongaku | 音楽 | ongakukai | 音楽会 |
| nyuujooken | 入場券 | nyuujooryoo | 入場料 |

## BUSINESS COLUMN

## MARRIAGE: THE DIVISION OF LABOR

*Kekkon seikatsu*, or Japanese married life, is characterized, as is much of Japanese social custom, by predetermined and rigid roles, which for married couples dictate a sharp division of labor between the sexes. Whether two people come to the decision to spend their lives together through the traditional *omiai* (arranged marriage) or for reasons of love (the latter considered by most of today's young Japanese to be the more desirable), the form the relationship takes as the honeymoon becomes memory is often similar.

The division between male and female roles coincides closely with respective ties to the workplace and the home. Although this may not differ greatly from many marital situations in the West, Japan stands out for the near total lack of flexibility afforded couples who may wish to depart from the norm.

The Japanese male's devotion to his company is a well-known phenomenon, and is considered to be one of the factors contributing to Japan's successful economic performance. His responsibilities at work, including the development of close-knit relations among co-workers, often keep him busy into the late hours of the evening. But as wives are virtually never included in an evening's socializing among fellow workers, couples are often left with only their Sundays to spend together.

And although many young women take jobs upon completion of schooling, both society and their employers expect, first, that they will marry someday and, second, that they will leave the job at that time. Particularly in large companies, a woman is often required to resign upon betrothal. It is generally thought that she could not possibly take proper care of her husband and home while also working full time, and if she somehow manages to do so, well, then she is most likely failing in her responsibilities at work.

The division between work and home life runs deep, so much so that it can be difficult for non-Japanese, even though they may pride themselves on being familiar with local customs, to fully understand the extent of it. There is the story of one Westerner, who after years as the sole foreigner employed by a Japanese company and countless evenings of socializing with fellow workers, proudly informed his boss and workmates of his decision to marry. The office decided to have a party for him. And when approached by the secretary responsible for organizing the affair, he responded that he was free on the evening being suggested but that he would have to check with his fiancee regarding her schedule. This led to an embarrassing pause, with the flustered secretary retreating while mumbling something about verifying the date with others. He immediately realized he had committed a faux pas, but in his years in Japan he still had not become accustomed to the idea of a party to celebrate his upcoming wedding without his fiancee being included in the festivities.

It may be that this episode played a small part in helping to break down the ways in which the relationship between husband and wife are divided so sharply between work and the home. For there is no doubt that many young Japanese couples are seeking greater flexibility in their lives, and in how they as a couple relate to the rest of Japanese society.

**by John Rivoir**
(MA candidate, International Relations, the London School of Economics)

# UNIT 20

*INVITATION*

招待

しょうたい

## MODEL CONVERSATION

## SITUATION

*Nakamura, the president of Chiyoda Advertising, invites Kelly and General Manager Doi to an expensive Japanese-style restaurant. When they arrive a hostess shows them to a private room where Nakamura is waiting.*

| | | |
|---|---|---|
| Nakamura | **1 Aa, Doi-buchoo, Kerii-san, yoku irasshaimashita.** | Ah, General Manager Doi and Mr. Kelly, welcome! |

**maneku**/II/ — to invite
**maneki/omaneki** ⟨polite⟩ — invitation

| | | |
|---|---|---|
| Doi | **2 Nakamura-san, kyoo wa omaneki, arigatoo gozaimasu.** | Mr. Nakamura, thank you very much for the invitation today. |

**ohutari** — two people, you (in this case)
**koso** — ⟨emphasis particle⟩
**oide** ⟨polite⟩ — coming, visiting
**kyooshuku** /**na**/ — to be thankful (for), be sorry
**otonari** ⟨polite⟩ — next (location)
**suwaru** /II/ — to sit down, take a seat
**raku**/**na**/ — easy
**oraku ni (shite kudasai)** — (please) make yourself at home

| | | |
|---|---|---|
| Nakamura | **3 Iie, iie, ohutari koso, oisogashii tokoro o oide kudasaimashite, kyooshuku desu. Sa, doozo.** *(pointing to a seat)* **Doi-buchoo, doozo achira e, Kerii-san wa sono otonari e osuwari ni natte kudasai. Doozo oraku ni (nasatte kudasai).** | Not at all. I'm so happy you could come (even though) you're so busy. Please (come in). Mr. Doi, please take a seat there, and Mr. Kelly, sit next to (Mr. Doi). Please make yourself at home. |

*(Doi and Kelly take their seats)*

| | | |
|---|---|---|
| Doi | **4 Kerii-san wa konna tokoro wa hajimete deshoo?** | Mr. Kelly, this is the first time you've been to such a restaurant (lit. place)? |

**rippa** /**na**/ — splendid, wonderful
**ooki na** — big, large
**tokonoma** — *tokonoma*, an alcove

| | | |
|---|---|---|
| Kelly | **5 Hai, soo desu. Nakanaka rippa na heya desu nee, ooki na tokonoma mo atte.** | Yes, that's right. This is a really nice room and such a big *tokonoma*! |

| | |
|---|---|
| **Nihon-huu** | Japanese-style |
| **zashiki** | *tatami* mat parlor |
| **mono** | things, articles |
| **ii mono** | very good (thing) |

| | | |
|---|---|---|
| Nakamura | **6 Nihon-huu no zashiki mo ii mono desu yo.** | Japanese-style parlor are very nice, you know. |

| | |
|---|---|
| **kimochi** | feeling, mood |
| **ochitsuku**/II/ | to relax, feel comfortable |

| | | |
|---|---|---|
| Kelly | **7 Hontoo desu nee. Kimochi ga ochitsukimasu nee.** | (That's) true. It's really very comfortable. |

| | |
|---|---|
| **shi** | and |
| **ii shi** | (is) good and |
| **niwa** | garden |
| **omise-shimasu** 〈humble〉 | to show (you) |

| | | |
|---|---|---|
| Nakamura | **8 Koko wa tatemono mo ii shi, niwa mo ii kara, ato de omise-shimasu yo.** | And the building is nice and there is a splendid garden as well. I'll show you later. |

| | |
|---|---|
| **zehi** | by all means, without fail |

| | | |
|---|---|---|
| Kelly | **9 Zehi onegai-shimasu.** | By all means, please do. |

*(meals are served)*

| | |
|---|---|
| **demo** | even |

| | | |
|---|---|---|
| Nakamura | **10 De wa, hajimemashoo. Kerii-san wa osake demo ii desu ka.** | Well, shall we begin. Mr. Kelly, is *sake* all right (for you)? |

| | |
|---|---|
| **soo da** | they say that, it is said that |

| | | |
|---|---|---|
| Doi | **11 Tomu wa osake ga daisuki desu yo. Yoku nomi ni iku soo desu.** | Tom likes *sake* very much. I've heard he ofen drinks *sake*. (lit. It is said that he often goes to drink.) |

| | | |
|---|---|---|
| | **tsureru** / I / | to take (animate object) |
| | **tsurete iku** | to take someone and go |
| | **daibu** | great many, rather, considerably |
| Kelly | **12 Yamaguchi-san ga iron na tokoro e tsurete itte kuremasu kara, osake mo daibu benkyoo-shimashita.** | Mr. Yamaguchi takes me to various places, so I've studied *sake* drinking very thoroughly. |
| | **Nihon-ryoori ni wa** | for Japanese meals |
| | **yahari** | after all |
| | **au** / II / | to match, suit, go very well with |
| Nakamura | **13 Soo desu ka. Nihon-ryoori ni wa yahari sake ga aimasu kara nee. Maa, doozo moo ip-pai.** | Is that so? After all *sake* goes very well with Japanese meals! Please have one more. |
| | **utsukushii** | beautiful |
| | **utsuwa** | tableware |
| Kelly | **14 Arigatoo gozaimasu. Nihon-ryoori wa utsukushii desu nee, tabemono mo utsuwa mo.** | Thank you very much. Japanese meals are beautiful, both the meal and the tableware! |
| | **me** | eyes |
| | **tanoshimu** / II / | to enjoy |
| Doi | **15 Soo. Ryoori wa me de mo tanoshimu tte iimasu yo.** | Yes. It is said that we also enjoy meals with the eyes as well. |
| | **kuchi** | mouth |
| | **enryo/goenryo** 〈polite〉 | reserve, modesty |
| | **goenryo naku** | freely, without restraint |
| Nakamura | **16 Saa, kuchi de mo tanoshinde kudasai. Doozo goenryo naku.** | Well, please enjoy the taste as well (lit. enjoy with your mouth too). Feel free to help yourself. |
| Kelly | **17 De wa, itadakimasu.** | Well, I'm going to have some. |
| | *(After dinner)* | |
| Doi | **18 Doomo kyoo wa gochisoosama deshita.** | Thank you. Today was a real treat. |

| | | |
|---|---|---|
| | **somatsu/osomatsu /na/** ⟨modest⟩ | humble, poor |
| Nakamura | **19 Iyaa, osomatsu deshita.** | No, it was nothing. |
| | **ippai** | full |
| Kelly | **20 Moo onaka ga ippai desu. Gochisoosama deshita.** | I'm full. It was a real feast. |

## ADDITIONAL VOCABULARY

| | | |
|---|---|---|
| 1 | **sofaa** | sofa |
| | **kakeru** / I / | to sit on |
| | **A: Doozo, sono sofaa ni kakete kudasai.** | Please sit on that sofa. |
| | **B: Arigatoo gozaimasu.** | Thank you very much. |
| 2 | *(at a restaurant)* | |
| | **yoyaku (-suru)/goyoyaku** ⟨polite⟩ | reservation |
| Maid | **Irasshaimase. Goyoyaku ga gozaimasu ka.** | Welcome, sir. Do you have a reservation? |
| | **shootai (-suru)/goshootai** ⟨polite⟩ | invitation |
| Kelly | **Iie, Chiyoda Kookoku no Nakamura-san no shootai de kimashita.** | No. I came through the invitation of Mr. Nakamura from Chiyoda Advertising. |
| | **sayoo** | such, like that |
| | **sayoo de gozaimasu ka** ⟨polite⟩ | is that so? |
| | **oseki** ⟨polite⟩ | seat, room (in this case) |
| Maid | **Sayoo de gozaimasu ka. De wa oseki ni goannai-itashimasu.** | Is that so? I'll show you to his room. |

**3**

| | | |
|---|---|---|
| | **nani mo nai** | there is nothing |
| | **meshiagaru** /II/ ⟨respectful⟩ | to eat, drink |
| Host | **Nani mo gozaimasen ga, doozo meshiagatte kudasai.** | It's (really) nothing, but please have some. |
| Guest | **Iyaa, subarashii gochisoo desu ne. Itadakimasu.** | Oh, this is a fine dish, isn't it? I'll have some. |

**4**

| | |
|---|---|
| **nan to/te iimasu ka** | what do you call? |
| **nihongo de** | in Japanese |
| **A: Kore wa nihongo de nan te iimasu ka.** | What do you call this in Japanese? |
| **sakazuki** | *sake* cup |
| **B: Sakazuki tte iimasu.** | We call it *'sakazuki.'* |
| **A: Ja, sore wa?** | How about that one? |
| **tokkuri** | *sake* bottle |
| **B: Sore wa tokkuri tte iimasu.** | We call that 'tokkuri.' |

**5**

| | |
|---|---|
| **aji** | taste, flavor |
| **A: Aji wa ikaga desu ka.** | Do you like the taste? |
| **B: Totemo ii aji desu ga, boku ni wa chotto amai desu yo.** | This is delicious, but it's a little sweet for me. |

**6**

| | |
|---|---|
| **suku** /II/ | to become vacant, empty |
| **A: Onaka ga suita kara, tabe ni ikimasu ga, issho ni ikaga desu ka.** | I'm hungry so I'm going to go eat something. How about us going together? |
| **sekkaku desu ga** | it's very kind, but |

| | |
|---|---|
| **B: Sekkaku desu ga, mada onaka ga suite inai kara...** | It's very kind of you to ask but I'm not (very) hungry yet... |

**7** Additional restaurant terms

| | | | |
|---|---|---|---|
| **hashi/ohashi** | chopsticks | **fooku** | fork |
| **sara/osara** | dish | **naihu** | knife |
| **chawan/ochawan** | (rice) bowl | **supu(u)n** | spoon |
| **wan/owan** | (soup) bowl | **napukin** | napkin |

## GRAMMATICAL NOTES

### 1 SOO DA

**Soo da** added to a sentence with an informal ending is used to repeat second-hand information and means 'it is said,' 'they say' or 'I heard.'

Examples: **Shachoo wa raigetsu Amerika e iku *soo desu.***
"They say the president is going to America next month."
**Kerii-san to Aoki-san wa issho ni eega o mi ni itta *soo desu.***
"I heard Mr. Kelly and Miss Aoki went to see a movie together."
**Ashita ame ga huru *soo desu.*** "I heard it will rain tomorrow."

### 2 SHI

**Shi** usually occurs between two clauses and is used to connect them with the meaning of 'and' or 'and what's more.' The verb, adjective or copula followed by **shi** is normally informal.

Examples: **Kono ryoori wa yasui *shi*, oishii n desu.**
"These dishes are cheap and delicious."
**Kinoo wa shiryoo o seeri-shita *shi*, hookoku mo kakimashita.**
"Yesterday I put the data in order and what's more, I wrote a report."
**Kerii-san wa osake mo nomu *shi*, biiru mo nomimasu.**
"Mr. Kelly drinks *sake* and (what's more he drinks) beer as well."
**Boku wa amai mono wa kirai da *shi*, tabeta koto wa nai n desu.**
"I don't like sweet food and haven't eaten any (either)."

### 3 O + verb stem

The polite prefix **o** + a verb stem is used as a polite noun. This often occurs with **kudasai** or **kudasaimasen ka** as a polite request.

Examples: **Shooshoo *omachi kudasai*.** "Please wait a while."
**Kore o yoku *oyomi kudasaimasen ka*.**
"Would you please read this carefully."
**Kono kusuri o *onomi kudasai*.** "Please take this medicine."

On the other hand, when this polite noun is followed by an irregular verb **suru**, it becomes a humble verb, which generally refers to an action by the speaker.

Examples: **Asu ku-ji goro oukagai-*shimasu*.** "I'll call on you about nine tomorrow."
**Seekyuusho wa sugu otodoke-*shimasu*.** "I'll deliver the bill soon."
**Kono keekaku wa watakushi ga buchoo ni ohanashi-*shimashita*.**
"As for this plan, I talked to the general manager about it."

When a polite noun is combined with the respectful verb **nasaru**, the combination becomes honorific.

**Kono mondai ni tsuite, shachoo to ohanashi-*nasaimashita* ka.**
"Did you talk with the president about this problem?"

A frequently used respectful/honorific verb is a combination of polite noun + **ni naru**.

Examples: **Kono mondai ni tsuite shachoo ga ohanashi *ni narimasu*.**
"The president will talk (to you) about this problem."
**Eki kara koko made oaruki *ni narimashita* ka.**
"Did you walk from the station to this place?"
**Mainichi kono kusuri o onomi *ni natte* kudasai.**
"Please take this medicine every day."
**Doi-san wa oide *ni narimasen* deshita.**
"Mr. Doi did not come."

## 4 NI WA

A noun + **ni wa** means 'in the case of' or 'for...'

Examples: **Kono hon wa kodomo *ni wa* muzukashii to omoimasu.**
"I think this book is difficult for children."
**Eego no benkyoo wa doitsujin *ni wa* yasashii soo desu.**
"I heard that studying English is easy for Germans."
**Kono mondai wa wagasha *ni wa* totemo juuyoo desu.**
"This problem is very important for our company."

WARNING: **Ni wa** cannot be used to mean 'for the sake of.'

## 5 -HUU

-**Huu** is a suffix that means '-style' or 'looking like ...' and always occurs directly after a noun.

| | |
|---|---|
| **Amerika-huu** | 'American style' |
| **Chuugoku-huu no doresu** | 'Chinese-style dress' |
| **bijinesuman-huu no gaikokujin** | 'foreigner that looks like a businessman' |

## 6 KOSO

**Koso** is used to emphasized preceding word.

Examples: **Okane *koso* ichiban daiji na mono da.**
"*Money* is the most important thing."
**Kotoshi *koso* ano daigaku ni hairitai n desu.**
"I want to enter into that university *this year*."

**Koso** is often used in formal/polite conversation to express the speaker's modesty.

**Kyoo wa gokuroosama deshita.**
"Thank you very much for your trouble today."

**Iie, anata *koso* gokuroosama deshita.** "No. *you're* the one who had trouble."
**Doomo shitsuree-shimashita.** "I'm sorry."
**Iie, watakushi *koso* shitsuree-shimashita.**
"No, *I* should be the one to apologize."

**7 DEMO**

A noun + **demo** means 'even if' and is used to express that something isn't the best selection, but still acceptable. For example:

**Koocha onegai-shimasu.** "May I have a cup of tea?"
**Koocha wa arimasen ga, koohii wa arimasu yo.**
"We don't have tea, but we have coffee."
**Jaa, koohii *demo* ii desu.** "Well, even coffee is all right."

## PRACTICE

**1** Response drill

Example: Teacher: **Kerii-san wa yoku nomi ni ikimasu ka.**
"Does Mr. Kelly go drinking frequently?"
Student: **Ee, yoku nomi ni iku soo desu yo.**
"Yes, I've heard that he often goes drinking."

| | |
|---|---|
| **1) Yamaguchi-san wa kuruma o kaimashita ka.** | **Ee, katta soo desu yo.** |
| **2) Ashita ame ga hurimasu ka.** | **Ee, (ame ga) huru soo desu yo.** |
| **3) Doi-san no otaku wa rippa desu ka.** | **Ee, rippa da soo desu yo.** |
| **4) Myuujikaru-eega wa tanoshii desu ka.** | **Ee, tanoshii soo desu yo.** |
| **5) Yunyuu no tetsuzuki wa muzukashii desu ka.** | **Ee, muzukashii soo desu yo.** |
| **6) Kyoo no kaigi wa taisetsu desu ka.** | **Ee, taisetsu da soo desu yo.** |
| **7) Eega wa roku-ji kara desu ka.** | **Ee, roku-ji kara da soo desu yo.** |

**2** Transformation drill

Example: Teacher: **Koko wa tatemono ga ii desu.** "The building here is nice."
**Niwa mo subarashii desu.** "The garden is also splendid."
Student: **Koko wa tatemono ga ii shi, niwa mo subarashii desu.**
"The building here is nice and the garden is also splendid."

| | |
|---|---|
| **1) Kinoo wa eega o mimashita. Sanpo mo shimashita.** | **Kinoo wa eega o mita shi, sanpo mo shimashita.** |
| **2) Ano resutoran no ryoori wa oishii desu. Yasui desu.** | **Ano resutoran no ryoori wa oishii shi, yasui desu.** |

3) **Tanaka-san wa genki desu.**
**Yoku hatarakimasu.**
**Tanaka-san wa genki da shi, yoku hatarakimasu.**

4) **Yunyuu ni tsuite shiryoo o yomimashita.**
**Iron na hito no iken mo kikimashita.**
**Yunyuu ni tsuite shiryoo o yonda shi, iron na hito no iken mo kikimashita.**

5) **Chiba-san wa eego ga joozu desu.**
**Shigoto mo yoku dekimasu.**
**Chiba-san wa eego ga joozu da shi, shigoto mo yoku dekimasu.**

6) **Teeki-yokin wa anzen desu.**
**Rishi mo waruku arimasen.**
**Teeki-yokin wa anzen da shi, rishi mo waruku arimasen.**

7) **Kerii-san wa biiru o nomimasu.**
**Osake mo nomimasu.**
**Kerii-san wa biiru o nomu shi, osake mo nomimasu.**

**3** Response drill
Example: Teacher: **Soko e suwarimashoo ka.** "Shall I sit there?"
Student: **Ee, osuwari kudasai.** "Yes, please sit down."

1) **Koko ni namae o kakimashoo ka.** **Ee, okaki kudasai.**
2) **Nakamura-san ni aimashoo ka.** **Ee, oai kudasai.**
3) **Buchoo no iken o kikimashoo ka.** **Ee, okiki kudasai.**
4) **Ima kanjoo o haraimashoo ka.** **Ee, oharai kudasai.**
5) **Kono shiryoo mo misemashoo ka.** **Ee, omise kudasai.**

**4** Response drill
Example: Teacher: **Dare ga hookoku o kakimasu ka.** "Who will write the report?"
Student: **Watakushi ga okaki-shimasu.** "I'll write the report."

1) **Dare ga seekyuusho o todokemasu ka.** **Watakushi ga otodoke-shimasu.**
2) **Dare ga denpyoo o kakimasu ka.** **Watakushi ga okaki-shimasu.**
3) **Dare ga Nakamura-san ni aimasu ka.** **Watakushi ga oai-shimasu.**
4) **Dare ga Aoki-san o okurimasu ka.** **Watakushi ga ookuri-shimasu.**
5) **Dare ga Kerii-san o tetsudaimasu ka.** **Watakushi ga otetsudai-shimasu.**

**5** Transformation drill
Example: Teacher: **Osake ga ii desu yo. /nihon-ryoori/**
"*Sake* is good."/Japanese meals/
Student: **Nihon-ryoori ni wa osake ga ii desu yo.**
"*Sake* is good with Japanese meals."

1) **Nihongo wa muzukashii desu yo. /gaikokujin/**
**Gaikokujin ni wa nihongo wa muzukashii desu yo.**

2) **Yooshoku no hoo ga ii desu yo. /boku/**
**Boku ni wa yooshoku no hoo ga ii desu yo.**

3) **Taihen daiji na mondai desu yo. /Nihon/**
**Nihon ni wa taihen daiji na mondai desu yo.**

4) **Totemo tanoshii eega deshita yo. /watakushi/**
**Watakushi ni wa totemo tanoshii eega deshita yo.**

5) **Kono wain ga aimasu yo. /niku-ryoori/**
**Niku-ryoori ni wa kono wain ga aimasu yo.**

| | |
|---|---|
| **6) Kono eego wa yasashii to omoimasu yo. /Nakano-san/** | **Nakano-san ni wa kono eego wa yasashii to omoimasu yo.** |

6 Transformation drill

Example: Teacher: **Nihon no zashiki wa ii mono desu.**
"Parlors in Japan are very nice."
Student: **Nihon-huu no zashiki wa ii mono desu.**
"Japanese-style parlors are very nice."

| | |
|---|---|
| **1) Doitsu no biiru ga suki desu.** | **Doitsu-huu no biiru ga suki desu.** |
| **2) Tookyoo no ryoori no aji wa ikaga desu ka.** | **Tookyoo-huu no ryoori no aji wa ikaga desu ka.** |
| **3) Ano ginkoo no tatemono wa nan ni narimasu ka.** | **Ano ginkoo-huu no tatemono wa nan ni narimasu ka.** |
| **4) Huransu no yoohuku wa takai desu.** | **Huransu-huu no yoohuku wa takai desu.** |

7 Response drill

Example: Teacher: **Biiru wa arimasen ga, osake wa arimasu ga...**
"We have no beer, but we have *sake*..."
Student: **Osake de mo ii desu.** "*Sake* will be fine."

| | |
|---|---|
| **1) Koocha wa arimasen ga, koohii wa arimasu.** | **Koohii de mo ii desu yo.** |
| **2) Doitsugo no hon wa arimasen ga, eego no hon wa arimasu.** | **Eego no hon de mo ii desu yo.** |
| **3) Osushi wa tsukurimasen ga, osashimi wa tsukurimasu yo.** | **Osashimi de mo ii desu yo.** |
| **4) Ashita wa isogashii keredo, asatte wa hima desu yo.** | **Asatte de mo ii desu yo.** |
| **5) Aoki-san wa shigoto o shite imasu ga, Kerii-san wa nani mo shite imasen.** | **Kerii-san de mo ii desu yo.** |

## EXERCISE

Translate the following sentences into Japanese:

1) The garden of this Japanese-style restaurant is famous and splendid.
2) Mr. Kelly usually goes to that cafeteria, when he feels hungry.
3) It is said President Nakamura invited Mr. Doi and Mr. Kelly to a splendid restaurant in Akasaka.
4) I think you had better enjoy Japanese meals with your eyes as well.
5) What do you call this in Japanese? We call that a *tokonoma.*
6) This kind of work is easy for American businessmen.

7) Won't you go and eat something? Thank you very much, but I'm full right now.
8) What kind of wine goes well with this meal?
9) Who takes Mr. Kelly out to drink *sake*? Mr. Nakano often takes him to Shinjuku.
10) They say Ms. Aoki likes musical films very much.

## FOR REFERENCE

### 〔MODEL CONVERSATION〕

| | | |
|---|---|---|
| Nakamura | **Aa, Doi-buchoo, Kerii-san, yoku irasshaimashita.** | ああ、土井部長、ケリーさん、よく いらっしゃいました。 |
| Doi | **Nakamura-san, kyoo wa omaneki, arigatoo gozaimasu.** | 中村さん、きょう は お招き、 ありがとう ございます。 |
| Nakamura | **Iie, iie, ohutari koso, oisogashii tokoro o oide kudasaimashite, kyooshuku desu. Sa, doozo. Doi-buchoo, doozo achira e, Kerii-san wa sono otonari e osuwari ni natte kudasai. Doozo oraku ni (nasatte kudasai).** | いいえ、いいえ、お二人 こそ、お忙しい ところ を おいで くださいまして、恐縮 です。さあ、どうぞ。 土井部長、どうぞ あちら へ、ケリーさん は その お隣り へ お座り に なって ください。 どうぞ お楽に (なさって ください)。 |
| Doi | **Kerii-san wa konna tokoro wa hajimete deshoo?** | ケリーさん は こんな ところ は はじめて でしょう? |
| Kelly | **Hai, soo desu. Nakanaka rippa na heya desu nee, ooki na tokonoma mo atte.** | はい、そう です。 なかなか 立派 な 部屋 です ねえ、 大き な 床の間 も あって。 |
| Nakamura | **Nihon-huu no zashiki mo ii mono desu yo.** | 日本風 の 座敷 も いい もの です よ。 |
| Kelly | **Hontoo desu nee. Kimochi ga ochitsukimasu nee.** | 本当 です ねえ。 気持ち が 落ちつきます ねえ。 |
| Nakamura | **Koko wa tatemono mo ii shi, niwa mo ii kara, ato de omise-shimasu yo.** | ここ は 建物 も いい し、 庭 も いい から、あと で お見せします よ。 |
| Kelly | **Zehi onegai-shimasu.** | ぜひ お願いします。 |
| Nakamura | **De wa, hajimemashoo. Kerii-san wa osake demo ii desu ka.** | で は、 始めましょう。 ケリーさん は お酒 でも いい です か。 |
| Doi | **Tomu wa osake ga daisuki desu yo. Yoku nomi ni iku soo desu.** | トム は お酒 が 大好き です よ。 よく 飲み に いく そう です。 |
| Kelly | **Yamaguchi-san ga iron na tokoro e tsurete itte kuremasu kara, osake mo daibu benkyoo-shimashita.** | 山口さん が いろん な ところ へ 連れて いって くれます から、お酒 も だいぶ 勉強しました。 |
| Nakamura | **Soo desu ka. Nihon-ryoori ni wa yahari sake ga aimasu kara nee. Maa, doozo moo ip-pai.** | そう です か。 日本料理 に は やはり 酒 が 合います から ねえ。 まあ、どうぞ もう 一杯。 |
| Kelly | **Arigatoo gozaimasu. Nihon-ryoori wa utsukushii desu nee, tabemono mo utsuwa mo.** | ありがとう ございます。 日本料理 は 美しい です ねえ、食べ物 も 器 も。 |

| | | |
|---|---|---|
| Doi | **Soo. Ryoori wa me de mo tanoshimu tte iimasu yo.** | そう。 料理 は 目 で も 楽しむ って 言います よ。 |
| Nakamura | **Saa, kuchi de mo tanoshinde kudasai. Doozo goenryo naku.** | さあ、口 で も 楽しんで ください。 どうぞ ご遠慮 なく。 |
| Kelly | **De wa, itadakimasu.** | で は、いただきます。 |
| Doi | **Doomo kyoo wa gochisoosama deshita.** | どうも きょう は ごちそうさま でした。 |
| Nakamura | **Iyaa, osomatsu deshita.** | いやあ、お粗末 でした。 |
| Kelly | **Moo onaka ga ippai desu. Gochisoosama deshita.** | もう おなか が いっぱい です。 ごちそうさま でした。 |

**〔ADDITIONAL VOCABULARY〕**

**1** **A: Doozo, sono sofaa ni kakete kudasai.** どうぞ、その ソファー に かけて ください。
**B: Arigatoo gozaimasu.** ありがとう ございます。

**2**

| | | |
|---|---|---|
| Maid | **Irasshaimase. Goyoyaku ga gozaimasu ka.** | いらっしゃいませ。ご予約 が ございます か。 |
| Kelly | **Iie, Chiyoda Kookoku no Nakamura-san no shootai de kimashita.** | いいえ、千代田広告 の 中村さん の 招待 で きました。 |
| Maid | **Sayoo de gozaimasu ka. De wa oseki ni goannai-itashimasu.** | さよう で ございます か。 で は お席 に ご案内いたします。 |

**3**

| | | |
|---|---|---|
| Host | **Nani mo gozaimasen ga, doozo meshiagatte kudasai.** | 何 も ございません が、どうぞ 召し上がって ください。 |
| Guest | **Iyaa, subarashii gochisoo desu ne. Itadakimasu.** | いやあ、すばらしい ごちそう です ね。 いただきます。 |

**4** **A: Kore wa nihongo de nan te iimasu ka.** これ は 日本語 で 何 て 言います か。
**B: Sakazuki tte iimasu.** さかずき って 言います。
**A: Ja, sore wa?** じゃ、それ は？
**B: Sore wa tokkuri tte iimasu.** それ は とっくり って 言います。

**5** **A: Aji wa ikaga desu ka.** 味 は いかが です か。
**B: Totemo ii aji desu ga, boku ni wa chotto amai desu yo.** とても いい 味 です が、僕 に は ちょっと 甘い です よ。

**6** **A: Onaka ga suita kara, tabe ni ikimasu ga, issho ni ikaga desu ka.** おなか が すいた から、食べ に 行きます が、一緒 に いかが です か。
**B: Sekkaku desu ga, mada onaka ga suite inai kara...** せっかく です が、まだ おなか が すいて いない から...

**7** Additional restaurant terms

| | | | |
|---|---|---|---|
| **hashi/ohashi** | 箸/お箸 | **fooku** | フォーク |
| **sara/osara** | 皿/お皿 | **naihu** | ナイフ |
| **chawan/ochawan** | 茶碗/お茶碗 | **supu(u)n** | スプ(ー)ン |
| **wan/owan** | 碗/お碗 | **napukin** | ナプキン |

## BUSINESS COLUMN

## BUSINESS AND BOOZE

In Japan, they say, "The wheels of business are oiled with booze." Saturday nights in stations see perfectly respectable businessmen totter about trains and platforms like ants blasted with insecticide. Unlike in the West, drunkenness is far from being a taboo in Japan, where even fairly heavy drinking can be a mandatory part of sealing business relationships.

Bound by rigorous codes of social behavior, the Japanese often find it difficult to unwind. Breaking the ice is a process that only begins when the cubes start dropping into a glass. Alcohol is virtually the only pretext for spontaneous behavioral outbursts there is; a hangover is the worker's only reasonable excuse for lateness or even absenteeism. Drinking is as steeped in unshakably respectable tradition as Japanese *sake*.

According to 1983 statistics, Japan's per capita annual alcohol intake stood at 5.07 liters, as opposed to 8.1 in the U.S. and a chart-busting 13.1 in France. But considering that Japanese women drinkers are very few, the figures apply mainly to men and hint at a powerful lot of drinking. Traditional patterns are changing as more women turn to social drinking, a fact likely to sway consumption figures in the future.

If waning, the traditional Japanese drinking method is to tank up before eating, the first chopstick-scoop of rice being a signal to stop the flow. The custom may be quaint, but drinking on an empty stomach largely explains why the Japanese have come to view and accept exaggerated drunkenness and even vomiting as inevitable side effects.

When not in ordinary bars and taverns, drinking can run up an astronomical tab. Plush hostess bars, for instance, are unabashedly exorbitant, because what is lavished on these is company money. Padding out 'entertainment' expenses when filing tax returns is a widely accepted Japanese corporate practice.

With Oriental complexions reddening even after the first glass, Westerners often believe that the Japanese "can't take it." Trying to keep up with some of the hardier members of a '*hashigo-zake*' (ladder-drinking) session may rather drastically prove this notion to be fallacious. *Hashigo-zake* involves carousing through the varied establishments of the *mizu-shoobai*—the water trade—with any or all brews from *sake* and *shoochuu* to whisky and cocktails consumed along the way. '*Chanpon*' or mixing drinks, shunned Occidentally as the surest way to a wicked hangover or a premature burial, is the norm. Regardless of your own poison, a glass poured from a companion's bottle should be drunk.

The salaryman's homeward session around a bottle of Suntory whisky with colleagues is the final duty for the working day. For most this is fairly moderate affair, but a resident lush is a common office fixture. Even a confirmed dipsomaniac benefits from the country's life employment system, whereas elsewhere his workday incompetence would cost him his job.

As a foreigner, even strangers will offer you Japanese *sake* as the opening gambit for tippling. Refusals can be indelicate, particularly when addressed to future business associates. Being antisocial, teetotalism doesn't pay in the Japanese business world, so your excuse for it had better be medical. Best of all, however, is the fun of drinking your way to better business. And remember, when you say "Bottoms up," it's "Kanpai!"

**by Nick Bornoff** (Copywriter, journalist, film critic for the Japan Times)

## REVIEW SECTION IV (UNIT 16-20)

**1** **Complete the following sentences using the correct particles:**

1) **Kerii-san wa Aoki-san (　　) shigoto (　　) tetsudatte moraimashita.**
"Mr. Kelly had Ms. Aoki help him with his work."
2) **Kerii-san wa Nakano-san (　　) eego (　　) oshiete agemasu.**
"Mr. Kelly teaches English to Mr. Nakano."
3) **Kono shorui (　　) namae o katakana (　　) kaite kudasai.**
"Please write your name in *katakana* on this form."
4) **Nodo (　　) kawaita kara, biiru (　　) nomitai n desu.**
"I want to drink beer because I'm thirsty."
5) **Aoki-san wa tokidoki boku ni nihongo (　　) oshiete kuremasu.**
"Ms. Aoki sometimes teaches me Japanese."
6) **Kyoo wa oisogashii tokoro (　　) yoku irasshaimashita.**
"Thank you for coming, while you're so busy."
7) **Ano hito wa eego (　　) joozu da (　　), shinsetsu ja arimasen.**
"Although that person is good in English, he isn't kind."
8) **Ano ryooriya wa ryoori ga oishii (　　), yasui n desu.**
"The meals at that restaurant are delicious and cheap."
9) **Nihon-ryoori wa me (　　) tanoshimu (　　) iimasu yo.**
"They say you enjoy Japanese meals with the eyes as well."
10) **San-ji ni kaigi (　　) hajimemasu kara, sore (　　) ni kaette kite kudasai.**
"I'll open the meeting at three, so please come back by that time."

**2** Change the following formal verbs into corresponding informal verbs:
Example: Teacher: **Kimasen deshita.** "(Someone) didn't come."
Student: **Konakatta.**

| | | | |
|---|---|---|---|
| **aimashita** | **atta** | **agemasen deshita** | **agenakatta** |
| **arimasu** | **aru** | **herimashita** | **hetta** |
| **agemasen** | **agenai** | **huemasen** | **huenai** |
| **benkyoo-shimasen** | **benkyoo-shinai** | **kawakimasu** | **kawaku** |
| **demashita** | **deta** | **komimasen** | **komanai** |
| **hairimasen** | **hairanai** | **kuremashita** | **kureta** |
| **hatarakimasu** | **hataraku** | **magarimasen deshita** | **magaranakatta** |
| **ikimasen deshita** | **ikanakatta** | **moraimashita** | **moratta** |
| **imashita** | **ita** | **narimasu** | **naru** |
| **iimashita** | **itta** | **norimasen deshita** | **noranakatta** |
| **irimasen** | **iranai** | **norikaemasu** | **norikaeru** |
| **kakarimasen** | **kakaranai** | **orimashita** | **orita** |
| **kakimasu** | **kaku** | **urimasu** | **uru** |
| **kanpai-shimashita** | **kanpai-shita** | **yobimashita** | **yonda** |
| **kikimasen** | **kikanai** | **yomimasen** | **yomanai** |
| **machimashita** | **matta** | **tetsdaimasu** | **tetsudau** |
| **mimashita** | **mita** | **tsukurimasen** | **tsukuranai** |
| **misemashita** | **miseta** | **hirakimashita** | **hiraita** |
| **oshiemashita** | **oshieta** | **dekimasen deshita** | **dekinakatta** |

| | | | |
|---|---|---|---|
| **setsumee-shimasen** | **setsumee-shinai** | **haraimasu** | **harau** |
| **tsukimasu** | **tsuku** | **sagarimasen** | **sagaranai** |
| **ukagaimasen** | **ukagawanai** | **oroshimashita** | **oroshita** |
| **dekakemashita** | **dekaketa** | **soodan-shimasen** | **soodan-shinai** |

**3** Response drill

Example: Teacher: **Tanaka-san wa kimasu ka.** "Will Mr. Tanaka come?"
Student: **Ee, kuru deshoo.** "(He) is probably coming."

1) **Chiba-san wa shiryoo o kuremasu ka.** **Ee, kureru deshoo.**
2) **Aoki-san wa tetsudaimashita ka.** **Ee, tetsudatta deshoo.**
3) **Buchoo wa kaigi ni shusseki-shimasen ka.** **Ee, shusseki- shinai deshoo.**
4) **Kerii-san wa hookoku o kakimashita ka.** **Ee, kaita deshoo.**
5) **Aoki-san wa osake o nomimasu ka.** **Ee, nomu deshoo.**
6) **Kachoo wa denpyoo o mimashita ka.** **Ee, mita deshoo.**
7) **Kerii-san wa han o tsukutte moraimashita ka.** **Ee, tsukutte moratta deshoo.**

**4** Response drill (distinguishing between adjectives and **na** nouns)

Example: Teacher: **Kono shigoto wa muzukashii desu ka.** "Is this work difficult?"
Student: **Ee, muzukashii shigoto desu.** "Yes, it's a difficult work."

1) **Kono shigoto wa kantan desu ka.** **Ee, kantan na shigoto desu.**
2) **Kono shigoto wa yasashii desu ka.** **Ee, yasashii shigoto desu.**
3) **Kono shigoto wa mendoo desu ka.** **Ee, mendoo na shigoto desu.**
4) **Kono shigoto wa abunai desu ka.** **Ee, abunai shigoto desu.**
5) **Kono shigoto wa anzen desu ka.** **Ee, anzen na shigoto desu.**
6) **Kono shigoto wa daiji desu ka.** **Ee, daiji na shigoto desu.**
7) **Kono shigoto wa tanoshii desu ka.** **Ee, tanoshii shigoto desu.**
8) **Kono shigoto wa raku desu ka.** **Ee, raku na shigoto desu.**
9) **Kono shigoto wa rippa desu ka.** **Ee, rippa na shigoto desu.**
10) **Kono shigoto wa tsumaranai desu ka.** **Ee, tsumaranai shigoto desu.**
11) **Kono shigoto wa taihen desu ka.** **Ee, taihen na shigoto desu.**
12) **Kono shigoto wa omoshiroi desu ka.** **Ee, omoshiroi shigoto desu.**

**5** Response drill

Example: Teacher: **Nani ka tanomimashita ka.** "Did you order something?"
Student: **Iie, nani mo tanomimasen.** "No. I ordered nothing."

1) **Kyoo dare ka kimashita ka.** **Iie, dare mo kimasen.**
2) **Ashita doko ka e ikimasu ka.** **Iie, doko e mo ikimasen.***
3) **Kerii-san ni nani ka moraimashita ka.** **Iie, nani mo moraimasen.**
4) **Dare ka ni soodan-shimasu ka.** **Iie, dare ni mo soodan-shimasen.**

*Note that a question word + **ka** is sometimes followed by a particle, while for a question word + **mo**, the particle occurs between the question word and **mo** .

## Let's learn KANA

### 1 KATAKANA

*Katakana* is normally used for writing foreign names and borrowed words. It is also sometimes used to write the Japanese words for names of animals, fish and plants. The pronunciation for borrowed words approximates the original sound but is strongly affected by Japanese speech habits.

**KATAKANA** Chart

| | | | | | | | | | | | | | | | |
|---|---|---|---|---|---|---|---|---|---|---|---|---|---|---|---|
| ア | カ | ガ | サ | ザ | タ | ダ | ナ | ハ | バ | パ | マ | ヤ | ラ | ワ | ン |
| a | ka | ga | sa | za | ta | da | na | ha | ba | pa | ma | ya | ra | wa | n |
| イ | キ | ギ | シ | ジ | チ | (ヂ) | ニ | ヒ | ビ | ピ | ミ | | リ | | |
| i | ki | gi | shi | ji | chi | ji | ni | hi | bi | pi | mi | | ri | | |
| ウ | ク | グ | ス | ズ | ツ | (ヅ) | ヌ | フ | ブ | プ | ム | ユ | ル | | |
| u | ku | gu | su | zu | tsu | zu | nu | hu | bu | pu | mu | yu | ru | | |
| エ | ケ | ゲ | セ | ゼ | テ | デ | ネ | ヘ | ベ | ペ | メ | | レ | | |
| e | ke | ge | se | ze | te | de | ne | he | be | pe | me | | re | | |
| オ | コ | ゴ | ソ | ゾ | ト | ド | ノ | ホ | ボ | ポ | モ | ヨ | ロ | ヲ | |
| o | ko | go | so | zo | to | do | no | ho | bo | po | mo | yo | ro | o | |
| | キャ | ギャ | シャ | ジャ | チャ | (ヂャ) | ニャ | ヒャ | ビャ | ピャ | ミャ | | リャ | | |
| | kya | gya | sha | ja | cha | ja | nya | hya | bya | pya | mya | | rya | | |
| | キュ | ギュ | シュ | ジュ | チュ | (ヂュ) | ニュ | ヒュ | ビュ | ピュ | ミュ | | リュ | | |
| | kyu | gyu | shu | ju | chu | ju | nyu | hyu | byu | pyu | myu | | ryu | | |
| | キョ | ギョ | ショ | ジョ | チョ | (ヂョ) | ニョ | ヒョ | ビョ | ピョ | ミョ | | リョ | | |
| | kyo | gyo | sho | jo | cho | jo | nyo | hyo | byo | pyo | myo | | ryo | | |

Notes: 1) Long vowels are indicated by 〔ー〕.
Example: スキー (sukii) 'ski'

2) Double consonants are indicated by a small 〔ッ〕 which appears before the double consonant.
Example: ネット (netto) 'net'

3) A sound consisting of consonant + '**y**' + vowel (e.g. **kya**) is indicated by a regular *katakana* character followed by a smaller one.
Example: キャ in キャバレー (kyabaree) 'cabaret'
Carefully study the second group of *katakana* in the chart above for this form.

4) In order to express certain foreign sounds, other *katakana* combinations not included in the chart may be used.
Examples:

| | | | | | |
|---|---|---|---|---|---|
| ウィ in ウィーン | (Wiin) | 'Wien' | デュ in デュエット | (duetto) | 'duet' |
| ウェ in ウェア | (weá) | 'wear' | トゥ in トゥナイト | (tunaito) | 'tonight' |
| ウォ in ウォッカ | (wokka) | 'vodka' | ドゥ in ドゥーデン | (duuden) | 'Duden' |

| | | | | | | |
|---|---|---|---|---|---|---|
| シェ in シェアー | (sheaa) | 'share' | ファ in ファン | (fan) | 'fan' |
| ジェ in ジェット | (jetto) | 'jet' | フィ in フィクション | (fikushon) | 'fiction' |
| チェ in チェック | (chekku) | 'check' | フェ in フェア | (fea) | 'fair' |
| ティ in ティー | (tii) | 'tea' | フォ in フォロー | (foroo) | 'follow' |
| ディ in ディナー | (dinaa) | 'dinner' | | | |

## READING PRACTICE

1) Names of Countries

| | | | |
|---|---|---|---|
| アイスランド | Iceland | アメリカ | America |
| アルゼンチン | Argentina | エジプト | Egypt |
| イギリス | U.K. | イタリア | Italy |
| インド | India | オーストリア | Austria |
| オーストラリア | Australia | カナダ | Canada |
| キューバ | Cuba | サウジアラビア | Saudi Arabia |
| シリア | Syria | スイス | Switzerland |
| スウェーデン | Sweden | スペイン | Spain |
| シンガポール | Singapore | ソビエト | Soviet (Soviet Union) |
| タイ | Thailand | チリ | Chile |
| トルコ | Turkey | ドイツ | Germany |
| ニュージーランド | New Zealand | ノルウェー | Norway |
| ビルマ | Burma | ブラジル | Brazil |
| フランス | France | ポーランド | Poland |
| ポルトガル | Portugal | メキシコ | Mexico |
| ユーゴスラビア | Yugoslavia | ヨルダン | Jordan |

2) Names of Cities

| | | | |
|---|---|---|---|
| アテネ | Athens | アムステルダム | Amsterdam |
| アンカラ | Ankara | イスタンブール | Istanbul |
| オスロ | Oslo | カラカス | Caracas |

| | | | |
|---|---|---|---|
| ケンブリッジ | Cambridge | コロンボ | Colombo |
| サイゴン | Saigon | サンフランシスコ | San Francisco |
| シカゴ | Chicago | ジュネーブ | Geneva |
| ストックホルム | Stockholm | セントルイス | St. Louis |
| ダッカ | Dacca | チューリッヒ | Zurich |
| デトロイト | Detroit | デンバー | Denver |
| トリポリ | Tripoli | トロント | Toronto |
| ナポリ | Naples | ニース | Nice |
| ニューヨーク | New York | ハーグ | The Hague |
| パリ | Paris | バンコック | Bangkok |
| ブタペスト | Budapest | ブリュッセル | Brussels |
| プラハ | Prague | ヘルシンキ | Helsinki |
| ベルリン | Berlin | ペンシルバニア | Pennsylvania |
| ホノルル | Honolulu | ホンコン | Hong Kong |
| マドリード | Madrid | マルセーユ | Marseilles |
| ミュンヘン | Munich | メルボルン | Melbourne |
| モスクワ | Moscow | モナコ | Monaco |
| モントリオール | Montreal | ラスベガス | Las Vegas |
| リヨン | Lyon | ロサンジェルス | Los Angeles |
| ロンドン | London | ワシントン | Washington |

3) Foods

| | | | |
|---|---|---|---|
| ランチ | lunch | ディナー | dinner |
| ステーキ | steak | スープ | soup |
| ビーフ | beef | ポーク | pork |
| サンドイッチ | sandwich | ハンバーガー | hamburger |
| パン | bread | バター | butter |
| チーズ | cheese | ケチャップ | ketchup |
| ソース | sauce | マヨネーズ | mayonnaise |
| ジュース | juice | アイスクリーム | ice cream |
| デザート | dessert | コーヒー | coffee |
| ビール | beer | ウイスキー | whisky |
| カクテル | cocktail | ワイン | wine |
| サラダ | salad | フルーツ | fruit |

4) Office terms

| | | | |
|---|---|---|---|
| デスク | desk | テーブル | table |
| タイプライター | typewriter | ワードプロセッサー | word processor |
| ペン | pen | コピー・マシン | coping machine |
| テレックス | telex | ファクシミリ | facsimile |
| エレベーター | elevator | トイレット | toilet |

5) Business terms

| | | | |
|---|---|---|---|
| アイデア | idea | アフター・サービス | after-sales service |
| インタビュー | interview | インフレ | inflation |
| オイル・ダラー | oil dollar | オートメーション | automation |
| ガイドライン | guide-line | カルテル | cartel |
| ギャランティ | guarantee | クレーム | claim |
| コール・レート | call rate | コミッション | commission |
| コミュニケーション | communication | コングロマリット | conglomerate |
| コンピュータ | computer | サービス | service |
| システム | system | スケジュール | schedule |
| スタグフレーション | stagflation | スタンス | stance |
| ストライキ | strike | スワップ | swap |
| ダウ・ジョーンズ | Dow-Jones | チャーター | charter |
| ディーラー | dealer | ディスインフレ | disinflation |
| ディスカウント | discount | データ・バンク | data bank |
| トラスト | trust | ノウ・ハウ | know-how |
| パスポート | passport | パッケージ | package |
| パニック | panic | ブーム | boom |
| プラン | plan | プラント | plants |
| プレミアム | premium | プロジェクト | project |
| ペイ | pay | マーケット | market |
| マージン | margin | マキシマム | maximum |
| マネー・サプライ | money supply | ミニマム | minimum |
| モデル・チェンジ | model change | モラトリアム | moratorium |
| ユーザンス | usance | リスク | risk |
| レイ・オフ | lay-off | レート | rate |
| レジュメ | résumé | レセプション | reception |

## 2 HIRAGANA

*Hiragana* is used for the endings of verbs and adjectives, all forms of copula, particles and some Japanese words not written in *kanji* or *katakana*. Japanese sentences therefore, are usually a combination of *hiragana*, *kanji* and *katakana*.

**HIRAGANA** chart

| | | | | | | | | | | | | | | | |
|---|---|---|---|---|---|---|---|---|---|---|---|---|---|---|---|
| あ | か | が | さ | ざ | た | だ | な | は | ば | ぱ | ま | や | ら | わ | ん |
| *a* | *ka* | *ga* | *sa* | *za* | *ta* | *da* | *na* | *ha* | *ba* | *pa* | *ma* | *ya* | *ra* | *wa* | *n* |
| い | き | ぎ | し | じ | ち | (ぢ) | に | ひ | び | ぴ | み | | り | | |
| *i* | *ki* | *gi* | *shi* | *ji* | *chi* | *ji* | *ni* | *hi* | *bi* | *pi* | *mi* | | *ri* | | |
| う | く | ぐ | す | ず | つ | (づ) | ぬ | ふ | ぶ | ぷ | む | ゆ | る | | |
| *u* | *ku* | *gu* | *su* | *zu* | *tsu* | *zu* | *nu* | *hu* | *bu* | *pu* | *mu* | *yu* | *ru* | | |
| え | け | げ | せ | ぜ | て | で | ね | へ | べ | ぺ | め | | れ | | |
| *e* | *ke* | *ge* | *se* | *ze* | *te* | *de* | *ne* | *he* | *be* | *pe* | *me* | | *re* | | |
| お | こ | ご | そ | ぞ | と | ど | の | ほ | ぼ | ぽ | も | よ | ろ | を | |
| *o* | *ko* | *go* | *so* | *zo* | *to* | *do* | *no* | *ho* | *bo* | *po* | *mo* | *yo* | *ro* | *o* | |
| | きゃ | ぎゃ | しゃ | じゃ | ちゃ | (ぢゃ) | にゃ | ひゃ | びゃ | ぴゃ | みゃ | | りゃ | | |
| | *kya* | *gya* | *sha* | *ja* | *cha* | *ja* | *nya* | *hya* | *bya* | *pya* | *mya* | | *rya* | | |
| | きゅ | ぎゅ | しゅ | じゅ | ちゅ | (ぢゅ) | にゅ | ひゅ | びゅ | ぴゅ | みゅ | | りゅ | | |
| | *kyu* | *gyu* | *shu* | *ju* | *chu* | *ju* | *nyu* | *hyu* | *byu* | *pyu* | *myu* | | *ryu* | | |
| | きょ | ぎょ | しょ | じょ | ちょ | (ぢょ) | にょ | ひょ | びょ | ぴょ | みょ | | りょ | | |
| | *kyo* | *gyo* | *sho* | *jo* | *cho* | *jo* | *nyo* | *hyo* | *byo* | *pyo* | *myo* | | *ryo* | | |

Note: 1) The kana for syllables **yi**, **ye**, **wi**, and **we** are no longer used in modern Japanese. However, **wo**「を」is used for the object particle '**o**', the topic particle '**wa**' is written as「は」, and the direction particle '**e**' is written as「へ」for historical reasons.

2) The **ji** and **zu** syllables are normally written as「じ」and「ず」, but in exceptional cases, as「ぢ」and「づ」.

3) Like *katakana*, double consonants are indicated by a small〔っ〕.
Example: きっと (kitto) certainly'

4) Unlike *katakana*, long vowels are written as:
aa ああ ii いい uu うう ee えい, ええ oo おう, おお.

| | | | | | | |
|---|---|---|---|---|---|---|
| Examples: | zeekin | 'tax' | ぜいきん | ee | 'yes' | ええ |
| | koojoo | 'factory' | こうじょう | ookii | 'big' | おおきい |

## READING PRACTICE

1) あ — a　い — i　う — u　え — e　お — u

| | | | |
|---|---|---|---|
| あい | love | あう | to meet |
| あおい | blue | いい | good |
| いえ | house | いいえ | no |
| おい | nephew | おおい | many |

2) か — ka　き — ki　く — ku　け — ke　こ — ko

| | | | |
|---|---|---|---|
| あかい | red | あき | autumn |
| えき | station | けいえい | management |
| かく | to write | かかく | price |
| けいかく | plan | くうき | air |

3) が — ga　ぎ — gi　ぐ — gu　げ — ge　ご — go

| | | | |
|---|---|---|---|
| あご | jaw | がいこく | foreign contry |
| かいがい | overseas | ぐあい | condition |
| えいが | movie | かいぎ | meeting |
| げき | drama, play | ごかい | misunderstanding |

4) さ — sa　し — shi　す — su　せ — se　そ — so

| | | | |
|---|---|---|---|
| あさ | morning | あし | foot |
| あす | tomorrow | あそこ | over there |
| すき | like | けさ | this morning |
| きそく | regulation | せき | seat |

5) ざ — za　じ — ji　ず — zu　ぜ — ze　ぞ — zo

| | | | |
|---|---|---|---|
| ざいかい | financial world | じか | current price |
| けいざい | economics | ぜい | tax |
| かぞく | family | かず | number |
| かじ | fire | ぜせい | correction |

6) た — ta　ち — chi　つ — tsu　て — te　と — to

| | | | |
|---|---|---|---|
| たかい | expensive | ちかい | near |
| あつかう | to handle | あいて | partner |
| とき | time | つき | moon |
| いた | board | ていき | time deposit |

7) だ — da　ぢ — ji　づ — zu　で — de　ど — do

| | | | |
|---|---|---|---|
| だいがく | university | そで | sleeve |
| どこ | where? | だす | to put |
| かど | corner | うで | arm |
| でぐち | exit | どい | Mr. Doi |

8) な — na　に — ni　ぬ — nu　ね — ne　の — no

| | | | |
|---|---|---|---|
| ない | there is not | にく | meat |
| きぬ | silk | ねこ | cat |
| なかの | Nakano | なに | what? |
| このこ | this child | にかい | second floor |

9) は — ha　ひ — hi　ふ — hu　へ — he　ほ — ho

| | | | |
|---|---|---|---|
| はい | yes | ひとつ | one unit |
| ふたつ | two units | へた | unskilled |
| ほか | other | ふかい | deep |
| はなし | story | へいたい | soldier |

10) ば — ba　び — bi　ぶ — bu　べ — bu　ぼ — bo

| | | | |
|---|---|---|---|
| ばか | fool | くび | neck |
| ぶた | pig | かべ | wall |
| ぼく | I | ばあい | case |
| こうほうぶ | The P.R. Dept. | べいこく | United States |

11) ま — ma　み — mi　む — mu　め — me　も — mo

| | | | |
|---|---|---|---|
| あまい | sweet | かみ | paper |
| むかし | olden days | むすめ | girl |
| きもち | feeling | まめ | bean |
| みぎ | right | めい | niece |

| | | | | | |
|---|---|---|---|---|---|
| 12) | や — ya | ゆ — yu | よ — yo | | |
| | やま | mountain | | ゆき | snow |
| | よい | good | | よゆう | space |
| | やおや | vegetable store | | およぐ | to swim |
| 13) | ら — ra | り — ri | る — ru | れ — re | ろ — ro |
| | あらし | storm | | となり | the next door |
| | るす | away from home | | しつれい | rudeness |
| | ふろ | bath | | ひろい | wide |
| | あります | there is | | かるい | light |
| 14) | わ — wa | ん — n | | | |
| | でんわ | telephone | | ほんとう | truth |
| | わかる | to understand | | こんや | this evening |
| 15) | きゃ — kya | きゅ — kyu | きょ — kyo | | |
| | ぎゃ — gya | ぎゅ — gyu | ぎょ — gyo | | |
| | おきゃく | guest | | きゅうよ | pay |
| | きょうと | Kyoto | | せいぎょ | control |
| 16) | しゃ — sha | しゅ — shu | しょ — sho | | |
| | じゃ — ja | じゅ — ju | じょ — jo | | |
| | かいしゃ | company | | しゅるい | kind |
| | ひしょ | secretary | | きんじょ | neighborhood |
| 17) | ちゃ — cha | ちゅ — chu | ちょ — cho | | |
| | ぢゃ — ja | ぢゅ — ju | ぢょ — jo | | |
| | ちゃいろ | brown | | ちゅうい | attention |
| | しゃちょう | president | | | |
| 18) | にゃ — nya | にゅ — nyu | にょ — nyo | | |
| | こんにゃく | food name | | どうにゅう | introduction |
| | にょじつ | truly | | | |

| | | | | | |
|---|---|---|---|---|---|
| 19) | ひゃ — hya | ひゅ — hyu | ひょ — hyo | | |
| | びゃ — bya | びゅ — byu | びょ — byo | | |
| | ぴゃ — pya | ぴゅ — pyu | ぴょ — pyo | | |
| | ひゃく | 100 | | だいひょう | representative |
| | びょうき | sick | | | |
| 20) | みゃ — mya | みゅ — myu | みょ — myo | | |
| | みゃく | pulse | | みょうあん | excellent idea |
| 21) | りゃ — rya | りゅ — ryu | りょ — ryo | | |
| | りゃくご | abbreviation | | りゅうこう | fashion |
| | こうりょ | consideration | | | |

## GENERAL REVIEW (from the Model Conversation of UNIT 1)

**1**
1) わたくし、トム・ケリー です。
2) ああ、ケリーさん、わたくし は アジアでんき の なかの です。
3) なかのさん です か。はじめまして。
4) はじめまして、どうぞ よろしく。
5) こちら こそ。どうぞ よろしく。
6) りょこう は いかが でした か。
7) かいてき でした。
8) そう です か。では、ホテル へ あんない します。
9) ありがとう ございます。
10) リムジン です か。
11) いいえ、タクシー です。
12) とうきょうホテル、おねがい します。
13) ぎんざ です ね。
14) ええ、そう です。

# APPENDICES

## 1. VERB INFLECTIONS

| Class | | Non-past Informal | Non-past Formal | Gerund (**-te** form) | Past Informal | Negative Non-Past Informal | Meaning |
|---|---|---|---|---|---|---|---|
| I **-RU** verbs | | **-ru**<br>**ageru** | **-masu**<br>**agemasu** | **-te**<br>**agete** | **-ta**<br>**ageta** | **-nai**<br>**agenai** | to give |
| II **-U** verbs | **-ku** | **-ku**<br>**kaku** | **-kimasu**<br>**kakimasu** | **-ite**<br>**kaite** | **-ita**<br>**kaita** | **-kanai**<br>**kakanai** | to write |
| | **-gu*** | **-gu**<br>**isogu** | **-gimasu**<br>**isogimasu** | **-ide**<br>**isoide** | **-ida**<br>**isoida** | **-ganai**<br>**isoganai** | to hurry |
| | **-bu** | **-bu**<br>**yobu** | **-bimasu**<br>**yobimasu** | **-nde**<br>**yonde** | **-nda**<br>**yonda** | **-banai**<br>**yobanai** | to call |
| | **-mu** | **-mu**<br>**yomu** | **-mimasu**<br>**yomimasu** | **-nde**<br>**yonde** | **-nda**<br>**yonda** | **-manai**<br>**yomanai** | to read |
| | **-nu**** | **-nu**<br>**shinu** | **-nimasu**<br>**shinimasu** | **-nde**<br>**shinde** | **-nda**<br>**shinda** | **-nanai**<br>**shinanai** | to die |
| | **-su** | **-su**<br>**hanasu** | **-shimasu**<br>**hanashimasu** | **-shite**<br>**hanashite** | **-shita**<br>**hanashita** | **-sanai**<br>**hanasanai** | to tell |
| | **-ru** | **-ru**<br>**hairu**<br>**aru** | **-rimasu**<br>**hairimasu**<br>**arimasu** | **-tte**<br>**haitte**<br>**atte** | **-tta**<br>**haitta**<br>**atta** | **-ranai**<br>**hairanai**<br>**nai***** | to enter<br>to be, have |
| | **-tsu** | **-tsu**<br>**matsu** | **-chimasu**<br>**machimasu** | **-tte**<br>**matte** | **-tta**<br>**matta** | **-tanai**<br>**matanai** | to wait |
| | vowel | **-u**<br>**au** | **-imasu**<br>**aimasu** | **-tte**<br>**atte** | **-tta**<br>**atta** | **-wanai**<br>**awanai** | to meet |
| III **-ARU** verbs | | **-aru**<br>**irassharu** | **-aimasu**<br>**irasshaimasu** | **-atte**<br>**irasshatte** | **-atta**<br>**irasshatta** | **-aranai**<br>**irassharanai** | to be, come |
| Irregular | | **kuru**<br>**suru** | **kimasu**<br>**shimasu** | **kite**<br>**shite** | **kita**<br>**shita** | **konai**<br>**shinai** | to come<br>to do |

* Verbs ending in **-gu** will be introduced in Vol. 3.

** There is only one verb ending in **-nu** in modern Japanese: **shinu**, 'to die.'

*** The verb **aru** 'to be, have' has no negative form. For this verb the adjective **nai** 'there is not, does not exist' is used.

I. **-RU** verb chart

| | | | | | |
|---|---|---|---|---|---|
| **akeru** | to open | **hareru** | to clear up | **oriru** | to get off |
| **azukeru** | to deposit | **hueru** | to increase | **shiraberu** | to check |
| **dekakeru** | to go out | **kakeru** | to sit | **taberu** | to eat |
| **dekiru** | to complete, | **kureru** | to give (to | **todokeru** | to deliver |
| | can do | | the speaker) | **tsukareru** | to be tired |
| **hajimeru** | to begin | **norikaeru** | to transfer | **tsureru** | to take |

II. **-U** verb chart

| | | | | | |
|---|---|---|---|---|---|
| **aruku** | to walk | **kumoru** | to become | **osu** | to push |
| **dasu** | to send | | cloudy | **owaru** | to finish |
| **hajimaru** | to start | **magaru** | to turn | **sagaru** | to decrease |
| **harau** | to pay | **mairu*** | to come | **suwaru** | to sit down |
| **hashiru** | to run | **maneku** | to invite | **tanomu** | to ask, order |
| **heru** | to decrease | **mawasu** | to send | **tanoshimu** | to enjoy |
| **hiraku** | to open | **meshiagaru** | to eat, drink | **tetsudau** | to help |
| **huku** | to blow | **morau** | to receive | **todoku** | to reach |
| **huru** | to fall | **motsu** | to have, hold | **torikesu** | to cancel |
| **itadaku** | to recieve | **naru** | to become | **tsukiau** | to go out |
| **itasu*** | to do | **nomu** | to drink | | (drinking) |
| **iu** | to say | **noru** | to get on | **tsukuru** | to make |
| **kaeru** | to return | **ochitsuku** | to calm down | **tsuzuku** | to continue |
| **kakaru** | to take, cost | **oku** | to put | **uketoru** | to receive |
| **kawaku (nodo ga)** | to become | **okuru** | to send | **uru** | to sell |
| | thirsty | **omou** | to think | **yamu** | to stop |
| **kiniiru** | to be pleased | **orosu** | to withdraw | **yaru** | to do |
| **komu** | to be crowded | **oru*** | to be | | |

III. **-ARU** verb chart

| | | | |
|---|---|---|---|
| **gozaru*** | to have, there is | **nasaru** | to do |

IV. **-SURU** verb chart

| | | | | | |
|---|---|---|---|---|---|
| **chikoku-suru** | to come late | **kesseki-suru** | to be absent | **shusseki-suru** | to attend |
| **chuumon-suru** | to order | **kyoka-suru** | to permit | **soodan-suru** | to consult |
| **gaishutsu-suru** | to be out | **nyuukin-suru** | to deposit | **yokin-suru** | to deposit |
| **gochisoo-suru** | to treat | **sanpo-suru** | to take a walk | **yoyaku-suru** | to reserve |
| **hassoo-suru** | to send | **seeri-suru** | to arrange | | |
| **hookoku-suru** | to report | **shootai-suru** | to invite | | |

* In modern Japanese these verbs are very rarely used in their formal forms.

## 2. ADJECTIVES

| | | | | | |
|---|---|---|---|---|---|
| **abunai** | dangerous | **mijikai** | short | **suppai** | sour, acidic |
| **amai** | sweet | **muzukashii** | difficult | **tanoshii** | pleasant |
| **atsui** | hot | **nagai** | long | **tsumaranai** | uninteresting |
| **chikai** | near | **nigai** | bitter | **tsumetai** | cold |
| **hayai** | early | **oishii** | delicious | **umai** | good, skillful |
| **hidoi** | bad | **osoi** | late, slow | **utsukushii** | beautiful |
| **karai** | hot, spicy | **shiokarai** | salty | **yasashii** | easy, simple |
| **katai** | hard, tough | **shoppai** | salty | **yawarakai** | soft, tender |
| **mazui** | bad-tasting | **subarashii** | wonderful | | |

## 3. COPULA INFLECTIONS AND NA NOUNS

| | Formal | | Informal | |
|---|---|---|---|---|
| | Non-past | Past | Non-past | Past |
| Affirmative | **desu** | **deshita** | **da** | **datta** |
| Negative | **ja arimasen** | **ja arimasen deshita** | **ja nai** | **ja nakatta** |

| | | | | | |
|---|---|---|---|---|---|
| **anzen /na/** | safe | **iroiro /na/** | various | **mendoo /na/** | troublesome |
| **benri /na/** | easy-to-use | **iron na*** | various | **ooki na*** | big, large |
| **betsu /na/** | separate | **jama /na/** | be interrupted | **osomatsu /na/** | humble, poor |
| **daiji /na/** | important | **joozu /na/** | be skilled | **raku /na/** | easy |
| **daijoobu /na/** | safe, OK | **kaiteki /na/** | pleasant | **rippa /na/** | splendid |
| **daisuki /na/** | favorite | **kantan /na/** | simple | **shinsetsu /na/** | kind |
| **dame /na/** | bad | **katte /na/** | selfish | **suki /na/** | favorite |
| **genki /na/** | well, fine | **kekkoo /na/** | fine, good | **taihen /na/** | awful |
| **heta /na/** | unskillful | **kirai /na/** | dislike | **taisetsu /na/** | important |
| **hima /na/** | be free | **kyooshuku /na/** | thankful | **yuumee /na/** | famous |
| | | | | **yuushuu /na/** | excellent |

* **Iron na** and **ooki na** are never used with a copula.

## 4. PARTICLES

| Particle | Meaning/Function | Examples | Unit |
|---|---|---|---|
| **de** | by means of | Mainichi basu **de** jimusho e ikimasu.<br>"I go to the office by bus everyday." | 11 |
| **demo** | even | Omizu **demo** ii (desu) kara nani ka kudasai.<br>"Please (give me) something to drink. Even water will do." | 20 |
| **de mo** | something similar | Eega ni **de mo** ikimasen ka.<br>"Will you go to the movies (or something similar) with me?" | 14 |
| **keredo/ kedo** | although <contrary reasoning> | Washoku wa suki da **kedo**, sashimi wa kirai desu.<br>"Although I like Japanese food, I don't like *sashimi.*" | 17 |
| **koso** | <emphasis> | Ashita **koso** dekiru to omoimasu.<br>"I think it'll be completed *tomorrow.*" | 20 |
| | <speaker's modesty> | Watakushi **koso** sumimasen deshita.<br>"I should be the one to apologize." | 20 |
| **made** | to, as far as <destination> | Nichiyoobi ni uchi **made** irasshatte kudasai.<br>"Please come to my house on Sunday." | 11 |
| **...mo ...mo** | both... and... | Niku **mo** sakana **mo** daisuki desu.<br>"I like both meat and fish." | 14 |
| **ni** | to do <purpose> | Kerii-san wa tomodachi ni ai **ni** ikimashita.<br>"Mr. Kelly went to see his friend." | 19 |

| | | | |
|---|---|---|---|
| **ni wa** | for | Boku **ni wa** daiji na mondai desu yo.<br>"It is important for me." | 20 |
| **node** | because <reasoning> | Yoku hataraita **node,** tsukaremashita.<br>"I worked hard, so I was tired." | 17 |
| **o** | through <location> | Kono michi **o** ikimashoo ka.<br>"Shall we go along this street?" | 11 |
| **to/tte** | <quotative> | Kanai wa sore wa takai **to** iimashita.<br>"My wife said that is expensive." | 13 |
| **to** | with | Sono mondai ni tsuite kachoo **to** hanashite mimasu.<br>"I'll try to talk with our chief about that problem." | 17 |
| **yori** | than | Kesa wa itsu mo **yori** hayaku tsukimashita.<br>"This morning I arrived earlier than usual." | 14 |

## 5. INTERROGATIVES

| Interrogative | Meaning | Examples | Unit |
|---|---|---|---|
| **dochira (no hoo)** | which one? | Osake to biiru to **dochira (no hoo)** go suki desu ka.<br>"Which do you like better, *osake* or beer?" | 11 |
| | where? | **Dochira (no hoo)** ni dekakemasu ka.<br>"Where are you going?" | |
| | who? | **Dochira** (sama) desu ka.<br>"Who are you?" | |
| **donata** | who?<br><polite> | **Donata** ga sono hon o motte ikimashita ka.<br>"Who took that book?" | 12 |
| **donna** | what kind of | **Donna** eega ga suki desu ka.<br>"What kind of movies do you like?" | 13 |
| **ikutsu** | how many units? | Ano shina o **ikutsu** chuumon-shimashoo ka.<br>"How many of those goods in question shall we order?" | 15 |
| **nan-ban-sen** | what the track Nq. | **Nan-ban-sen** de omachi-shimashoo ka.<br>"At what track shall I wait for you?" | 11 |
| **nan-bon** | <question counter> | **Nan-bon** gurai biiru o onomi ni narimasu ka.<br>"About how many bottles of beer can you drink?" | 14 |
| **nan-bai** | | Osatoo wa **nan-bai** desu ka.<br>"How many spoonfuls of sugar shall I put in?" | 14 |
| **nan-mai** | | Repooto o **nan-mai** gurai kakimashita ka.<br>"About how many sheets have you written for the report?" | 18 |
| **nan de** | by what means? | Eki kara wa **nan de** ikimashoo ka.<br>"How shall I go from the station?" | 11 |

# ANSWERS

## 〔EXERCISE〕

### UNIT 11

**1**
1) (Depaato no mae ni) hoteru ga arimasu.
2) (Ginkoo no migi ni) hoteru ga arimasu.
3) (Kooen no ushiro ni) gakkoo ga arimasu.
4) (Eki no hidari ni) depaato ga arimasu.
5) (Denwa wa) yuubinkyoku no mae ni arimasu.
6) Iie, (ginkoo no mae wa) eki desu.
7) Hai, soo desu.
8) (Byooin no hidari ni) otearai ga arimasu.

**2**
1) Tomu Kerii wa senshuu Amerika kara hikooki de kimashita.
2) Shinbashi made basu de itte, kokuden ni norikaemashoo.
3) Sumimasen ga, ano ookii biru wa Jetoro desu ka.
4) Ashita no asa Ajia Denki e itte, Doi-san ni aimasu.
5) Kono michi o itte, ginkoo no kado o migi e magatte kudasai.
6) Kono hen ni chikatetsu no eki wa arimasen kara, takushii de itte kudasai.
7) Tanaka-san no kaisha wa ano hoteru no ushiro no biru (*or* tatemono) (no naka) ni arimasu.
8) Yamaguchi-san wa Tookyoo-eki no midori no madoguchi de kippu o kaimashita.
9) Chiba-san wa ni-bansen de Shinkansen ni notte, Kyooto e ikimashita.
10) Shinjuku de densha o orite, basu ni norikaemashita.

### UNIT 12

**1**

| (As a host or hostess) | (As a guest) |
|---|---|
| 1) Chiba-san, yoku irasshaimashita. | Oisogashii tokoro o ojama-shimasu. |
| 2) Doozo kochira e. | Osoreirimasu. *or* Shitsuree-shimasu. |
| 3) Chiba-san, Koohii wa ikaga desu ka. | Iie, kekkoo desu. |
| 4) Ocha wa ikaga desu ka. | Arigatoo gozaimasu. |

**2**
1) Jimusho wa Ginza de, uchi wa Shibuya desu.
2) Yakusoku wa arimasen ga, buchoo wa irasshaimasu ka.
3) Ashita no asa juu-ji han made ni (anata no) kaisha e ukagaimasu.
4) Nakamura-shachoo wa senshuu Nyuuyooku e irasshaimashita.
5) Dono gurai Igirisu ni irasshaimashita ka.
6) Watakushi wa san-nen gurai Rondon ni orimashita.
7) Watakushi wa Rondon no Nihon no ginkoo de hataraite orimashita.
8) Tanaka-san wa Chiba-san no shookai de (watakushi no) jimusho e irasshaimashita.
9) Doi-buchoo ni yoroshiku.
10) Yamaguchi-san no hookoku wa taihen sankoo ni narimashita.

## UNIT 13

**2**
1) Kerii-san wa Yamaguchi-san ni "Tadaima" to iimashita.
2) Kinoo aishii shijoo ni tsuite no hookokusho o yonde mimashita ga, wakarimasen deshita.
3) Doi-buchoo wa taisetsu na deeta o shirabete imasu.
4) Watakushi wa Buraun-san kara Amerika no rekishi ni tsuite no hon o moraimashita.
5) Watakushi wa Buraun-san ni totemo takai nooto o agemasu.
6) Nakamura-san wa benri na waaporu o (watakushi ni) kuremashita.
7) Wagasha no yakuin wa dandan huete imasu.
8) Nani o kaite imasu ka. Eegyoo ni tsuite no hookoku o kaite imasu.
9) Chiba-san wa iroiro na shiryoo o kuremashita. Shinsetsu na kata desu.
10) Amerika no denki-seehin no shijoo o shirabete mimashoo.

## UNTI 14

**2**
1) Chiba-san wa "Kanpai" to iimashita.
2) Watakushi wa tenpura mo sukiyaki mo suki desu ga, (o) sushi ga ichi-ban suki desu.
3) Ano shokudoo ni wa oishii tabemono (or ryoori) wa arimasen.
4) Nakamura-san no okusan wa biiru mo sake mo nomimasen.
5) Kerii-san to Buraun-san to Sumisu-san no uchi (or naka) de dare ga ichiban nihongo ga joozu desu ka.
6) Tookyoo Hoteru to Kyooto Hoteru to dochira (no hoo) ga hurui desu ka.
7) Nakano-san wa Kerii-san ni "Anata wa (o) sushi o tabemasu ka" to kikimashita.
8) Kerii-san wa "Biiru ip-pon to nama-biiru ip-pai onegai-shimasu" to iimashita
9) Chiba-san wa jikan ga arimasen deshita kara, koohii o nomimasen deshita.
10) Onaka ga sukimashita. Yuubinkyoku no ushiro no yuumee na resutoran e ikimashoo.

## UNIT 15

1) Kerii-san wa baabon no on-za-rokku to piinattsu o chuumon-shimashita.
2) Nihon no keeki wa yoku narimasu deshoo.
3) Nakamura-san ni atte kara, Jetoro e ikimasu.
4) Tookyoo ni wa ikutsu gurai daigaku ga arimasu ka.
5) Yamaguchi-san ni yoku gochisoo ni narimasu kara, konban wa watakushi ga haraimasu.
6) Moo tenpura o tabemashita ka. Iie, mada desu.
7) Kinoo no kanjoo wa dare ga haraimashita ka. Doi-buchoo ga haraimashita.
8) Kono resutoran no wain ga (taihen) suki desu. Ee, (taihen) oishii desu nee.
9) Tanaka-san wa taitee kaisha no hitotachi to tsukiaimasen.
10) Chiba-san kara deeta o moratte kara, jimusho ni kaette kudasai.

## UNIT 16

**2**
1) Buraun-san wa senshuu han 〔*or* hanko (o), inkan〕 o tsukutte moraimashita.
2) Nakano-san ga (watakushi ni) yunyuu no tetsuzuki o oshiete kuremasu.
3) Watakushi wa Kerii-san ni Ginza no chizu o kaite agemashita.
4) Chiba-san wa Yokohama Ginkoo no jidoo-hurikomi ni shite imasu kara, gasu-ryookin ya denki-ryookin no shiharai wa mondai arimasen.
5) Watakushi wa Tookyoo Ginkoo ni juuman-en azuketai n desu.

6) Inkan [*or* han (koo)] mo tsuuchoo mo asoko no teeburu no ue ni arimasu.
7) (Watakushi wa) Aoki-san ni kono shorui o kaite moraitai n desu.
8) Otetsudai-shimashoo ka. Iie, kekkoo desu. Watakushi ga dekimasu yo.
9) Doi-buchoo wa atarashii waapuro o (watakushi ni) katte kuremashita.
10) Nihon de wa teeki-yokin no riritsu wa nen yon-ten ni paasento gurai desu.
11) Nihon de ichi-ban anzen na kabu wa nan desu ka. Watakushi mo (sore ni tsuite) oshiete morai tai n desu yo.
12) Kabu wa taitee abunai desu kara, kaitaku arimasen.
13) Kogitte de haraimasu ka. Iie, genkin de haraimasu.
14) Ano ginkoo ni ikura-gurai roon (*or* shakkin) ga arimasu ka. gojuuman-en gurai desu.
15) Riritsu wa ikura gurai desu ka. Nen 12.5 paasento desu yo.

**UNIT 17**

**1** 1) tsuzukimasu 2) hatarakimasu 3) tetsudaimasu 4) kakimasu 5) oroshimasu 6) narimasu 7) haraimasu 8) kaerimasu 9) tabemasu 10) agemasu

**2** 1) Shachoo wa kaigi ni shusseki-shinai to omoimasu.
2) Kyoo wa zuibun tsukareta kara, sugu uchi ni kaerimasu.
3) Jetoro e itte, shijoo-choosa no shiryoo o shirabeta hoo ga ii desu yo.
4) Kachoo ga buchoo no keekaku ni hantai-suru to wa omoimasen.
5) Kerii-san wa watakushi ni Yamaguchi-san no iken o kiku to iimashita.
6) Sukiyaki wa totemo suki desu ga, ano resutoran no sukiyaki wa tabetaku arimasen.
7) Shachoo wa kono keekaku wa nanajuuman-en gurai kakaru to iimashita.
8) Tanaka-san ga kite kara, kaigi o hajimeta hoo ga ii to omoimasu.
9) Tomodachi no yakusoku o torikesanai hoo ga ii desu yo.
10) Osoku natta keredo, Aoki-san wa matte imashita.

**UNIT 18**

1) Keeribu no Tanaka-san ga kitara, kono denpyoo o agete kudasai.
2) Watakushi wa huransugo mo doitsugo mo benkyoo-shita koto ga arimasu.
3) Kachoo no kyoka o morawanakattara, okane o haraimasen yo.
4) Kerii-san wa Asakusa e itta koto ga nai kara, tsugi no nichiyoobi ni Aoki-san ga annai-shite agemasu.
5) Kinoo Akasaka no ryooriya e ittara, Doi-buchoo ga irasshaimashita.
6) Kono denpyoo o eegyoobu e mawashimashoo ka.
7) Dare ga kono tsutsumi o shachoo no tsukue no ue ni okimashita ka. Watakushi desu. Sore wa kyoo Kankoku kara todokimashita.
8) Denpyoo ni han o oshita koto ga arimasu ka. Iie, han o oshita koto wa arimasen.
9) Kami wa nan-mai irimasu ka. Go-mai kudasai.
10) Ashita mo isogashikattara, Yokohama no kaigi ni shusseki-shimasen.

**UNTI 19**

**1** 1) yamimashita 2) hidoi tenki desu *or* ii tenki ja arimasen 3) hutte imasu 4) hutte imasu *or* hurimashita 5) hukimasu 6) huranai

**2** 1) Ima ohima deshitara, (go) issho ni shokuji o shi ni (*or* nani ka tabe) ni ikimasen ka.

2) Kinoo wa nichiyoobi deshita ga, kono shiryoo (*or* deeta) o shirabe ni jimusho e kimashita.
3) Doi-san no ikitsuke no ryooriya wa Kabukiza no mae ni arimasu (*or* mae desu).
4) Kesa Aoki-san wa chikoku-suru to omotte, eki kara kaisha made hashitte kimashita.
5) Kyoo shiryoo (or deeta) o seeri-shiyoo to omoimasu.
6) Kyoo wa ii tenki da kara, sanpo-shiyoo to omoimasu.
7) Hidoi tenki datta kara, kinoo wa Jetoro no Chiba-san ni ai ni ikimasen deshita.
8) Buchoo no iken o kikoo to omotte imasu ga. . .
9) Moo juuichi-ji sugi desu kara, (otaku made) okurimashoo ka.
10) Ashita haretara (*or* ii tenki dattara), Kamakura e ikoo to omoimasu.

**UNIT 20**
1) Kono ryooriya no niwa wa yuumee da shi, subarashii n desu yo.
2) Kerii-san wa onaka ga suitara, taitee ano shokudoo e ikimsu.
3) Nakamura-shachoo wa Doi-san to Kerii-san o Akasaka no rippa na restoran e shootai-shita soo desu.
4) Nihon-ryoori o me de mo tanoshinda hoo ga ii to omoimasu.
5) Kore o nihongo de nan to iimasu ka. Tokonoma to iimasu.
6) Konna shigoto wa Amerika no bijinesuman ni wa yasashii n desu.
7) Nani ka tabe ni ikimasen ka. Arigatoo gozaimasu. Demo ima onaka ga ippai desu.
8) Donna wain ga kono ryoori ni aimasu ka.
9) Dare ga Kerii-san o nomi ni tsurete ikimasu ka. Nakano-san ga yoku Shinjuku e tsurete ikimasu.
10) Aoki-san wa myuujikaru eega ga daisuki da soo desu.

〔**REVIEW SECTION III**〕

**1** 1) de 2) de, o, ni 3) o, o 4) de 5) ni, to 6) ni
7) to, to, ga 8) ga, de 9) kara (*or* ni), ni 10) mo

**2** 1) atsui 2) ookii 5) benri

〔**REVIEW SECTION IV**〕

**1** 1) ni, o 2) ni, o 3) ni, de 4) ga, o 5) o
6) o 7) ga, keredo 8) shi 9) de, to 10) o, made

# INDEX

To the right of the word entry is the volume number in which the indexed word first appears followed in bold face by references to page number and section of the units in which the word is listed.
Example: **aru** ①46, 6 / **50, 1** / **117, 4** ②**24, 2**
This shows that the word, **aru**, initially appears in Vol. 1 on page 46, item 6 of the MODEL CONVERSATION; on page 50, item 1 of the GRAMMATICAL NOTES; on page 117, item 4 of the GRAMMATICAL NOTES; and in Vol. 2 on page 24, item 2 of the GRAMMATICAL NOTES.
Numbers are not listed in this section. For Chinese derived numerals see the vocabulary section of Unit 6 and the chart in Unit 7 (Vol. 1). Japanese derived numbers are explained in Unit 15.
All verbs are listed in their citation form.

## A



## B



## C

## D



## E

## F



## G



## H

## I



## J



## K

## M



## N

# O

## P



## R



## S